Perpetual Motion

THE ILLUSTRATED HISTORY OF THE PORT AUTHORITY OF NEW YORK & NEW JERSEY

BY JOE MYSAK WITH JUDITH SCHIFFER

GENERAL
PUBLISHING
GROUP
Los Angeles

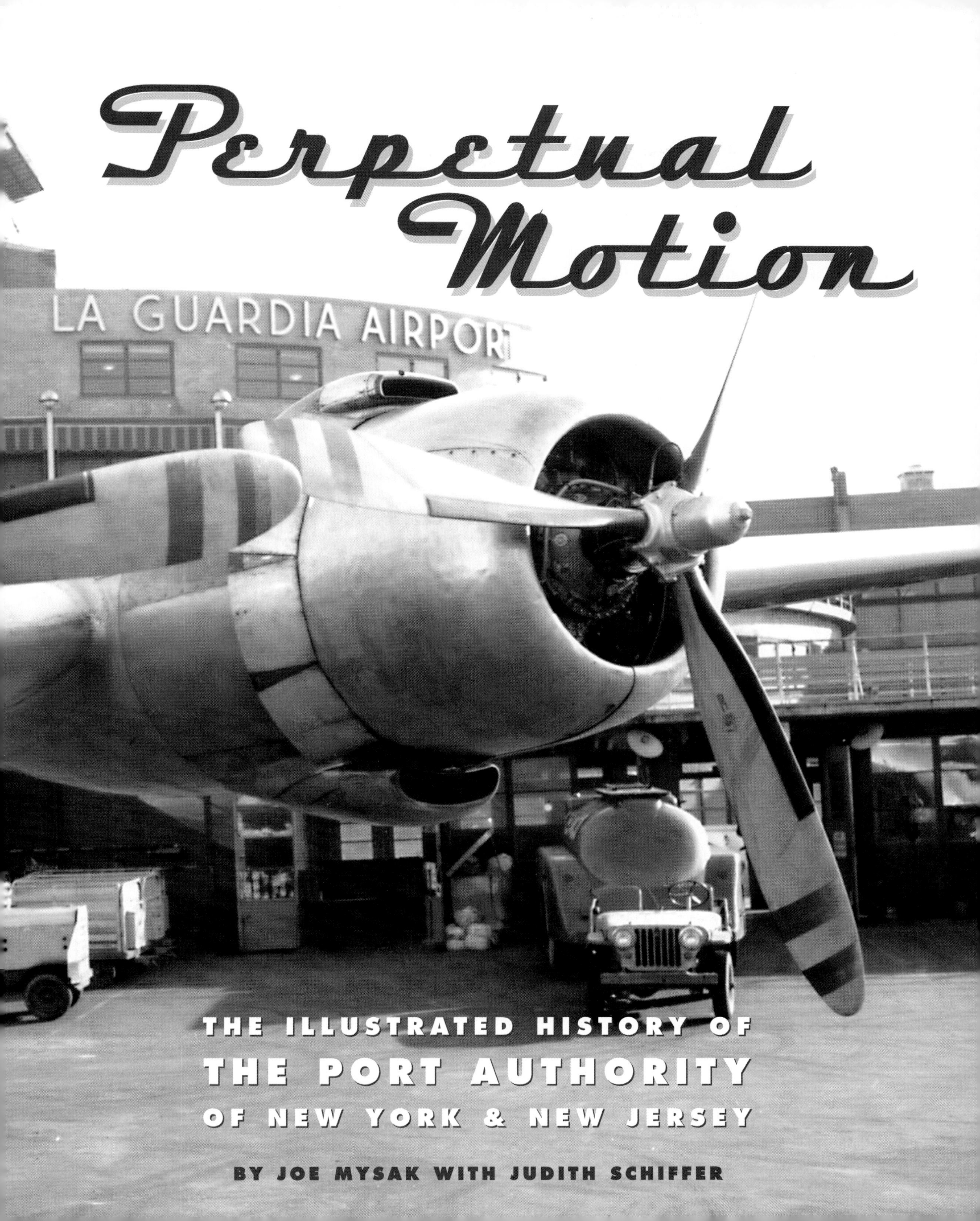

Perpetual Motion

THE ILLUSTRATED HISTORY OF THE PORT AUTHORITY OF NEW YORK & NEW JERSEY

BY JOE MYSAK WITH JUDITH SCHIFFER

Publisher: *W. Quay Hays*
Editorial Director: *Peter L. Hoffman*
Art Director: *Susan Anson*
Production Director: *Trudihope Schlomowitz*
Color and Pre-Press Manager: *Bill Castillo*
Production Artists: *Regina Troyer, Gaston Moraga*
Production Assistants: *Tom Archibeque, David Chadderdon, Gus Dawson*
Assistant Editor: *Dana Stibor*
Copy Editors: *Mark Lamana, Amy Spitalnick*

For information:

General Publishing Group, Inc.
2701 Ocean Park Boulevard, Suite 140
Santa Monica, CA 90405

Library of Congress Cataloging-in-Publication Data

Mysak, Joe
Perpetual Motion : the illustrated history of the Port Authority
of New York and New Jersey / by Joe Mysak with Judith Schiffer.
p. cm.
Includes index.
ISBN 1-57544-004-0
1. Port Authority of New York and New Jersey—History. 2. Tobin, Austin J. 3. Executives—United States—Biography. I. Title.
HE554.N7M97 1996
353.97470087'71—dc20 96-36410
CIP

Printed in the USA by RR Donnelley & Sons Company
10 9 8 7 6 5 4 3 2 1

GENERAL PUBLISHING GROUP
Los Angeles

Table of Contents

Acknowledgments

In any work like this, there are numerous people to thank, particularly George Marlin, Mark Hatfield, Lysa Meduri, and Gwendolyn Williams. I also wish to thank Cathy Pavelec, Barbara Frink, and Lillian Kropf, who aided me in the research. Kathy Bincoletto smoothed the way.

I especially want to thank Austin C. Tobin, the son of the Port Authority's longest-serving executive director, who has not only been a friend for the 16 years I have covered the municipal finance industry, but also an invaluable source.

Thanks, too, to John H. Allan, my mentor, not a few of whose 1960s vintage clips from the New York Times I came across in my research, and to Jack Doran of Reuters.

Finally, thanks as always to Susan Merett, my long-suffering wife, who had to get used to an entirely new shtick, replacing my history of the municipal bond market in general and the centennial history of the Daily Bond Buyer in particular.

—*Joe Mysak*

Staff in the Port Authority's Office of Corporate Communications were valuable contributors to *Perpetual Motion*. Joseph R. Liccardo, editor of the agency's employee publication *P.A. Today*, did extensive research and editing, and provided historical vignettes compiled from archival material and the Port Authority's newsletters. Fred G. Shaw was an integral part of the editorial team. His efforts were crucial to the book's historical accuracy. He did much of the fact-checking, identification, and organizing of the photos and editing of photo captions. Well-versed in recent Port Authority events, Gwendolyn Williams researched the contemporary chapters and located their photos. Harry Czinn jumped in at the eleventh hour to critique the last set of galleys. We received able assistance from Robert Chernoff of Records Management, who located archival materials; Brenda Jimenez, who typed many a draft; and Vernon Joseph, who made endless copies.

We are inestimably grateful to the late Bruce Rossomando, Supervisor of the Port Authority's Photographic Services and his staff-photographer Jerry Rosen, Diane Wilson, now retired, and Albert J. Belva, who provided the magnificent photos used in this volume.

Our sincere appreciation goes to the Port Authority's Director of the Office of Corporate Communications, Mark O. Hatfield, Jr., for initiating the project and for his unfailing support. Thanks also to General Counsel Jeffrey S. Green, and to acting Chief Economist, Eugene Spruck, for their insightful comments.

Political scientist Jameson Doig of Princeton University was kind enough to read portions of the manuscript. We relied heavily on his extensive research on the Port Authority for some of the early chapters and the section on "The Battle for a Consolidated Bus Station in Manhattan" in Chapter VI. We also used Geoffrey Arend's series on "Great Airports" as sources for the sections on LaGuardia, Newark International, and John F. Kennedy International airports.

GPG's book editor, Peter Hoffman, was a joy to work with. Thanks go to him and his team, especially art director, Susan Anson, for designing this beautiful book.

—*Judith Schiffer*

Foreword

GOVERNOR GEORGE E. PATAKI
STATE OF NEW YORK

GOVERNOR CHRISTINE TODD WHITMAN
STATE OF NEW JERSEY

THE PORT AUTHORITY'S BANNER WAVES OVER THE WORLD TRADE CENTER'S PLAZA, A SYMBOL OF BISTATE COOPERATION AND PROGRESS.

For more than three quarters of a century, the Port Authority has played a pivotal role in defining and managing the complex transportation needs of the New York–New Jersey region.

Through the Port Authority Compact of 1921, New York and New Jersey embraced a bistate philosophy essential to the region's future economic health. This sparked a new era of growth with a series of improvements of monumental scale and historic importance that we often take for granted today.

The legacy of the Port Authority is one of innovation, cooperation, and enterprise. It has met the challenges of the 20th Century with extraordinary success, and in the process created some of the largest and most impressive public facilities constructed in this century. Under our direction, the agency now looks to the greater challenges of the 21st century.

In the Port Compact, the two states pledged their "faithful cooperation in the future planning and development of the Port of New York." As a result, the region's marine, rail, and trucking terminals now supply America with every imaginable commodity, all growing exponentially around an infrastructure largely designed and constructed by the agency. Its tunnels and bridges are landmarks of engineering and technology. Its shippers pioneered containerization, revolutionizing the handling of cargo worldwide, and its airports have grown from fledgling operations to become the collective epicenter of American aviation.

During the last 75 years, the Port Authority has invested billions of dollars in the land, marine, and air terminals within the bistate region. It is an agency that not only addresses the technical challenges of erecting great public facilities, but mediates the myriad provincial concerns of both states and their diverse communities.

The story of the Port Authority is more than one of steel and concrete. It is the story of the people of the New York–New Jersey region—their needs, their creativity, their diversity, their shared human experience. It is also the story of those who looked into the future and saw the possibility of building on a scale befitting a metropolitan community which represents an America bustling with vitality, industry, and excitement.

New Jersey's Governor Walter E. Edge, and Governors Alfred E. Smith and Charles S. Whitman of New York were among the advocates who led the campaign to create an effective governing body to both develop the port area and protect its commerce. In 1921, the Port Authority officially came into being under the Governor of New York, Nathan L. Miller, and the Governor of New Jersey, Edward T. Edwards. Today, the Port Authority is redefining itself based on their founding principals and the essential mission of transportation and trade. On behalf of these forword-looking leaders, as well as all who have served since its inception, we salute the achievements of the first 75 years and together we challenge The Port Authority of New York and New Jersey to renew and fulfill its commitment to our bistate region.

Introduction

The Diamond Jubilee of the Port Authority of New York and New Jersey provides an opportunity to document some 75 years of remarkable and often trailblazing achievements. The Port Authority was, and still is, more than just an agency overseeing the operation of tunnels, bridges, airports, and terminals in the New York–New Jersey region. It solved many long-standing problems between the two states, enabling the citizens of the region—and the nation—to benefit from some of the finest transportation facilities ever built.

This unique agency was created three-quarters of a century ago by young men schooled in the Progressive rebellion against the corruption of the Tweed Ring and Tammany Hall. Believing that governance should be separated from politics, they sought to create an organization that was insulated from the political environment but subject to its direction. In this way, the agency could strive to achieve goals that would benefit the region.

The Port Authority is a unique government agency. Rather than receiving tax dollars to build and operate its facilities, it raises its own revenues by collecting tolls, fees, and rents, and issuing its own bonds. A bistate agency, the Port Authority is governed by a board of commissioners appointed by the governors of New York and New Jersey.

The founders of the Port Authority believed that a corporate-style board composed of regional leaders from the public and private sectors would enable the agency to resist the changing tides of politics and build great public works that could take a decade or more to construct. The commissioners are appointed by the governors to six-year terms and serve without pay.

The structure of the agency proved essential to its dynamism. It is unlikely that an ordinary government bureaucracy would have built the Lincoln Tunnel and the George Washington Bridge during the depths of the Great Depression, developed airfields when commercial aviation was out of reach of the average person, or built a World Trade Center when lower Manhattan was being written off as a commercial dead zone. The Port Authority defied conventional wisdom and took chances. Of course, in taking huge risks, one is bound to make some wrong turns. But the agency's failures pale when weighed against its achievements and innovations.

Adapting to new demands and circumstances, the Port Authority has evolved over the years. It has had to grapple with how to balance the contradictory needs of different groups of citizens. For each achievement there is often a repercussion.

During the past 75 years, the Port Authority has created some of the world's finest and most enduring engineering and architectural marvels. Its mission has been to improve the region's transportation infrastructure while creating jobs and fostering commerce. It is an agency in perpetual motion, much like the bustling metropolitan area that it serves. This book provides a glimpse at the Port Authority's proud history and remarkable achievements.

THE EMBLEM OF THE PORT AUTHORITY OF NEW YORK AND NEW JERSEY INCORPORATES THE SEALS OF BOTH STATES.

THE PORT AUTHORITY OF NEW YORK AND NEW JERSEY CELEBRATED ITS 75TH ANNIVERSARY IN 1996.

The Birth of a Great Port

BEFORE THE PORT AUTHORITY

A VIEW FROM THE 1920S: THE HUDSON AND EAST RIVERS CONVERGING INTO NEW YORK BAY, WITH THE BROOKLYN AND MANHATTAN BRIDGES CONNECTING MANHATTAN AND BROOKLYN (AT THE UPPER RIGHT). THE SKYLINE WAS EMERGING. TALL SLIM SPIRES OVERLOOK A HARBOR BUSTLING WITH LUXURY LINERS, STEAMERS, AND FERRIES. THE GOTHIC-STYLE WOOLWORTH BUILDING (EXTREME LEFT) WAS THE TALLEST IN THE WORLD AT 792 FEET HIGH; THE ORNATE SINGER BUILDING (CENTER) WAS THE SECOND TALLEST AT 612 FEET. (COURTESY OF THE SOUTH STREET SEAPORT MUSEUM)

ISLAND FOR SALE

Manhattan's debut in maritime history dates back to 1524, when a Florentine navigator, Giovanni da Verrazano, was commissioned by the king of France to find a new route to the Indies. He sailed into what is now New York Harbor on the three-masted vessel *Dauphine* and was met by some 30 canoes, no doubt one of the most extraordinary meetings in the annals of exploration. Verrazano took soundings of the bay, which he recorded was fed by "a very big river," then dutifully sailed on to find the ever-elusive western route to the Orient, with its promise of the spices, silks, and gold so prized by Europeans. With a failed mission to find the Indies, this early explorer would probably be quite surprised to learn that his name would nevertheless be given to the Verrazano Narrows and the great bridge that spans it.

THE DUTCH COLONY OF NIEUW AMSTERDAM AT THE TIP OF MANHATTAN ISLAND ABOUT 1650 WITH BROOKLYN ON THE FAR SHORE.

Although Verrazano returned to France with amazing stories of "people clothed with the feathers of birds" and hills filled with minerals, King Francis I did not grasp the significance of the discovery, and it remained for the Dutch to establish a settlement there. In September 1609, a Dutch East India Company ship, *The Half Moon*, landed on a beautifully wooded island nestled in a bay brimming with fish and wildlife. Henry Hudson, an English navigator commissioned by the Dutch with the same mission to find a new passage to the Orient, guided the small ship through bitter arctic storms to this serene harbor, which one crewman logged as "a very good land to fall in with." Although the local inhabitants of the North American coast were usually friendly and willing to trade, the crew of *The Half Moon* received a hostile reception on Staten Island. One crewman was killed by an arrow, and the others were lucky to escape with their lives.

Like Verrazano, Hudson also failed to find the Indies, but the majestic river and huge bay, both of which he charted, would ultimately bear his name. The Dutch, sufficiently intrigued by the wealth of fur pelts and hides that could be acquired in the New World, considered establishing a settlement on Manhattan, even if it didn't offer the exotic treasures of the Far East. In one of the most questionable real estate transactions in history, Peter Minuit, leader of a small Dutch colony, purchased Manhattan Island in 1626 from a group of local Native Americans for a box of trinkets worth about 60 guilders. It's amazing to think that such enormously valuable property was purchased for so paltry a price.

On this bucolic island a city of skyscrapers would eventually rise, a great port with a history rich in colorful characters—entrepreneurs, pirates, scallywags, and heroes. It would grow from a simple trading post to a megalopolis that stretches not only across rivers and a harbor but across state lines as well—today's Port of New York and New Jersey.

THE EVER-EVOLVING PORT

Before 1950, Manhattan's waterfront was extraordinarily active, with ships docked at the foot of virtually every street and hundreds more plying the waters for their turn at the wharves. Stevedores, crews, and passengers milled about in a profusion of activities that mingled with the sundry sounds of a bustling metropolis. Unlike today's sprawling marine terminals, which are sequestered behind security fences and acres of marshaling yards, the early docks were an integrated part of the city, the logical outgrowth of an intricate marine transportation system.

As an island sheltered in a temperate bay, Manhattan could use virtually its entire periphery for docks, which is why it was established as a port. With the East River on one side and the Hudson on the other, Manhattan had two ideal inland corridors for domestic shipping, and the Atlantic Ocean was its link with the rest of the seaboard and the world. Prior to the era of planes, trains, and motor vehicles, ships were the only practical mode for transporting large and heavy cargo and passenger loads. Thanks to its geography, Manhattan was virtually destined to grow into one of the world's great ports.

The transition from city docks to discrete marine terminals was in large part accelerated by the demands of the two world wars. Materiel for the war effort brought the need for heightened security, and for handling cargo and personnel on a scale never before imagined. In addition, for decades Manhattan had become more densely populated and its real estate grew to be too expensive for solely marine terminal use.

In the 1800s there was already a migration of shipping facilities to the outer boroughs, particularly Brooklyn and several locations in northern New Jersey, as immigrants settled into what were then the suburbs of Manhattan. Indeed, these areas eventually spawned independent shipping operations to serve their own growing populations, not simply to meet the demands in Manhattan.

By the mid-1800s Brooklyn was handling many times the tonnage of its island neighbor, particularly at Red Hook, where the entrepreneur William

A STREETSCAPE TAKEN BY VICTOR PREVOST IN 1853 FROM THE COLLECTION OF THE MUSEUM OF THE CITY OF NEW YORK. THE PHOTOGRAPH, PRINTED FROM A DELICATE WAX NEGATIVE, IS A VIEW INTO A LOST WORLD.

THIS IS THE SOUTHERNMOST TIP OF LOWER MANHATTAN, LOOKING NORTH. IN THE FOREGROUND, THE SOMEWHAT LUNAR LANDSCAPE WAS FORMED BY LANDFILL STRETCHING 100 YARDS FROM CASTLE CLINTON (THEN KNOWN AS THE CASTLE GARDEN ENTERTAINMENT CENTER) TO THE ORIGINAL SHORELINE. THE FORTRESS HOUSED 28 GUNS.

TO THE RIGHT ARE THE PROMENADE AND RETAINING WALL, WITH THE SPIRES OF TRINITY CHURCH IN THE FOREGROUND AND ST. PAUL'S CHAPEL IN THE BACKGROUND. TO THE LEFT, THE OFFICES OF STEAMSHIP COMPANIES WERE LOCATED IN THE BRICK BUILDINGS ALONG BATTERY PLACE. AT THE EDGE OF THE PHOTO ARE MASTS FROM THE SHIPS DOCKED ALONG WEST STREET.

WHEN THIS PICTURE WAS TAKEN, THE POPULATION OF MANHATTAN ISLAND WAS A HALF MILLION. THE CIVIL WAR WAS EIGHT YEARS AWAY. THE PORT WAS FILLED WITH BUSTLING DOCKS AND PIERS, AND THE ONLY WAY TO GET TO BROOKLYN OR NEW JERSEY FROM MANHATTAN WAS OVER THE WATER. CONSOLIDATION OF THE GREATER CITY OF NEW YORK WAS 53 YEARS AWAY, THE CREATION OF THE PORT AUTHORITY 68 YEARS AWAY.

Beard bought waterfront property and devised a clever way to develop it. Most international ships in those days came to New York Harbor laden with ballast stones, the weight of which kept them stable on the high seas. Ballast was used when ships had little cargo aboard, a necessity for most ships coming to New York Harbor because the region at that time was primarily an exporter of goods. Before the ships could be loaded with cargo, however, they had to dump their ballast or have it carted away at considerable

expense. Beard invited ships to dump their ballast at Red Hook, and in the process they created a 4,000-foot-long breakwater that was 300 feet wide. Tons of stone imported from virtually every corner of the world formed an extraordinary landfill that still shelters the Brooklyn waterfront, a legacy that helped Brooklyn to blossom into a great port in its own right.

Brooklyn's waterfront boomed and the city grew rapidly, becoming "America's pantry" by importing, processing, and exporting sugar, grains,

LOOKING SOUTHWEST, THIS IS THE WORLD INTO WHICH THE PORT AUTHORITY WAS BORN. THE ROUND, FLAT STRUCTURE ON THE LEFT IS CASTLE GARDEN, WHICH IN TWO YEARS WOULD BE TURNED INTO THE NEW YORK AQUARIUM BY THE NOTED NEW YORK ARCHITECTURAL FIRM OF McKIM, MEAD & WHITE. DIRECTLY AHEAD LIES THE CONTINENT—NEW JERSEY AND THE REST OF AMERICA. THE LARGE STRUCTURE ON THE RIGHT IS THE WHITEHALL BUILDING. NOTICE THE ELEVATED RAILWAY LINE SNAKING AROUND THE BATTERY, AND THE PIERS DIRECTLY AHEAD. MORE THAN 50 PIERS WERE SITUATED ON THE WEST SIDE OF MANHATTAN SOUTH OF 14TH STREET.

TODAY THE BATTERY IS ONE OF THE MOST PEACEFUL PLACES IN NEW YORK CITY. NOT SO AT THE TURN OF THE CENTURY. WEST STREET AT THE HEIGHT OF RUSH HOUR TODAY IS CALM COMPARED TO THE 1890s TO THE 1930s, WHEN THE DISTRICT RESEMBLED A MOB SCENE FROM SUNRISE TO SUNSET. HEADING FOR THOSE 50 PIERS WERE SHIPS AND FERRIES CARRYING TENS OF THOUSANDS OF NEW JERSEYANS TO WORK. THE HARBOR WAS CROWDED WITH TUGS, FERRIES, BARGES, SCHOONERS, STEAMERS, NAVY SHIPS, PASSENGER LINERS, AND YACHTS—SHIPS AND BOATS OF EVERY KIND. ON SHORE IT WAS EVEN MORE HECTIC, AS THOUSANDS OF WAGONS, CARTS, TROLLEYS, AND EVENTUALLY TRUCKS AND CARS GREETED THE NEW ARRIVALS AT THE PIERS AND CAUSED GRIDLOCK. (COURTESY OF THE MUSEUM OF THE CITY OF NEW YORK)

meat, fish, spices, coffee, molasses, and other useful products. Traffic across the East River was increasing rapidly as the population in both cities swelled. With the opening of the Brooklyn Bridge in 1883, the first nonmarine link to Manhattan came just in time to meet the demands of the industrial revolution and its numerous manufactured products. With deliveries and trips between the two boroughs now as simple as crossing a bridge, growth followed on both shores.

CASTLE GARDEN, THE ROUND, FLAT STRUCTURE IN THE CENTER OF THE PHOTO, BECAME THE NEW YORK AQUARIUM IN 1896. IMMIGRANTS AWAITING ENTRY INTO NEW YORK WERE PROCESSED AT CASTLE GARDEN BEFORE FACILITIES WERE ESTABLISHED ON ELLIS ISLAND DIAGONALLY ACROSS THE BAY. THE AQUARIUM MOVED TO THE BRONX ZOO IN 1941 AND EVENTUALLY TO CONEY ISLAND. (COURTESY OF THE MUSEUM OF THE CITY OF NEW YORK)

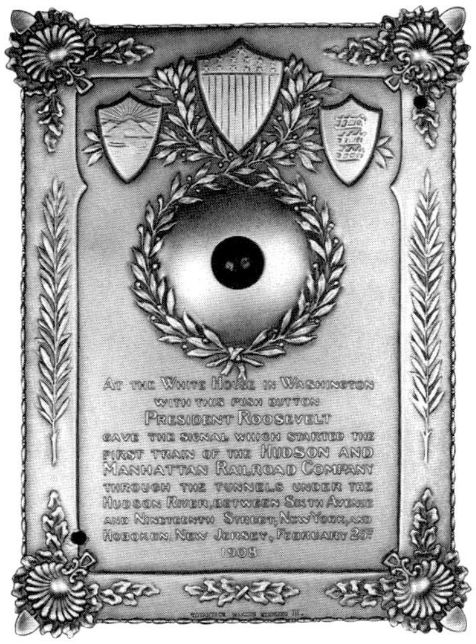

PRESIDENT THEODORE ROOSEVELT PRESSED THIS BUTTON TO GIVE THE SIGNAL THAT STARTED THE FIRST TRAIN OF THE HUDSON & MANHATTAN RAILROAD.

THE 1908 DEDICATION CEREMONY FOR THE HUDSON & MANHATTAN RAILROAD.

THE HUDSON AND MANHATTAN TUBES

As far back as 1869, an architect named DeWitt Clinton Haskin proposed a trans-Hudson railway during an era when subways and subaqueous tunnels were as technologically ambitious as a trip to the moon. The technique of using airlocks and pressure to bore tunnels under water was pioneered on the Hudson and Manhattan Railroad tubes in the late 1800s, but not without considerable risk and some loss of life. In 1901, lawyer William Gibbs McAdoo took on the task of completing the tubes after numerous construction delays and a lack of funding. He would become president of the H&M Railroad, leading it through a tortuous route of financial, technical, and legal problems.

On February 25, 1908, McAdoo proudly telegraphed a message to President Theodore Roosevelt: "The first special train of the Hudson & Manhattan Railroad Company under the Hudson River awaits your signal and pleasure." When Roosevelt pressed a button at the White House, the system's lights went on, electric engines purred, and 800 dignitaries rode from 19th Street in Manhattan to Hoboken Terminal in New Jersey. New York Governor Charles Hughes shook hands with New Jersey Governor John Franklin Fort as the train passed red, white, and blue lights, which marked where the two states met beneath the river. The *New York Times* hailed the completion of the underwater tubes as "a feat greater than the building of the Panama Canal." The same construction methods would later be used to build the Holland and Lincoln Tunnels; the Port Authority and the engineering world owe much to Haskin and his ambitious and ingenious ideas.

CITY HALL IN JERSEY CITY CELEBRATED THE OPENING OF ITS NEW HUDSON & MANHATTAN RAILROAD SECTIONS IN 1909.

HUDSON TUNNELS,
19TH St. & 6TH Ave. Station, Uptown Side

THE 19TH STREET STATION WAS WHERE 800 DIGNITARIES BOARDED THE FIRST HUDSON & MANHATTAN TRAIN TO HOBOKEN IN 1908. TOPPED WITH ORNATE CAPITALS, THE COLUMNS MET GRACEFUL ARCHES THAT FORMED A CLASSICAL CHAMBER.

STATION ATTENDANTS, A NEWSSTAND, WHITE TILE WALLS, AND A MEN'S CLOTHING STORE WERE AMONG THE AMENITIES TO BE FOUND AT THE 19TH STREET ENTRANCE. NOTE THE SPITTOON FOR THOSE WHO CHEWED TOBACCO.

HERALD SQUARE CIRCA 1910 WAS A HODGEPODGE OF TROLLEYS, AN EL, AND THE ENTRANCE TO THE H&M TUBES BORDERING A SMALL TRIANGULAR PARK THAT WAS, APPARENTLY, OFF-LIMITS TO PEDESTRIANS.

AN H&M TRAIN CIRCA 1908.

THOMPSON-STARRETT
COMPANY
BUILDING CONSTRUCTION

CRÈME
ELCAVA
THIS TRAIN FOR
23RD ST.
NEXT STATION
PENNSYLVANIA RY
HEGEMAN & CO.
HEARN Dry Goods 14th St.
LARGE STOCKS—QUICK SELLING PRICES
WANAMAKER'S
CHINA AND
GLASSWARE
Dress Goods

ONE OF THE ORIGINAL HUDSON & MANHATTAN CARS CONTAINED ADVERTISING SIGNS, ELECTRIC CEILING FANS, HANDHOLD BARS, AND INTERIOR HEATING. THESE CARS WERE BUILT ON A SMALLER AND MORE INTIMATE SCALE THAN NEW YORK SUBWAY CARS.

INTRODUCED IN 1965, THE PA-1 CARS WERE SLEEK AND MODERN, WITH AIR-CONDITIONING, FLUORESCENT LIGHTS, PADDED SEATS, AND COLORFUL INTERIORS. PATH WOULD ULTIMATELY OFFER THE WORLD'S FIRST FULLY AIR-CONDITIONED FLEET OF RAPID TRANSIT CARS.

Whose River Is It, Anyway?

THE CREATION OF THE PORT AUTHORITY

THE SIGNING OF THE COMPACT AFTER DECADES OF FUSSING, FEUDING, AND FIGHTING. NEW YORK AND NEW JERSEY FINALLY FOUND A SOLUTION TO THE DISPUTE OVER REGIONAL TRANSPORTATION. "WITH AN ONION AND A POTATO AND SOME MEAT WE MADE OUR STEW! AND DID IT STEW! AND DID WE STEW," WROTE JULIUS HENRY COHEN ABOUT THE CREATION OF THE PORT AUTHORITY. AFTER YEARS OF POLITICAL NEGOTIATION THE COMPACT WAS SIGNED IN 1921 IN THE GREAT HALL OF THE NEW YORK CHAMBER OF COMMERCE ON LIBERTY STREET IN DOWNTOWN MANHATTAN.

There was little harmony and cooperation between New York and New Jersey during the 19th century as they frequently fought over political and jurisdictional rights on the mighty Hudson. In 1834, they resolved their boundary dispute by splitting the river down the middle, but this imaginary borderline could not stem the commercial conflict that would stretch well into the next century.

Matters became worse with the advent of World War I, when congestion in New York Harbor became almost unmanageable. The harbor was inundated with ships transporting soldiers and materiel for the war effort across the Atlantic. For New Jersey this congestion exacerbated an already trying situation. Most of the railroads coming in from the West had terminals on the Jersey side of the Hudson. Cargo had to be transferred to barges for a trip that took anywhere from 18 minutes to a half hour to reach the docks in Manhattan and Brooklyn, where most steamships called. After navigating through the chaos of the harbor, the barges would often have to wait for space at the piers.

Then there was the matter of freight rates, which New Jerseyans claimed were unfair to them. The Interstate Commerce Commission considered New York and New Jersey to be in the same district, and treated them equally in terms of the rates they could set. This issue became the direct impetus for creation of the Port Authority.

In 1917, New Jersey's waterfront cities petitioned the ICC, claiming that setting equal rail-freight rates for both states was discriminatory. They argued that although the rail lines terminated in New Jersey, most cargo had to be hauled at extra expense from New Jersey across the Hudson River to the New York side, where the majority of steamship lines called. New Jersey rates, they said, should be cheaper, to attract more ships to their side of the river.

Newspapers at the time called New Jersey's move a bid to "split the harbor." If the ICC did lower rates on their side of the harbor, it might induce certain industries to relocate. New York felt that it was entitled to all the commerce that flowed from its investments in the Erie Canal, and wanted to prevent the development of competitive shipping facilities on the western bank of the river. The state opposed the move, claiming that it would result in a disruptive reorganization of the port.

The leaders of the New York Chamber of Commerce, particularly Chairman Eugenius H. Outerbridge and Julius Henry Cohen, saw the New York Harbor Case as more than a squabble, but rather an opportunity to develop a unified port. They understood that cooperation between the two states would ultimately benefit both. After much to-do, the ICC reached the same conclusion.

The two states had flirted with cooperation before—two parallel commissions had been collaborating on constructing a trans-Hudson tunnel or bridge since 1906.

Nonetheless, getting the states to agree on how to "cooperate for their mutual benefit" took considerable prodding on the part of the ICC, and the leadership of three determined governors, New York's Charles Whitman and Alfred E. Smith, and New Jersey's Walter Edge.

JULIUS HENRY COHEN, THE FIRST GENERAL COUNSEL OF THE PORT AUTHORITY, WROTE THE LEGISLATION THAT LED TO THE FORMATION OF THE AGENCY.

For Cohen, the basic question was "How could the two states be bound?" since the Constitution forbids the making of any treaties or compacts between states without the consent of Congress. The 1834 treaty between the two states that settled their jurisdictional dispute had been accomplished by compact. Cohen set out to supplement that landmark agreement, and to create a bistate agency for the port.

The plan was promptly attacked by machine politicians on both sides of the Hudson, who felt threatened by a new governmental agency involved in public works over which they had little control or patronage power. Legislation creating the Port Authority was vehemently opposed by New York Mayor John Hylan and several New Jersey mayors, and was twice vetoed by Edge's successor, Edward Edwards, before it was enacted by a veto override vote of the New Jersey Legislature. After years of political squabbling and negotiation, legislation was finally passed and ratified by Congress in 1921 that created the Port of New York Authority.

The compact gave the Port Authority a broad mandate to develop and modernize the entire port district, a bistate region of about 1,500 square miles which includes portions of 17 counties and 108 towns. The Authority could buy, build, lease, or operate any terminal or transportation facility in the region. It could issue bonds and levy user fees, but could not tax or pledge either state's credit. In essence, as long as the commissioners and the two states agreed, the Port Authority could embark on any project in the port district that fit the rubric "improving commerce and trade."

How the Authority Got Its Name

THE PORT OF NEW YORK AUTHORITY WAS PATTERNED AFTER THE PORT OF LONDON AUTHORITY, FOUNDED IN 1908. IT WAS, IN FACT, THE FIRST AMERICAN AGENCY TO USE THE WORD AUTHORITY IN ITS NAME, A PRACTICE THAT WAS QUICKLY ADOPTED BY MANY OTHER PORTS.

JULIUS HENRY COHEN TOLD THE STORY OF HOW THE LONDON BODY GOT ITS NAME: IT SEEMS THAT LORD DEVENPORT AND LLOYD GEORGE WERE WORKING ON THE PROPOSED ACT OF PARLIAMENT, BY WHICH THEY EXPECTED TO CONSOLIDATE A GROUP OF LONDON PORT BODIES. FOR THE NAME, COMMISSION, BOARD, AND AGENCY WERE ALL REJECTED BECAUSE THEY SEEMED TOO COMMON. LLOYD GEORGE SAID, "LET'S WAIT UNTIL WE FINISH THE WHOLE BILL AND THEN WE MAY GET AN INSPIRATION." WHEN THEY HAD COMPLETED THE BILL THEY FOUND THAT NEARLY EVERY PARAGRAPH BEGAN WITH THE WORDS "AUTHORITY IS HEREBY GIVEN." SO LLOYD GEORGE SAID, "LET'S CALL IT THE PORT OF LONDON AUTHORITY."

A TESTIMONIAL DINNER AT THE WALDORF-ASTORIA ON JUNE 30, 1942, WITH PORT AUTHORITY GENERAL COUNSEL JULIUS HENRY COHEN (LEFT) AND COMMISSIONER CHARLES S. WHITMAN.

The Original Movers and Shakers

CHARLES S. WHITMAN

While serving a second term as governor of New York, Whitman played a leadership role in the creation of the Port Authority. He advocated the principle of cooperation in the Port District, which led to the establishment of the New York–New Jersey Port and Harbor Commission. He was appointed a commissioner of the Port of New York Authority by New York Governor Herbert H. Lehman in 1935, and reappointed for a full six-year term in 1936.

JULIUS HENRY COHEN

Cohen, a lawyer, conceived and wrote the legislation required for the creation of the Port Authority in language that was acceptable to both states. The compact entered into between New York and New Jersey that established the agency was essentially his creation.

Later, as general counsel for the Authority, Cohen designed and defended its various bond indentures. In essence, he set up a circulatory system through which the Authority's life's blood, cash, would flow. Cohen told the story of his life in *They Builded Better Than They Knew* (1946), a series of fascinating portraits focusing on the "good government" reform movement in turn-of-the-century New York, but also including chapters on two other founders of the Port Authority, Eugenius H. Outerbridge ("the handsomest man I ever knew...His mustache was always in curl, a sure sign that the owner is interested in his personal appearance"), and Alfred E. Smith ("confirming evidence of the truth that you can be a politician and yet accomplish great public good").

WALTER EDGE

An early supporter of bistate cooperation, Edge, the newly elected governor of New Jersey, in 1917 called the Port of New York a "national institution," and called for a "far-sighted interstate commission, which is oblivious to sectional prejudices and intent upon developing an important section of the country along broad lines."

EUGENIUS H. OUTERBRIDGE

An ardent advocate of bistate friendship and cooperation, Outerbridge was a signer of the original port compact on April 30, 1921. He subsequently served as the first chairman of the Port of New York Authority, a post he held until March 1924. The Outerbridge Crossing, which links Staten Island and New Jersey, bears his name. Built by the agency in the 1920s, it is a fitting monument to his vision of bistate achievement.

GEORGE SILZER

As governor of New Jersey, Silzer supported the Port Authority's bridge program and was influential in gaining public support for building the George Washington Bridge in Upper Manhattan. He was appointed commissioner in 1926 and elected chairman immediately thereafter.

HOWARD S. CULLMAN

When New York Governor Alfred E. Smith invited Cullman to serve as commissioner of the Port of New York Authority in 1927, he responded, "Sure. What is it?" He served as chairman of the Board of Commissioners from 1945 to 1955, and honorary chairman until 1969, when he retired. At that time, his fellow commissioners conferred upon him the title of honorary chairman emeritus, a title he held until his death in 1972.

ALFRED E. SMITH

A four-term governor of New York, Smith served on the first Board of Commissioners of the Port of New York Authority from 1921 to 1923, between his first and second terms as governor. Smith, who signed the 1921 compact, was strongly committed to the creation of the Port Authority. In colorful speeches, he detailed the adventures of a fictitious "Mr. Potato," whose journey from farm to grocery dramatized the lack of unified terminal facilities, as well as wasteful routing and rehandling of cargo. Smith's leadership and style gained widespread support for a bistate philosophy that would ultimately benefit the entire region.

ESSEX
UNION
MIDDLESEX
HUDSON
STATEN ISLAND
Montclair
Nutley
Rutherford
Lyndhurst
North Arlington
Bloomfield
Belleville
West Orange
Orange
East Orange
Livingston
Kearny
Harrison
South Orange
Maplewood
Irvington
Newark
Millburn
Summit
Springfield
Union
Cranford
Westfield
Roselle
Elizabeth
Linden
Rahway
Iselin
Avenel
Woodbridge
Carteret
Fords
Perth Amboy
Bayonne
Jersey City
Hoboken
Secaucus
North Bergen
Union City
Weehawken
NEWARK INTERNATIONAL AIRPORT
PORT NEWARK
ELIZABETH PORT AUTHORITY MARINE TERMINAL
HOWLAND HOOK MARINE TERMINAL
AUTO MARINE TERMINAL
GLOBAL MARINE TERMINAL
MILITARY OCEAN TERMINAL
SOUTH BROOKLYN MARINE TERMINAL
GREENVILLE FLOAT YARD (NYCH)
OAK ISLAND YARD
DOREMUS AVENUE AUTO TERMINAL
ARLINGTON YARD
PORT READING YARD
TELEPORT
EXPRESSRAIL TRANSFER
E-RAIL TERMINAL
65TH STREET INTERMODAL TERMINAL
50TH STREET FLOAT BRIDGE (NYCH)
NORTH JERSEY INTERMODAL TERMINAL (CROXTON)
RESOURCES INTERMODAL TERMINAL
NORTH BERGEN TERMINAL
JOURNAL SQUARE TRANSPORTATION CENTER
PENN STATION-NEWARK (PATH-AMTRAK-NJ TRANSIT)
NEWARK LEGAL CENTER
ESSEX CO. RESOURCE RECOVERY FACILITY
MEADOWLANDS SPORTS COMPLEX
EAGLE ROCK RES
SOUTH MOUNTAIN RESERVATION
BRANCH BROOK PARK
WEEQUAHIC PARK
GALLOPING HILL PARK
LENAPE PARK
WARINANCO PARK
LIBERTY STATE PARK
CLOVE LAKES PARK
LATOURETTE PARK
GREAT KILLS PARK
MILLER FIELD
ELLIS I
LIBERTY I
GOVERNORS I
HOFFMAN I
SWINEBURN I
HOLLAND TUNNEL
LINCOLN TUNNEL
GOETHALS BRIDGE
BAYONNE BRIDGE
OUTERBRIDGE CROSSING
VERRAZANO-NARROWS BRIDGE
EDISON BRIDGE
VICTORY BRIDGE
PULASKI SKYWAY
NEW JERSEY TPKE
NEW JERSEY TPKE EXTENSION
GARDEN STATE PKWY
STATEN ISLAND EXPWY
WEST SHORE EXPWY
RICHMOND PKWY
GOWANUS EXPWY
Passaic River
Hackensack River
Rahway River
Arthur Kill
Kill van Kull
NEWARK BAY
UPPER NEW YORK BAY
LOWER NEW YORK BAY
The Narrows
Gravesend Bay
NJ
NY

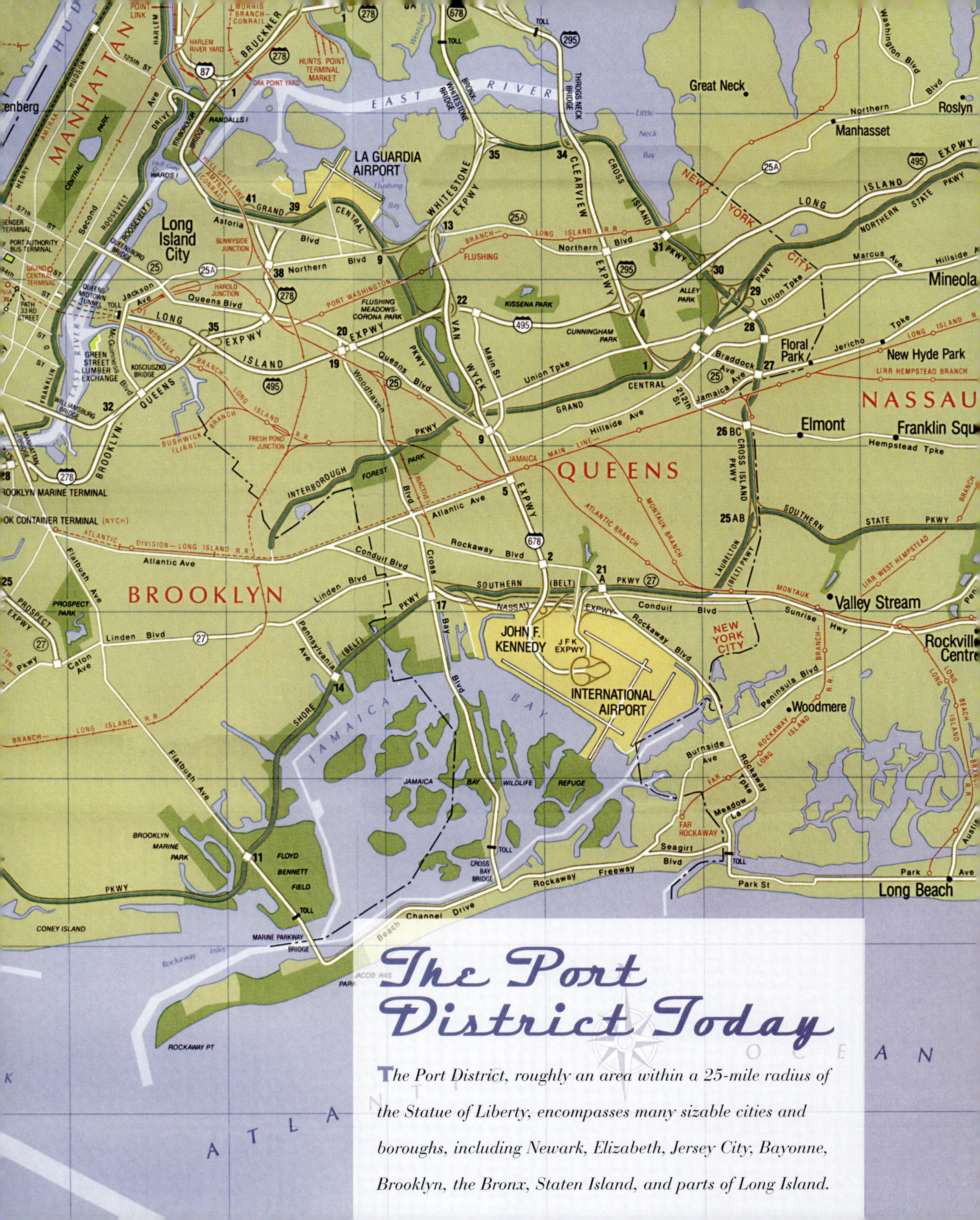

The Port District Today

The Port District, roughly an area within a 25-mile radius of the Statue of Liberty, encompasses many sizable cities and boroughs, including Newark, Elizabeth, Jersey City, Bayonne, Brooklyn, the Bronx, Staten Island, and parts of Long Island.

The Tempo of the '20s

LOCATED NEAR THE ENTRANCE TO NEW YORK HARBOR, THE OUTERBRIDGE CROSSING CONNECTS PERTH AMBOY, NEW JERSEY, AND TOTTENVILLE, STATEN ISLAND. IT IS THE OUTERMOST CROSSING IN THE PORT DISTRICT, BUT THAT'S NOT WHY IT'S CALLED WHAT IT IS. THE BRIDGE WAS NAMED AFTER EUGENIUS H. OUTERBRIDGE, FIRST CHAIRMAN OF THE PORT AUTHORITY.

The Port Authority was born in an exciting decade that redefined and enhanced virtually every element of urban and suburban life, just as the agency's own facilities would revolutionize commuting between Gotham and its bedroom communities. Often portrayed as a decade of good fortune and good times in America, the 1920s was actually a blessed reprieve between the Great War and the Great Depression. America was poised for prosperity by 1921, the year the Port Authority was formed. The new agency's founders and employees lived in an era when whole tracts of landscape would be transformed, reconfigured, urbanized, and paved at a pace never witnessed before.

The 1920s was one of those rare periods when everything seemed to accelerate, thrusting society forward into a spectacular renaissance. Rising out of the ashes of war and a deadly medical plague, the Spanish Flu (which claimed more lives than the war itself), a golden era was about to emerge.

Factories applied the growing technologies of mass production, used so effectively during the war, to make countless domestic products, all designed to woo consumers with a growing taste for things modern. And a whole new service industry—advertising—blossomed around the concept of capturing target markets.

Radio provided the means to reach vast audiences. The simple crystal sets of the early '20s evolved into powerful receivers with mysterious glowing vacuum tubes, devices capable of driving loudspeakers and pulling in stations from many miles away. By the end of the decade the radio audience grew from a few hundred hobbyists to millions of listeners, making it possible even for farmers in the most remote stretches of the Northeast to tune into the latest news and entertainment from New York City.

Entertainment in the New York area was unbelievably diverse, a rich composite of vaudeville, film, opera, jazz, burlesque, sports, and multicultural art forms—all drawing audiences morning, noon, and night. The city's attractions pulled in crowds from far and near. The Great White Way of Broadway and its dazzling lights suggested a constellation of stars, and stars there were. Rudolph Valentino literally made women swoon in his signature role as *The Sheik*. Swashbuckling Douglas Fairbanks, star of *The Thief of Baghdad*, married America's sweetheart, Mary Pickford. Charlie Chaplin waddled across the flickering screen as the ever-lovable Tramp, and *Tarzan of the Apes* opened with live animals on stage. In 1922, *Toll of the Sea* debuted as the first Technicolor movie ever made, but the process was too expensive to be commercially practical.

DOUGLAS FAIRBANKS IN *THE THIEF OF BAGHDAD.*

Fabulous movie palaces like the Roxy, with marble staircases, rococo gilt, lavishly painted murals, plush velvet seats, thick carpets, and huge mirrors, gradually made way for the equally striking, if somewhat simpler, art deco theaters like Radio City. Harlem underwent a renaissance, also capitalizing on the relative prosperity of the decade. Jazz poured out of hundreds of new hot spots like the Cotton Club and Connie's Inn, attracting the downtown crowd with their gowns and tiaras, tuxes and top hats.

Babe Ruth, New York's own superstar, hit an incredible 59 home runs in 1921, the year that Westinghouse broadcast the first play-by-play coverage of the World Series. In 1923, Yankee Stadium, "the house that Ruth built," opened to accommodate the growing crowds of increasingly avid baseball fans.

Another Ruth was also loved in 1921—the new Baby Ruth candy bar. It was joined that year by the introductions of Mounds Bars, Wise Potato Chips, Band-Aid adhesive bandages, and the much admired (though fictitious) Betty Crocker. New products were sprouting up everywhere, with an emphasis on design, technology, and glamour. What household could exist without a sleek Electrolux, the first canister vacuum cleaner introduced in the United States? What woman could resist Chanel No. 5, with its promise of French cachet and romance? These were just a few of the many new products that debuted in 1921 and found their way into the country via the Port of New York. During the decade, a taste for things imported, particularly from Europe, held great allure to Americans.

IMMIGRANTS FLOWED THROUGH ELLIS ISLAND TO FIND A BETTER LIFE, MANY SETTLING IMMEDIATELY IN THE NEW YORK–NEW JERSEY REGION.

European immigants poured through Ellis Island, and frequently settled in the immediate New York–New Jersey area. Even if the streets weren't truly "paved with gold," war-weary Europeans eyed American cities as safer havens—and places where class was not destined by bloodlines. Situated between two great oceans and sharing just two borders with friendly nations, the United States was well insulated against the madness of conquest and tyranny endured on many other continents.

Immigrants provided a much needed workforce to build an entrepreneurial economy in a nation that was growing rapidly. A postwar recession in 1921, however, created stiff competition for jobs. Housing and services were severely taxed by the sudden surge in population. These factors inspired the Emergency Quota Act of 1921, which limited the number of immigrants who could enter the country.

The United States had become a world power, and a center of commerce, finance, agriculture, and industry that equaled or eclipsed most nations. Most of those activities were anchored or headquartered in the New York area, an economic concentration that fostered developments in the arts, education, and science. New York had become a major intellectual and commercial center—a world capital.

Manhattan's exuberance stretched skyward. No longer content to be just one of the world's big cities, New York sought to be the tallest, the biggest, the snazziest—the place to be. As an island, Manhattan had to build upward, not outward, to maximize the use of extremely expensive real estate. The Woolworth Building ruled the skies in 1921, a Gothic confection some 60 stories tall—a "cathedral of commerce" built for cash, without a cent of external financing. It was just one of several one-time tallest buildings that Manhattan had been sprouting like trees since the turn of the century.

By the end of the decade, the Bank of Manhattan Building at 40 Wall Street and the Chrysler Building in midtown vied for the "world's tallest" record, but each would hold the title only briefly. The Empire State Building was already laying its foundation for 110 stories—nearly twice as tall as the Woolworth. Included in the plan was a rooftop mast for mooring zeppelins, which, although ingenious, proved impractical due to high winds and the possibility of lightning strikes.

Commercial flight was still in its infancy, but ready to take off. The competition between Manhattan's incredible spires manifested the philosophy of the '20s—the sky is the limit.

Henry Ford had proved the concept of mass production by so efficiently making standardized parts that his company could produce a Model T automobile that the average consumer could afford. The Model T provided sturdy transportation that could handle the worst roads, be fixed with basic tools and a little determination, and even be converted to other uses, such as churning butter. Although 62 percent of the cars on the road in 1921 were Tin Lizzies, dozens of new automakers were selling Franklins, Moons, Maxwells, and Pierce Arrows, cars of higher quality targeted for the newly affluent. All of these cars created a huge demand for improved roads, bridges, and tunnels, which would reconfigure every city in the country, especially New York. America was on wheels, and there was no turning back.

THE FASHIONABLE FLAPPER BROKE ALL THE MOLDS TO ASSERT A NEW INDEPENDENCE.

Ford's "factory model" of efficiency became a philosophy that even found its way into the schools, where children were considered "end products." It now seemed that everything could be standardized, simplified, and rationalized. By the end of the decade, even art, fashion, and architecture embodied the ideal of mechanical perfection. The streamlined look, the geometrics of art deco design, the sleek surfaces of modernist sculptures, the uniform tones of lithographed art—all found an eager market that was moving away from the ornate toward the dictum "form follows function."

Women won the right to vote in 1920, and by 1921 they could serve on juries in 20 states. Although only 8 million women held jobs at the beginning of the decade (with more than half working as teachers and nurses), as the decade unfolded women started to outnumber men as secretaries, typists, and clerical workers in many offices, including those of the Port Authority. World War I had profoundly, although temporarily, altered the status of women. Females began to be hired in such traditionally male industries as munitions and metalworking. The number of female railroad workers had tripled by the 1920s, and in many cities women even worked as streetcar conductors.

Asserting their newfound independence, "flappers," with their rolled-down stockings, rising hemlines, and helmet-inspired cloche hats, thumbed their noses at the traditional mores and began to frequent speakeasies, as Prohibition took hold. Even fashionable women were seen drinking and smoking in public for the first time—a shocking display often vilified in the press.

The twenties did have a dark side as well. Under Prohibition, organized crime became big business, fueled by the vast profits made from the sale of illegal liquor. Criminal gangs, prostitution, loansharking, and labor racketeering took hold, and corrupt politicians and police officers were bought off wholesale. Gangsters like Al Capone became national celebrities.

On a lighter note, the 1920s were famous for a staggering number of fads. People played mah-jongg, and contract bridge was all the rage. Pie-eating contests, dance marathons, rocking-chair derbies, and cross-country car races were rampant. Shipwreck Kelly became famous for sitting on a flagpole for 559 hours.

PROHIBITION SEEMED LIKE A GOOD WAY TO STEM ALCOHOLISM, BUT IT SPAWNED A NEW PROBLEM—ORGANIZED CRIME.

The eccentric was also expressed in art, or rather anti-art. Based on the futility of life—a likely theme to come out of devastated postwar Europe—Dadaism inspired art exhibits that used broken windows, urinals, pigs in uniforms, and surrealistic incongruities to provoke emotions ranging from laughter to outrage. The Rorschach inkblot test, which presumed to assess the sanity of a world "gone mad," was well-timed with its introduction in 1921.

What really made the '20s different from any previous decade was the birth of mass culture. Radio, newspapers, glossy magazines, and movies brought Americans together in new and exciting ways. In 1921, Americans huddled around their radios as the 29th president, Warren G. Harding, announced in a live broadcast from the Tomb of the Unknown Soldier at Arlington National Cemetery that Armistice Day would become a national holiday. The first sports event to be broadcast, a boxing match, was aired that same year. Radio's first bandleader, Vincent Lopez, began his 1921 broadcast from New York City's Hotel Taft with "Lopez speaking..." And Americans listened again and again to the hit parade's number 1 song, "Second Hand Rose."

Mohawks in High Steel

A building boom that had been gaining momentum since the turn of the century reached its zenith in the 1920s. The bridges and skyscrapers under construction called for a new kind of worker, one who was, among other things, comfortable with heights. Among the most colorful of the bridge builders were the dozens of Mohawks from the Caughnawaga Reservation in Canada. They were profiled by Joseph Mitchell in the 1949 New Yorker *article "The Mohawks in High Steel." Mitchell described how the Mohawks came to specialize in what many called the most dangerous work in all construction, and the highest paid: "Men who want to do it are rare, and men who can do it are even rarer, and in good construction years there are sometimes not enough to go around." Working in four-man riveting teams, the Mohawks were among the hundreds of ethnic groups who came from points far and near to build the Port Authority bridges as well as other great public works.*

Telephones had been around for decades but did not become household fixtures until the '20s, when more and more families could afford them. You jiggled the handle on a standard stick phone and asked the operator to dial a three- to six-digit number for you—an indication of how few people had service. In small towns you could even ask for people by name—the operator knew all the residents. Though first tested in 1921, the dial telephone would not become widely available for many years.

Also in the '20s, traffic congestion became a real headache in the New York region, especially for drivers crossing the Hudson. Imagine the line of cars and trucks waiting to roll up the ramp to board a ferry. Most commuters parked their cars, took a ferry on foot, then relied on public transportation to reach their destinations on the other side of the river. The Hudson was choked with traffic, the Hudson & Manhattan Tubes packed with passengers, and local subways and trolleys were compared to sardine cans. A great outcry arose from hundreds of thousands of New Jersey commuters, who demanded a better way to get their vehicles to and from Manhattan. Bridges and tunnels needed to be built to unify two great states and their resources. This public challenge was promptly taken up during the '20s by the Port Authority, which would change the landscape of the New York region forever.

EUGENIUS H. OUTERBRIDGE, FIRST CHAIRMAN OF THE PORT AUTHORITY, WAS AN HONORED GUEST AT THE DEDICATION OF "HIS" BRIDGE ON JUNE 20, 1928. THE OUTERBRIDGE CROSSING OPENED TO TRAFFIC NINE DAYS LATER.

THE PORT AUTHORITY'S FIRST YEARS

The newly formed Port of New York Authority had to contend with a transportation industry dominated by privately run railroads. The fiercely entrepreneurial railroad moguls were not the type of men who would easily bow down to a governmental authority, so the agency's first few years were frequently dogged by frustration and failure.

The new Authority's first job was to develop a rational plan that would not only be approved by the public and the two states but also be accepted by the railroads. Owned privately and operated competitively, the 12 railroads serving the New York area had developed their terminal facilities without any coordinated regional plan in mind. After eight months of effort, under the leadership of Chairman Eugenius H. Outerbridge, the Port of New York Authority introduced its "Comprehensive Plan" in 1922. It was designed to remedy the problems of congestion and duplicated efforts that were the by-products of private-sector competition, the same selfish concerns that had threatened to split the port just a few years before.

A TOLL PLAZA AT THE OUTERBRIDGE CROSSING.

The plan proposed new rail lines, terminals, and feeder highways, as well as a tunnel between Jersey City and Brooklyn for the common use of all rail carriers. The document revealed the kinds of efficiencies that could be wrought with a little coordination and cooperation. But it also showed what can happen when an organization designed to bring about those noble goals is not given the power of enforcement. The Authority could not compel the railroads to cooperate, and their mutual mistrust killed the plan. The railroads and the Port Authority did, however, agree on the establishment of inland freight stations that would eliminate the duplication of each railroad having its own facility. Each railroad would transport cargo from the wharves to a central location, where truckers could deliver the goods to their ultimate destinations.

Trucks and automobiles rapidly eclipsed the rail stronghold on both cargo and passenger traffic. Recognizing this trend, in 1924 New York and New Jersey authorized the Port Authority to build its first two facilities—the Goethals Bridge and the Outerbridge Crossing, both spanning the Arthur Kill that separates New Jersey from Staten Island. The two bridges opened in 1928. The George Washington Bridge—then the world's longest and largest span—and the Bayonne Bridge opened three years later. All four bridges were completed ahead of schedule and within budget, a major coup for the agency that increased public confidence in its ability to get things done.

The First P.A. Police

On June 1, 1928, 40 young men signed up to become the original Port Authority Police Force. Screened from some 200 applicants, they were quickly trained to operate toll booths and fulfill many other functions at the Outerbridge Crossing and Goethals Bridge, which were scheduled to open only four weeks later.

Thirty-one of the new recruits were dubbed "PA Bridgemen" and nine were called "Bridgemasters," until 1935, when the titles were officially changed to Police Officer and Sergeant. A Bridgeman's starting salary was $2,200 a year for a standard 48-hour work week.

Having had no police experience, the 40 original recruits were placed in an intensive training program. The Port Authority, as well as consultants from the U.S. Army, the Red Cross, and local police departments created a crash program that would have the young men on the job just in time for the grand opening of both bridges at 5:00 A.M., June 29, 1928. Instruction included police methods, traffic control, first aid, fire-fighting techniques, and toll-collecting skills. The new P.A. officers held police authority in both New York and New Jersey.

THE FIRST CONSTRUCTIONS: THE STATEN ISLAND BRIDGES

When asked years later why the Port Authority began with the Outerbridge Crossing and the Goethals Bridge, instead of the Bayonne and George Washington Bridges, general counsel Julius Henry Cohen replied, "We wanted to begin with something where we were most likely to succeed, and the smaller enterprise was the better one for the purpose. If we succeeded, the George Washington Bridge would surely come later. And so it did." This was the turning point in the organization's history, when it was proven that a bistate public authority with no taxing power could actually accomplish a great deal.

UNDER THE OUTERBRIDGE CROSSING LOOKING ACROSS THE WATER TO NEW JERSEY THROUGH AN ARCHWAY OF BRIDGE SUPPORT PIERS.

STAGES OF CONSTRUCTION OF THE OUTERBRIDGE CROSSING.

DESIGNED BY JOHN ALEXANDER WADDELL, THE OUTERBRIDGE CROSSING IS ALMOST A TWIN TO THE SHORTER GOETHALS BRIDGE. THE STEEL-TRUSS CANTILEVER BRIDGES, SUPPORTED BY CONCRETE PIERS, SPAN THE HEAVILY TRAVELED SHIP CHANNEL OF THE ARTHUR KILL. A 135-FOOT CLEARANCE PERMITS TALL VESSELS TO SAIL UNDER EACH BRIDGE.

THE GOETHALS BRIDGE LOOKING WEST TO ELIZABETH, NEW JERSEY, FROM STATEN ISLAND. BOTH THE OUTERBRIDGE CROSSING AND THE GOETHALS BRIDGE WERE DEDICATED ON JUNE 20, 1928.

THE GOETHALS BRIDGE IS NAMED IN HONOR OF MAJOR GENERAL GEORGE W. GOETHALS, BUILDER OF THE PANAMA CANAL AND THE FIRST CONSULTING ENGINEER OF THE PORT AUTHORITY. THE BRIDGE CONNECTS ELIZABETH, NEW JERSEY, WITH HOWLAND HOOK, STATEN ISLAND.

Raising Billions

"Unless we could raise money—real money, the Port of New York Authority's future is bleak," Julius Henry Cohen wrote in his memoirs. "We needed millions of dollars. Hundreds of millions."

The hundreds of millions—the billions—were raised through the sale of municipal bonds. "The Port Authority would have achieved precisely nothing if we had not been able to sell Port Authority bonds to the public," observed Cohen.

Before it could succeed in the bond market, however, the Authority had to establish its credit. At first it did so with the help of state advances, with both New York and New Jersey lending the Authority 25 percent of the cost of its first two projects, the Outerbridge Crossing and the Goethals Bridge, while agreeing to take a junior lien on their revenues. The Port Authority sold its first 20-year bond issue in 1926. The same approach was used for the bonds issued for the construction of the Bayonne and George Washington Bridges. Each bond issue was backed solely by the toll revenues generated by a project.

Meanwhile, the Holland Tunnel, completed in 1927 under the auspices of the New York State Bridge and Tunnel Commission, and the New Jersey Interstate Bridge and Tunnel Commission, opened for business to notable success. Revenues were running 50 percent higher than projected during its first year of operation, and the tunnel began generating surpluses. Both commissions recommended in 1929 that New York and New Jersey begin work on as many as four more trans-Hudson tunnels, to be financed by the Holland Tunnel's millions in surpluses and cash advances by the states.

The Port Authority suggested that it be allowed to build a new trans-Hudson tunnel and that all interstate crossings be unified under a single agency that would standardize tolls. It also recommended that it be allowed to refinance the Holland Tunnel with a new bond issue, repay the states, and sell more bonds to raise money for the new tunnel. The bonds would be backed not only by anticipated toll revenues from the new Lincoln Tunnel, but also by a general reserve fund comprising all surplus toll revenues. The New York and New Jersey legislatures approved the plan in 1931.

The Holland Tunnel commissions thus merged with the Port of New York Authority, and the first version of the consolidated revenue bond was born, with "excess earnings from paying projects used to secure marginal facilities," as the New York Times *explained in 1952, when the Authority created a revenue bond backed by the net revenues of all of its facilities.*

No agency has more stoutly defended tax exemption of bond issues than the Port Authority. In 1938, the U.S. Supreme Court ruled that state and municipal salaries could be taxed. The Port Authority realized that this decision could be used as a springboard for taxing state and municipal bond interest as well as the revenues of state and municipal agencies. The Authority fought such a trend by forming the Conference on State Defense, an organization of state and municipal officials from throughout the country.

Arrayed against the municipal tax exemption were the Roosevelt Administration, many financial and legal interests, and the public. The arguments against the tax exemption ranged from it being an inefficient subsidy and a drag on the U.S. Treasury to it being a tax shelter for the very rich. The Port Authority and its allies argued that tax exemption saves municipalities money when they go to the market and sell bonds to raise funds. If, for example, the Port Authority sells bonds with an interest rate of 6 percent, comparable corporate bonds would pay from 7 to 9 percent.

The federal government tested its case against tax exemption for municipalities in a lawsuit, which was ultimately decided in favor of allowing tax exemption for municipal bonds. In 1944, the Circuit Court of Appeals affirmed this Tax Court ruling, and, a year later, the Supreme Court declined to review the case, thus affirming the Court of Appeals decision. Within 48 hours of the Supreme Court action, the Port Authority's 2 percent bonds "made the most sensational advance" in the market, according to The Bond Buyer. *"Municipal bond buyers feel that the threat of taxation is now pretty completely removed," the paper stated. Additional attacks on municipal tax exemption were waged in the 1950s and 1960s, and the Port Authority and the Conference on State Defense opposed every one.*

The Bubble Bursts

THE GREAT DEPRESSION

INSTALLING THE FOOTBRIDGE SECTIONS FROM THE NEW YORK SIDE OF THE GEORGE WASHINGTON BRIDGE.

While the golden era that followed World War I had been a welcome renaissance, the Great Depression that followed the boom of the '20s came as a complete shock. The New York region had been flying high during the 1920s, but the stock-market crash of 1929 brought on widespread calamity.

New York and its surrounding communities were still flush with the accomplishments of an economy that seemed irrepressible. Staffed by doormen, bellboys, and domestics, the swank apartment houses lining Fifth Avenue, Park Avenue, and Central Park were imitated on a smaller scale in the best neighborhoods of the outer boroughs. The elite areas were serviced by equally swank department stores and stylish specialty shops, their windows aglow with gems, furs, and the latest fashions.

Many families were overextended financially and paying huge interest payments on a house, a car, furniture, and household appliances, now considered necessities for the middle class. Consumers often held stock and bond portfolios, which made saving in a low-interest bank account seem foolish. Even those who did stash money in bank accounts, however, were about to learn that banks can also collapse when their investments turn sour. The run on the banks forced many financial institutions to bolt their doors to prevent rioting.

Companies accustomed to gearing up for the growing demand for their products were also overextended. When the Depression struck and the demand suddenly stopped, they were unable to unload their bloated inventories of Packards, blue-mirrored coffee tables, and silk evening gowns. Investors were unable to meet margin calls before the market crashed, and they lost their stocks and bonds. The abrupt fall from luxury to poverty wasn't just on paper, however—a number of distraught Wall Streeters opened the windows of skyscrapers and leapt from their posh offices to the streets below.

BORIS KARLOFF AS FRANKENSTEIN'S MONSTER IN THE 1931 FILM. MOVIES WERE A WAY FOR PEOPLE TO ESCAPE DURING THE DEPRESSION.

It was hard to believe that the golden age was over, but the signs were everywhere. Companies failed to meet their payrolls, factory doors were locked, the unemployed formed breadlines at soup kitchens that fed the hungry. For most people, the loss of a job meant not only the inability to pay their bills, but repossession of the items bought on credit and forfeiture of the payments already made. "Brother, Can You Spare a Dime" became the theme song for an era when professionals could be found selling apples on street corners or even sleeping on park benches. Ritzy apartments, hotels, and office buildings turned on their lights to make empty rooms look occupied, and many offered a free month's rent to woo those who could still afford accommodations. With the boom gone bust, the flapper's knee-high hemline fell to ankle length, and the fabric became more durable and businesslike. Some lights on the Great White Way dimmed to a flicker. Legitimate theaters, which formerly found lines of people waiting to see a live show, were now mostly empty.

But to save their sanity, many people would scrape together 20 cents for a movie ticket—which bought two movies, some film shorts, a few cartoons, singalongs, and the chance to win a door prize. During the thirties, the silent screen got noisy, as talkies became all the rage. Fred Astaire met Ginger Rogers, and the miseries of the Great Depression could be forgotten for a while as the audience enjoyed the glittering sets, perky songs, and screwball plots. Laurel and Hardy and the Marx Brothers helped audiences laugh their problems away, and Boris Karloff helped scare them away as Frankenstein's monster. James Cagney became America's tough guy, Claudette Colbert its captivating Cleopatra, and Clark Gable its matinee idol. And everyone fell in love with Shirley Temple when she sang "The Good Ship Lollypop" in the film *Bright Eyes*.

THE 1939 NEW YORK WORLD'S FAIR HELD THE PROMISE OF A BRIGHTER FUTURE, WHEN TECHNOLOGY WOULD SOLVE VIRTUALLY EVERY PROBLEM WITH EASE.

By the mid-1930s the worst was over, but the economy was still limping along, a shadow of its former self. It took Franklin Delano Roosevelt's New Deal and the growing threat of World War II to snap the nation out of its downward spiral. The Works Progress Administration (WPA) was formed to sponsor public works and create thousands of jobs. By 1935 the bread lines and apple sellers had virtually disappeared. Bands were playing in the clubs again and new shows were opening on Broadway. Folks were going out, decked in the latest fashions, to take in the vaudeville shows and variety acts popping up again all over town.

At home, people's ears were glued to the radio, listening to Bing Crosby croon on the NBC Kraft Music Hall and Benny Goodman playing his mellow clarinet on NBC's *Let's Dance*. In 1938, Orson Welles pulled a theatrical Halloween prank by broadcasting *The War of the Worlds* in the format of a news broadcast. Many area listeners believed that the Martian invasion of Grovers Mill, New Jersey, was real. Thousands were terrified. Many even armed themselves, and some took flight from local cities.

In 1939, the New York World's Fair exhibited the dreams of a new dawn, in which technology would reshape life and make everything wonderful again. Better living through chemistry, electricity, appliances, television, helicopters, streamlined cars, glistening cities, and all the other visions of a glowing future stood in stark contrast to the rumblings of totalitarianism and the specter of war rising across the Atlantic.

BRIDGING THE DEPRESSION

By the end of 1931, the Port Authority had constructed four bridges. The Bayonne Bridge and the George Washington Bridge opened to rave reviews. But in the midst of the Great Depression toll revenues declined. A serious crimp in cash flow made rationalization necessary for efficiency, cost control, and maintaining what were now essential components to the region's economy. The Holland Tunnel was transferred to the Port Authority via a $50 million payment financed by bonds. This created for the first time a unified grouping of bistate vehicular crossings. Along with it, a prudent financial pool was also devised to ensure the agency's continued stability.

CONSTRUCTION OF THE BAYONNE BRIDGE, LEFT TO RIGHT ACROSS SPREAD:

THE STEEL ARCH STARTS ITS RISE.

THE ARCH SOARS UPWARD TO THE SKY.

THE LACY NETWORK OF STEEL IN THE 325-FOOT-HIGH ARCH OF THE BAYONNE BRIDGE AS SEEN FROM THE CENTER OF THE ROADWAY.

NEARING COMPLETION OF THE ERECTION OF THE ARCH.

THE BAYONNE BRIDGE

The Bayonne Bridge was acclaimed "the most beautiful structure of steel" by the American Institute of Steel Construction when it opened in 1931. Linking New Jersey with Staten Island, it had taken three years and $13 million to build. Designed by the great bridge builder Othmar H. Ammann, the Bayonne Bridge is one of the longest steel arch spans in the world. Several alternatives were considered before the design was chosen. Cantilever proved to be the most expensive and least attractive. Although a suspension bridge was estimated at a half-million dollars less, the arch design provided the rigidity needed to accommodate rapid transit lines. The demand for mass transit did not materialize along this route, however, so rail tracks were not added.

Despite the bridge's graceful and beckoning appearance, traffic across it remained sparse during its first 15 years. But when the St. George Ferry Terminal caught fire in 1946, commuters to Staten Island and New Jersey, many of whom did not even know the bridge existed, began using it. "Thank goodness the Bayonne Bridge was here," said many patrons.

THREE YEARS, ONE MONTH, AND 28 DAYS AFTER THE GROUNDBREAKING CEREMONIES OF SEPTEMBER 18, 1928, THE BAYONNE BRIDGE OPENED TO TRAFFIC. THE 1,675-FOOT SPAN LINKS BAYONNE, NEW JERSEY, AND PORT RICHMOND, STATEN ISLAND (IN VIEW). INCLUDING ITS APPROACHES, THE BRIDGE IS MORE THAN A MILE AND A HALF LONG. RISING 150 FEET ABOVE THE KILL VAN KULL, IT ALLOWS VESSELS CALLING AT PORT NEWARK AND ELIZABETH TO PASS EASILY UNDERNEATH.

OPENING CEREMONIES

DEDICATION DAY PARADE FOR THE BAYONNE BRIDGE IN PORT RICHMOND, STATEN ISLAND.

TRAFFIC ON THE BAYONNE BRIDGE THE DAY AFTER ITS DEDICATION.

U50217

DECLARED "THE MOST BEAUTIFUL STRUCTURE OF STEEL OF 1931" BY THE AMERICAN INSTITUTE OF STEEL CONSTRUCTION, THE BAYONNE BRIDGE IS NOW A NATIONAL HISTORIC CIVIL ENGINEERING LANDMARK. THE WORLD'S LONGEST STEEL ARCH, IT IS JUST 25 INCHES LONGER THAN ITS AUSTRALIAN COUNTERPART, THE SYDNEY HARBOR BRIDGE, WHICH WAS BUILT ABOUT THE SAME TIME.

GROUNDBREAKING AT FORT LEE, NEW JERSEY.

THE GEORGE WASHINGTON BRIDGE

The great Austrian-American bridge builder Gustave Lindenthal had a dream. He wanted to build an immense bridge that would span the Hudson River, and he was dead set on building it in midtown Manhattan. One of Lindenthal's employees, Othmar H. Ammann, disagreed with the plan to situate the bridge in a spot that would require expensive approaches in already congested midtown. The bridge was intended to connect rail lines from New Jersey to the terminals along Manhattan's waterfront. Ammann contended that such a bridge would be politically controversial and so expensive that it would never be built.

Bridge Spirit Lived in Roebling, New Jersey

IN A PICTURESQUE LITTLE TOWN IN NEW JERSEY LIVE A GROUP OF MEN WHO REMEMBER WHEN THERE WAS NO PIZZA SHOP NEXT TO THE GENERAL STORE, AND YOU COULD GET A SHAVE IN THE BARBERSHOP FOR 15 CENTS AND A HAIRCUT FOR A QUARTER. THEY REMEMBER WHEN A VISIT TO THE DOCTOR COST A DOLLAR, AND IF YOU WERE REALLY SICK YOU WENT BY HORSE AND WAGON TO THE HOSPITAL IN TRENTON. THAT WAS ALL BACK WHEN THESE SAME MEN WERE BUSY WORKING AT THE ROEBLING PLANT, MAKING WIRE ROPE FOR THE GEORGE WASHINGTON BRIDGE.

IN A 1991 INTERVIEW FOR THE PORT AUTHORITY'S EMPLOYEE NEWSLETTER, *THE DIARY*, 91-YEAR-OLD GEORGE LICHVARCIK SPOKE ABOUT HIS BUDDIES WHO SETTLED IN ROEBLING MANY DECADES AGO, SOME OF WHOM WERE GATHERED AT THE CIVIC CENTER THAT DAY. "EVERYONE HERE HAS A PERSONAL CONNECTION TO THE GWB," HE SAID. "IN 1931 THINGS WERE TOUGH BECAUSE OF THE DEPRESSION. I WAS PAID 50 CENTS AN HOUR, AND SUPPORTED A WIFE AND TWO CHILDREN. IT WAS LUCKY FOR US THAT BREAD WAS ONLY FIVE CENTS."

"SPEAKING OF BREAD," ADDED FORMER ROEBLING WORKER GEORGE LUYBER, "I STARTED WORKING IN A BAKESHOP WHEN I WAS 14. THEN I WENT TO THE MILL TO BE A BRIDGE WORKER AND MADE SOME REAL DOUGH. I WASN'T FORTUNATE ENOUGH TO GET A HIGH-SCHOOL DIPLOMA OR A COLLEGE DEGREE. BUT I AM PROUD TO SAY THAT I WENT TO SCHOOL AT NIGHT TO LEARN MECHANICAL DRAWING AND HOW TO READ BLUEPRINTS. AFTERWARDS, I BECAME A LAYOUT MAN IN THE METAL SHOP. I BUNDLED THE WIRES FOR THE CABLES."

ED REED SAID, "DURING THE TIME THE BRIDGE WAS BEING CONSTRUCTED, SOMEONE IN THE PLANT CHARTERED A BUS TO TAKE US TO SEE WHAT WAS GOING ON. THEY EVEN ARRANGED FOR SOME OF US TO GO TO THE TOP OF THE TOWER. IT WAS A TRIP I'LL NEVER FORGET—RIDING UP ON A GALVANIZED PAN WITH FOUR CABLES AT EACH END. EVERY NOW AND THEN MY HEART WOULD SKIP A BEAT AND I WOULD SAY A HAIL MARY."

JOHN HUDSON RECALLED, "THE MEN WHO MADE THE WIRES FOR THE GWB HAD A HARD TIME BECAUSE THERE WAS A LOT OF PIECEWORK INVOLVED AND VERY FEW CONVENIENCES. THE GOING WAS TOUGH, BUT ALL OF US PITCHED IN TO GET THE JOB DONE. SOME MEN PUT THEIR KIDS THROUGH COLLEGE WHILE THEY WORKED ON THE BRIDGE."

How to Weave a Great Bridge

THE "HUDSON RIVER BRIDGE," AS THE GEORGE WASHINGTON BRIDGE WAS CALLED IN THE EARLY DAYS, WAS TWICE THE LENGTH OF ANY EXISTING SPAN, AND IT REQUIRED AN INTRICATE SYSTEM OF ACCESS ROADS TO HANDLE LARGE VOLUMES OF TRAFFIC.

THE BRIDGE'S TWO STEEL TOWERS, EMBEDDED DEEP IN ROCK AND CONCRETE, SOAR SOME 600 FEET INTO THE SKY, EACH AS TALL AS SOME OF MANHATTAN'S GREAT SKYSCRAPERS. THEY CONTAIN MORE THAN 43,000 TONS OF STEEL. ROPE CABLES WERE STRUNG FROM ANCHORAGES ON EACH SHORE AND DRAPED IN AN ARC BETWEEN THE TOWERS, LIKE A GIANT SILVER BRAID. WHEN 36 OF THEM HAD BEEN PLACED, CATWALKS WERE ERECTED TO PROVIDE WALKING PLATFORMS.

CABLE SPINNING REQUIRED TWO SPINNING WHEELS ON EACH SIDE OF THE RIVER THAT TRAVELED BACK AND FORTH TO CREATE STRANDS ABOUT THE DIAMETER OF A PENCIL. THE STRANDS WERE SPUN INTO FOUR GREAT CABLES, EACH A YARD IN DIAMETER. STEEL SUSPENDER ROPES WERE THEN HUNG FROM THE CABLES, EACH CONTAINING SOME 107,000 MILES OF WIRE.

WITHIN THIS SILVER WEB, STEEL SECTIONS WERE PUT IN PLACE TO FORM THE ROADWAY, WHICH PROGRESSED FROM EACH SHORE UNTIL THE LAST SECTION JOINED THE OTHERS IN THE MIDDLE. FINALLY, THE CONCRETE WAS POURED, THE LANES WERE LAID DOWN, AND THE BRIDGE WAS PAINTED.

Ammann proposed that the bridge be built farther uptown, at 179th Street, where it could stretch to the top of the Palisades. His plan called for a bridge that would serve motor vehicles and light rail. The uptown location would cross the Hudson at a high point in Manhattan, which would provide clearance for ships. Ammann's bridge would be a much easier political sell because it would not require the approval of Manhattan's business leaders, who opposed a midtown bridge, nor would it be necessary to persuade a dozen railroads to use it.

Unable to convince Lindenthal to abandon his plan, Ammann struck out on his own. As the research by Jameson Doig of Princeton University has shown, Ammann joined forces with George Silzer, the new Governor of New Jersey, to devise a campaign that would demonstrate the merits of the proposed bridge for commuting, recreation, and trucking.

At the time, Port Authority officials were only mildly receptive to taking on motor vehicle projects, but because of the successful public campaign waged by Ammann and Silzer, by 1925 there was widespread support on both sides of the Hudson for the "Fort Lee Bridge." The agency at last agreed to take responsibility for building and running the bridge, and employed Ammann as bridge engineer.

THE GWB'S NECKLACE OF LIGHTS CASTS AN ENDLESS ARRAY OF REFLECTIONS ACROSS THE HUDSON.

CONSTRUCTION OF THE NEW YORK ANCHORAGE AND THE ERECTION OF THE NEW YORK AND NEW JERSEY PORTALS.

CLOCKWISE FROM TOP LEFT:

ERECTION OF THE UPPER PORTAL IN NEW YORK, WHICH DWARFS THE JEFFREY'S HOOK LIGHTHOUSE (AT LOWER RIGHT). THE BRIDGE'S STEEL TOWERS ARE LOCATED ON A ROCKY POINT OF LAND IN FORT WASHINGTON PARK ON THE NEW YORK SIDE AND ON BEDROCK 100 FEET BELOW HIGH WATER ON THE NEW JERSEY SIDE.

LINKING THE TOWERS BY CABLE.

THE NEW YORK ANCHORAGE.

CLOCKWISE FROM TOP LEFT:

A HIGH-WIRE PERFORMANCE.

SECURING THE CABLE STRANDS FROM THE ANCHORAGE.

LOOKING UP AT THE ANCHORAGE SADDLES. THE CABLES ARE EMBEDDED IN THE CONCRETE OF THE ANCHORAGE.

FLOOR STEEL BEING LAID OVER THE CABLE TUNNEL AREA.

BACKGROUND: THE ROADWAY IN PLACE, AWAITING SURFACING.

GOING UP!

ATOP THE TOWER, PREPARING TO ERECT THE FOOTBRIDGE.

THE FIRST FOOTBRIDGE STRAND IS HOISTED UP THE NEW YORK TOWER. NOTE THE CAR FLOAT (AT TOP) IN THE RIVER BELOW.

CAGES TRAVELING ALONG CABLES STRUNG BETWEEN THE TOWERS ENABLE WORKMEN TO CONSTRUCT FOOTBRIDGES WHICH ARE USED AS WORKING PLATFORMS TO LAY THE MAIN SPAN CABLE—A TWO-YEAR JOB.

BACKGROUND: WORKING AT THE CABLE STRAND SHOES.

CLOCKWISE FROM TOP LEFT:

AS THE VERTICAL CABLES ARE HUNG, STEEL BEAMS ARE FASTENED TO THEIR BOTTOMS AND THE CONCRETE ROADWAY IS POURED. TO BALANCE THE PULL ON THE TOWER, WORK IS DONE FROM BOTH ENDS.

NOT FOR THE FAINTHEARTED, THE FOOTBRIDGES NOW TRAVERSE THE RIVER.

BOUND BY STEEL AND CONCRETE, THE TWO SHORELINES ARE BRIDGED.

Othmar Herman Ammann, Master Bridge Builder

PORT AUTHORITY CHIEF ENGINEER OTHMAR H. AMMANN SPEAKS AT DEDICATION DAY CEREMONIES FOR THE BAYONNE BRIDGE IN BAYONNE, NEW JERSEY, ON NOVEMBER 14, 1931.

Othmar Herman Ammann was, in the words of the Encyclopedia of New York City, *"the unrivaled master of the American steel bridge." Born in Schaffhausen, Switzerland, in 1879, he studied architecture before deciding to become an engineer. Urged by one of his former professors to go to America, "where the engineer has greater freedom in applying individual ideas and where young men may be put in charge of work that, in Europe, would only be given to a much older generation," Ammann emigrated when he was 25. He later became an American citizen.*

Arriving in New York in the spring of 1904, he found a job with an engineering company and worked on several major bridges, including the Queensboro. He joined the firm of Gustave Lindenthal in 1912, and the Port of New York Authority 13 years later.

During a career that spanned six decades, Ammann worked on most of America's greatest bridges, including the George Washington Bridge, the Triborough, the Golden Gate, and the Verrazano Narrows, which he designed in his 80s. He also played a prominent role in the design of the Mackinac Bridge in Michigan and the Delaware Memorial Bridge in Wilmington, as well as the Walt Whitman Bridge in Philadelphia. His engineering credits also include some of the other important river crossings in New York and New Jersey, such as the Bronx Whitestone Bridge and the Throgs Neck Bridge. It might be said that Othmar Ammann defined how the modern American bridge should look.

Ammann was chief engineer of the Port Authority. After 14 years with the agency, he returned to private practice in 1939 at the age of 60. Seven years later, he and partner Charles S. Whitney started the international consulting firm of Ammann and Whitney, which built bridges, highways, coliseums, floating dry docks, and airport terminals around the world. The firm developed structures for Saarinen's beautiful "bird in flight" terminal for TWA at Kennedy International Airport.

In his late 70s, Ammann returned as a consultant when the Port Authority decided to put a lower deck on his beloved George Washington Bridge. He had contemplated this feature in his original design more than 30 years earlier. He supervised the delicate job of jacking up the bridge's two main towers to correct the effects of hanging the second deck—like hanging a second load of wash on a clothesline, as one aide described it. Eighty-three years old at the completion of the project, Ammann was honored by the unveiling of a bronze bust that is now located on the concourse of the George Washington Bridge Bus Station.

Interviewed by the Engineering News-Record *in 1958, Ammann explained that it was not good enough for a bridge to be functional. It must also be beautiful. "Economics and utility are not the engineer's only concerns," he said. "He must temper his practicality with esthetic sensitivity. His structures should please the eye. In fact, an engineer designing a bridge is justified in making a more expensive design for beauty's sake alone. After all, many people will have to look at the bridge for the rest of their lives. Few of us appreciate eyesores, even if we should save a little money by building them."*

Despite his accomplishments, Ammann was, from all accounts, a self-effacing man who did not like egotists. "People are meant to work together," he said. "Nobody wants to see a one-man show."

Ammann died in 1965 at the age of 86, a year after the opening of his final triumph, the Verrazano Narrows Bridge, the world's longest suspension bridge. His long life was not nearly long enough according to one admirer, who said, "It's a pity that we cannot live another hundred years, for then it is probable that he would have built a bridge across the ocean."

THE GEORGE WASHINGTON BRIDGE WELCOMED ITS FIRST PATRONS ON OCTOBER 25, 1931. THE BRIDGE WAS COMPLETED IN FOUR YEARS AND ONE MONTH—SIX MONTHS AHEAD OF SCHEDULE AND AT A COST BELOW THE ORIGINAL ESTIMATE.

DESIGNED BY OTHMAR H. AMMANN, THE BRIDGE SOARS FROM 178TH STREET IN UPPER MANHATTAN TO A PALISADES CLIFF IN FORT LEE, NEW JERSEY. THE BRIDGE WAS A DEPARTURE FROM THE STANDARD DESIGNS OF 1931—NO STIFFENING MEMBERS WERE USED. AMMANN CALCULATED THAT BECAUSE OF THE LENGTH OF THE SPAN—DOUBLE THAT OF ANY BRIDGE AT THE TIME—THE DEAD LOAD WOULD BE SO GREAT THAT IT WOULD MAKE THE CABLES RIGID ENOUGH TO WITHSTAND MOVING LOADS AND WIND PRESSURE.

ARCHITECT CASS GILBERT HAD INTENDED THAT THE BRIDGE'S TWO TOWERS BE SHEATHED IN GRANITE, BUT WITH THE ONSET OF THE DEPRESSION, DESIGNER AMMANN DECIDED TO LEAVE THE STEELWORK EXPOSED.

GOVERNOR FRANKLIN D. ROOSEVELT TAKES TIME OUT FROM HIS PRESIDENTIAL CAMPAIGN TO DEDICATE THE GEORGE WASHINGTON BRIDGE ON OCTOBER 24, 1931.

THE DESIGNERS CREATED A BRIDGE THAT COULD BE ENLARGED TO ACCOMMODATE THE NEEDS OF A GROWING REGION. THE ORIGINAL SIX LANES WERE EXPANDED TO EIGHT IN 1946, AND A LOWER LEVEL WAS ADDED IN 1962, CREATING THE WORLD'S FIRST 14-LANE SUSPENSION BRIDGE. TRAFFIC CONTINUED UNABATED DURING CONSTRUCTION OF THE LOWER LEVEL, WHICH TOOK ONE YEAR TO BUILD.

"THE GEORGE WASHINGTON BRIDGE OVER THE HUDSON IS THE MOST BEAUTIFUL BRIDGE IN THE WORLD. MADE OF CABLES AND STEEL BEAMS, IT GLEAMS IN THE SKY LIKE A REVERSED ARCH. IT IS BLESSED....IT IS PAINTED AN ALUMINUM COLOR AND, BETWEEN WATER AND SKY, YOU SEE NOTHING BUT THE BENT CORD SUPPORTED BY TWO STEEL TOWERS. WHEN YOUR CAR MOVES UP THE RAMP THE TWO TOWERS RISE SO HIGH THAT IT BRINGS YOU HAPPINESS; THEIR STRUCTURE IS SO PURE, SO RESOLUTE, SO REGULAR THAT HERE, FINALLY, STEEL ARCHITECTURE SEEMS TO LAUGH." LE CORBUSIER: *WHEN THE CATHEDRALS WERE WHITE*, REYNAL & HITCHCOCK, 1947.

THE WORLD'S LARGEST AMERICAN FLAG FLIES AT THE GEORGE WASHINGTON BRIDGE.

The Inspiring George Washington Bridge

A future president opened it to the public. A plane once landed on it. A pair of rare falcons live on it. Once, a baby chose to be born there, delivered into the arms of a cop named Jack Dempsey. The George Washington Bridge is a place where cable, steel, and sky provide a canvas for wonder. As it passes its 65th year, the GWB endures as a stunning national landmark. It remains a unique source of inspiration for artists, writers, and musicians who have been moved by its beauty.

World-famous American composer William Schuman wrote a symphony in 1950 that he named after the bridge. He said the crossing had an "almost human personality," and said he was inspired by the impressions the bridge gave him as he crossed it and observed it at different times of the day.

Two beloved children's books feature the George Washington Bridge as a benevolent and awesome character. The Little Red Lighthouse and the Great Gray Bridge *made famous the tiny lighthouse that stands in the shadow of the span on the New York side. Written in 1942 by Hildegarde Swift and Lynn Ward, the book is still a favorite among children.* Tar Beach, *by Faith Ringgold, is about a girl who sits on the flat roof of her apartment building and dreams of flying over the glittering necklace lights of the bridge. The Public Television program* Reading Rainbow *filmed a segment at the bridge in order to help* Tar Beach *come alive for young audiences.*

Even the U.S. Postal Service has seen fit to attest to the uniqueness of the bridge. On September 6, 1952, it issued a stamp to portray the advancements made in one branch of civil engineering—bridge building—over the past century. In the lower left-hand corner of the stamp is an 1852 wooden-covered bridge; dominating the center-right area is the George Washington Bridge. Above the artwork is the official badge of the American Society of Civil Engineers.

The building of the George Washington Bridge was the subject of a newsreel. The bridge made its film debut in the 1943 Barbara Stanwyck/Gary Cooper movie Ball of Fire. *The bridge was such a standout performer that it has had an active film career ever since.*

Unfortunately, no official record exists of all the movies—or other forms of artistic expression—that have shown the bridge in different interpretations. But bridge fans report that the GWB can be spotted in the following films: How to Marry a Millionaire, The Butcher's Wife, One Good Cop, The House on 92nd Street, Desperately Seeking Susan, The Sunshine Boys, Willie and Phil, Times Square, The French Connection, Manhattan, *and* The In-Laws.

Even though it may be impossible to find all of the people who have been inspired by the creation of master bridge-builder Othmar Ammann, his daughter, Dr. Margot Ammann, has felt the bridge's almost humanlike qualities. She once said, "I am the sister of the George Washington Bridge."

COMPLETION OF THE BRIDGE HAD A PROFOUND EFFECT ON THE DEVELOPMENT OF NORTHERN NEW JERSEY, LEADING TO DENSE SUBURBANIZATION AND THE INCREASED USE OF CARS AND BUSES INSTEAD OF RAILROADS, TROLLEYS, AND FERRIES.

THIS 1931 PHOTO SHOWS THE GERMAN NAVAL TRAINING SHIP COMMANDER COUNT VON LUCKNER AT ANCHOR IN THE SHADOW OF THE GEORGE WASHINGTON BRIDGE. THE SHIP WAS SEIZED FROM GERMANY DURING WORLD WAR II.

TUNNELS

Before the Holland Tunnel was built, vehicles crossed from New York to New Jersey via ferries, which carried 30 million vehicles each year. But the rapid growth of midtown Manhattan as a center of commerce meant that a crossing was needed that would bring commuters and trucks from New Jersey and points west into the urban core. Bridges are easier and cheaper to build than tunnels, so they are the most practical choice for unpopulated areas. However, they require considerable land because they must gradually descend from midriver heights to join local roads, which takes up space in local neighborhoods. Tunnels are the better choice for built-up areas, such as midtown Manhattan and Jersey City, the town across the river to which the contemplated crossing would connect. Also, the New York side of the river did not meet the 200-foot elevation required for a bridge, so a tunnel was the answer. The Port Authority convinced the legislatures that a new tunnel should be financed by floating an issue of agency bonds, and not by pledging the credit of the states. The agency was soon authorized to build the Lincoln Tunnel linking midtown Manhattan to Union City.

CANAL STREET BEFORE THE BUILDING OF THE HOLLAND TUNNEL.

THE HOLLAND TUNNEL

Tunnels under the Hudson River were nothing new when the New York and New Jersey tunnel commissions decided to build the Holland Tunnel in 1913. Both the Pennsylvania Railroad and the Hudson & Manhattan already had tubes linking New York and New Jersey. The vehicular Holland Tunnel, it should be noted, is almost twice the diameter of the H&M tube, which was built for train traffic.

What was new—and untested—was the effect of car and truck exhaust on vehicle occupants, especially when they were stopped inside the tunnel. The American can-do attitude prevailed, with experts from Yale University and the United States Bureau of Mines designing a system of ventilator fans and air shafts to keep the air in the tunnel fresh and clean for its entire length of 9,250 feet. The *New York Times* later observed, "The tunnel engineers designed an automatic ventilation system that produced purer air under the Hudson than was to be found on heavily traveled surface streets."

President Calvin Coolidge formally opened the Holland Tunnel from the presidential yacht *Mayflower*, at anchor in the Potomac, by pressing a gold-and-platinum telegraph key that turned on the electricity in the tubes. President Woodrow Wilson had used the same key in 1915 to open the Panama Canal.

GROUND WAS BROKEN FOR THE TUNNEL AT THE ERIE RAILROAD SITE. AT LEFT IS CLIFFORD HOLLAND, JOINED BY MR. BOOTH AND MR. FLINN OF BOOTH & FLINN, LTD., ONE OF THE CONSTRUCTION CONTRACTORS FOR THE PROJECT.

THE ORIGINAL IDEA WAS TO BUILD A BRIDGE BETWEEN NEW JERSEY AND NEW YORK, BUT DUE TO TOPOLOGICAL CONDITIONS OF THE SITE, THE COST OF A BRIDGE WAS PROHIBITIVE. THE TUNNEL COST $54 MILLION, FAR LESS THAN WHAT ENGINEERS ESTIMATED A BRIDGE AT THE SAME SPOT WOULD HAVE COST.

CHIEF ENGINEER CLIFFORD MILBURN HOLLAND DESIGNED THE TUNNEL THAT BEARS HIS NAME.

HOLING THROUGH THE NORTH TUNNEL BETWEEN NEW YORK AND NEW JERSEY. THESE TWO BROTHERS WERE FOREMEN OF THE "RIVAL" GANGS OF SANDHOGS WORKING THEIR WAY UNDER THE RIVER FROM OPPOSITE ENDS.

PREPARING TO SET OFF A FINAL BLAST TO "HOLE THROUGH" IN THE TUNNEL'S NORTH TUBE IN 1924.

BUILDING A TUNNEL

Building a tunnel was slow, hot, dismal work. It was sloppy, it was wet, and it was dangerous. The workers on the Holland and Lincoln tunnels followed an enormous, 240-ton hydraulically powered "shield" under the riverbed. It was pushed forward with a set of jacks like an enormous cookie cutter. A team of sandhogs followed the shield, removing mud, blasting rock, and bolting together a series of iron rings, which formed the lining of the tunnel. The rings were then caulked, filled with concrete, and tiled.

On a good day, the sandhogs progressed about 40 feet. On a bad day, they hardly moved at all. The dangers of tunnel building included cave-ins and explosions from the premature ignition of dynamite, floods, and fires. On occasion, the compressed air being used in the tunnel's lower reaches blew open weak spots in the roof, endangering any workers who happened to be in the vicinity of possible projection through the riverbed to the surface. And then there were the bends, that potentially lethal reaction which became well-understood by the time the Port Authority got into tunnel construction.

MIDDLE LEFT: CAULKING THE TUNNEL TO KEEP WATER FROM SEEPING IN BEFORE LAYING THE CONCRETE OVER THE IRON RINGS.

LEFT: THE INTERIOR OF THE HOLLAND TUNNEL BEFORE ADDING FINISHING MATERIALS TO COVER THE IRON RINGS.

WHO WERE THE SANDHOGS? ALTHOUGH THE TRADE UNIONS WERE DOMINATED BY IRISH-AMERICANS, MANY ITALIAN IMMIGRANTS ALSO WORKED IN TUNNEL CONSTRUCTION. THIS PHOTOGRAPH, TAKEN DURING THE BUILDING OF THE H&M TUNNEL, SHOWS SEVERAL AFRICAN-AMERICAN LABORERS AS WELL. THE SANDHOGS HAD AN EXPRESSION THAT SUMMED UP THE DANGER INVOLVED IN TUNNEL WORK: THINK TWICE. YOU ONLY LIVE ONCE.

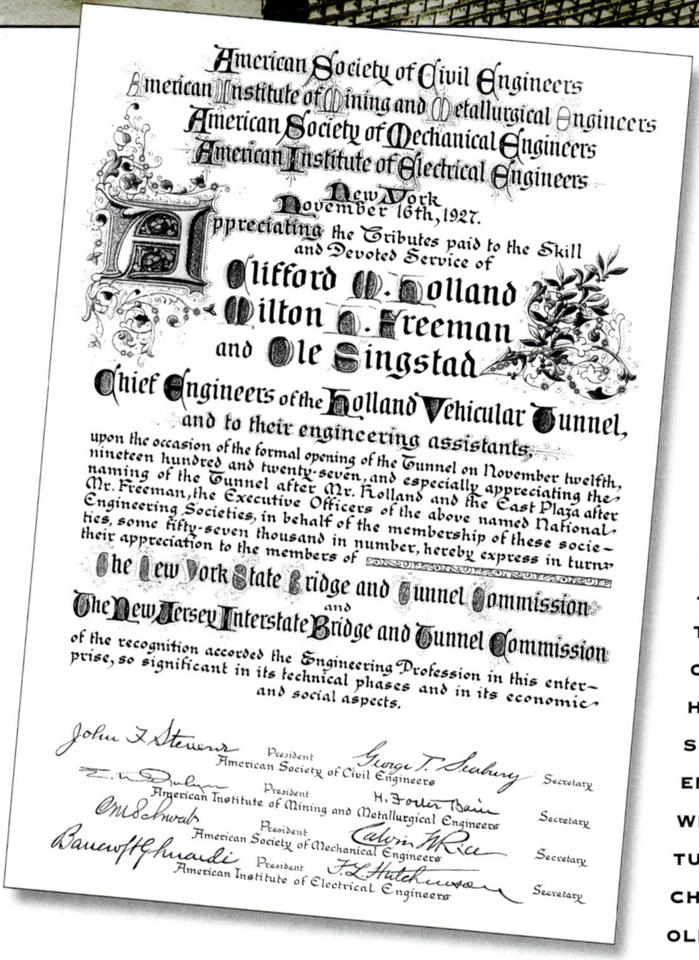

American Society of Civil Engineers
American Institute of Mining and Metallurgical Engineers
American Society of Mechanical Engineers
American Institute of Electrical Engineers

New York
November 16th, 1927.

Appreciating the Tributes paid to the Skill and Devoted Service of

Clifford M. Holland
Milton H. Freeman
and Ole Singstad

Chief Engineers of the Holland Vehicular Tunnel, and to their engineering assistants, upon the occasion of the formal opening of the Tunnel on November twelfth, nineteen hundred and twenty-seven, and especially appreciating the naming of the Tunnel after Mr. Holland and the East Plaza after Mr. Freeman, the Executive Officers of the above named National Engineering Societies, in behalf of the membership of these societies, some fifty-seven thousand in number, hereby express in turn their appreciation to the members of

The New York State Bridge and Tunnel Commission
and
The New Jersey Interstate Bridge and Tunnel Commission

of the recognition accorded the Engineering Profession in this enterprise, so significant in its technical phases and in its economic and social aspects.

John F. Stevens, President — George T. Seabury, Secretary
American Society of Civil Engineers

[illegible], President — H. Foster Bain, Secretary
American Institute of Mining and Metallurgical Engineers

C.M. Schwab, President — Calvin W. Rice, Secretary
American Society of Mechanical Engineers

Bancroft Gherardi, President — F.L. Hutchinson, Secretary
American Institute of Electrical Engineers

ABOVE: NEW YORK PLAZA ON DEDICATION DAY. CROWDS ASSEMBLE TO HEAR NEW JERSEY GOVERNOR A. HARRY MOORE'S SPEECH ON NOVEMBER 12, 1927. ON OPENING DAY 51,748 CARS PASSED THROUGH THE TUNNEL.

LEFT: A TRIBUTE TO THREE OF THE HOLLAND TUNNEL'S CHIEF ENGINEERS. CLIFFORD M. HOLLAND DIED JUST BEFORE THE "HOLING THROUGH" OF BOTH ENDS OF THE TUNNEL UNDER THE HUDSON RIVER. HE WAS SUCCEEDED BY CONSTRUCTION ENGINEER MILTON H. FREEMAN, WHO ALSO DIED BEFORE THE TUNNEL'S COMPLETION, AND CHIEF ENGINEER OF DESIGN OLE SINGSTAD. THE PLAZA ON THE NEW YORK END OF THE TUNNEL IS NAMED FREEMAN SQUARE IN HONOR OF FREEMAN. NORWEGIAN-BORN SINGSTAD FINISHED THE DAUNTING TASK AND WAS LARGELY RESPONSIBLE FOR DESIGNING THE VENTILATION SYSTEM.

TRAFFIC STREAMING INTO THE HOLLAND TUNNEL AT THE NEW YORK PLAZA IN 1931. AFTER THE TUNNEL WAS OPENED, MOTORISTS CAME FROM MANY MILES AWAY JUST TO DRIVE THROUGH, BRINGING ALONG CARLOADS OF PASSENGERS WHO REGARDED THE TRIP AS AN ADVENTURE.

GOVERNORS ALFRED E. SMITH OF NEW YORK (FIFTH FROM THE LEFT) AND A. HARRY MOORE OF NEW JERSEY (TO SMITH'S LEFT) WITH TUNNEL COMMISSIONERS AND OTHER OFFICIALS AT THE STATE-LINE MARKER.

BRIGADIER GENERAL GEORGE R. DYER, CHAIRMAN OF THE NEW YORK STATE BRIDGE AND TUNNEL COMMISSION, PAID THE FIRST TOLL AT MIDNIGHT ON NOVEMBER 12, 1927. HE IS SURROUNDED BY OTHER OFFICIALS. THE FIRST TOLLS WERE 25 CENTS FOR MOTORCYCLES, 50 CENTS FOR PASSENGER CARS, AMBULANCES, AND HEARSES, AND ONE DOLLAR FOR BUSES AND FOR TRUCKS BETWEEN FIVE AND 10 TONS.

Patrolling the Tunnel

When asked by the *Newark Star-Ledger* what police officers on patrol in Port Authority tunnels do to relieve the monotony, George A. Cole, who was on duty at the Holland Tunnel from 1927 to 1937, replied, "I memorized 'Casey at the Bat,' 'Dangerous Dan McGrew,' and enough other poems to give me a repertoire for an hour and forty-five minutes." The cops memorized speeches and played automobile license poker. Many counted license plates from different states—the most Cole ever saw in one day, he said, was thirty-two. And finally, there was singing. "Every tunnel cop sings—at the top of his voice," Cole said. "No one hears him, but it entertains him."

AN EMERGENCY VEHICLE AT THE HOLLAND TUNNEL, CIRCA 1928. HOLLAND TUNNEL PERSONNEL CONDUCTED PERIODIC FIRE AND DISASTER DRILLS TO PREPARE FOR EMERGENCIES.

CLEANING THE HOLLAND TUNNEL IN 1947. THE TUNNEL'S 4 MILLION CEILING TILES AND 3.1 MILLION WALL TILES ARE CLEANED IN STAGES WEEKLY.

ATTENDING THE MAY 17, 1934, GROUNDBREAKING PARTY FOR THE LINCOLN TUNNEL (THEN CALLED THE MIDTOWN HUDSON TUNNEL). ON THE NEW YORK SIDE WERE CHAIRMAN OF THE NEW YORK STATE BRIDGE AND TUNNEL COMMISSION GENERAL DYER, PORT AUTHORITY CHIEF ENGINEER AMMANN, NEW JERSEY GOVERNOR MOORE, AND NEW YORK CITY MAYOR LAGUARDIA.

THE LINCOLN TUNNEL

Soon after the Port Authority acquired the Holland Tunnel, New York and New Jersey authorized the agency to proceed with its plan to build what was then called the Midtown Hudson Tunnel. Creating a 1.5-mile-long structure, even above ground, would be no small accomplishment, but to build it under a river bed was a monumental task. Hundreds of huge iron rings, each weighing 21 tons, had to be assembled and bolted together on-site to form the lining of the tunnel.

The work of the sandhogs was dangerous, claustrophobic, and tedious. Just entering and exiting the tunnel took a long time. Crews entered air locks, one at a time, after which the doors at each end were sealed. An air pipe started hissing, and the mens' ears would pop as the air pressure climbed until it equaled that of the adjoining lock. The workers were then able to safely open the connecting door and crowd into the next section, where the entire ordeal would be repeated. Once at the forward end of the tunnel, the men had to work swiftly because they could handle the pressure only briefly. Compression and decompression had to be reached in safe, short increments.

Inside the tunnel, rock drills roared, tram cars rattled back and forth, and air lines hissed as the shields pushed the tunnel forward until it could be braced like the hull of a ship. In the din of construction, men bolted rings into place, poured cement behind the new lining to seal out the river, prepared for the next shove, and dynamited in front of the shield when the going got tough.

MANY UNDERWATER TUNNEL EXCAVATION TECHNIQUES, SUCH AS USING AIR LOCKS TO KEEP OUT THE WATER, WERE PIONEERED DURING THE BUILDING OF THE HUDSON & MANHATTAN RAILROAD TUBES IN THE LATE 19TH CENTURY. WORKING AMID COMPRESSED AIR CREATED BIZARRE CONDITIONS THAT ALTERED SOUNDS AND VOICES AND CAUSED CIGARETTES TO BURN AWAY IN SECONDS.

While one crew worked from the Jersey side, another proceeded toward them from the New York side. Alignment of both ends vertically and horizontally took considerable engineering skill and care. The first "hole through" was achieved on August 3, 1935, when a hydraulic engineer in the New Jersey end was pushed by his feet through an opening to meet the New York crew.

TUNNEL OPERATIONS IN WEEHAWKEN, NEW JERSEY, SHOWING THE FULL BORE OF THE TUNNEL LINING. THE BOLTING PLATFORM IN THE UPPER PORTION PROVIDED ACCESS TO THE BOLTS IN THE ARCH OF THE RING. THE CHUTE IN THE LEFT UPPER SECTION WAS USED TO DISPOSE OF MUCK TAKEN IN DURING A "SHOVE," WHEN A SECTION OF THE TUNNEL WAS PUSHED FORWARD. IN THE LEFT MIDDLE IS THE EMERGENCY GANGWAY.

POSITIONING AIR LOCKS WHERE THE CONCRETE BULKHEAD IS TO BE CONSTRUCTED, WEEHAWKEN.

SANDHOGS IN THE NEW YORK RIVER SHAFT CAISSON WELCOME THEIR COUNTERPARTS FROM THE SOUTH TUNNEL FROM NEW JERSEY, AS THEY EMERGE FROM THE 30-INCH "HOLING THROUGH" PIPE, THE FIRST CONNECTION BETWEEN THE TWO TUNNELING OPERATIONS.

BACKGROUND: INTERIOR OF THE LINCOLN TUNNEL'S NORTH TUBE STRUCTURAL STEEL SHELL AT WEEHAWKEN BEFORE BEING LINED WITH CONCRETE.

OPPOSITE PAGE, BOTTOM: LOOKING EAST FROM THE NEW YORK RIVER VENTILATION SHAFT. THE CONCRETE SIDEWALLS ARE IN PLACE. THE 8,216-FOOT-LONG TUBE WAS LINED WITH 18 INCHES OF CONCRETE BEFORE THE CEILING AND ROADWAY WERE BUILT. THE FINISHED CEILING CONSISTED OF 32 MILES OF CREAM-COLORED TILES, EACH SIX INCHES SQUARE AND STIPPLED TO ELIMINATE GLARE. SODIUM VAPOR LIGHTS, BRICK ROADWAYS, AND TWO OBELISKS TO STRADDLE THE TUNNEL'S ART DECO PORTALS AWAITED INSTALLATION.

ABOVE: LAYING FOUNDATIONS FOR THE ROADWAY.

LEFT: THE NEW JERSEY SHIELD DURING ASSEMBLY SHOWING THE FRONT OR CUTTING EDGE. NOTE THE STEEL CUTTING EDGE CASTINGS AND THE WORKING PLATFORMS.

LOOKING WEST OVER THE NEW YORK PLAZA EXCAVATION TO THE LOCATION OF THE PORTAL IN THE UPPER RIGHT CORNER OF THE CONSTRUCTION SITE.

BELOW: PROGRESS OF CONSTRUCTION OF THE NEW YORK PLAZA. THE PORTAL CAN NOW BE SEEN CLEARLY IN THE UPPER RIGHT.

THE WEEHAWKEN PORTAL SIX AND A HALF MONTHS BEFORE THE TUNNEL WAS TO OPEN.

NEW YORK GOVERNOR AVERELL HARRIMAN (RIGHT) AND NEW JERSEY GOVERNOR ROBERT MEYNER (SECOND FROM LEFT) TIGHTEN THE LAST BOLT IN THE FINAL RING OF THE $100 MILLION THIRD TUBE ON JUNE 28, 1956. PARTICIPATING WERE PORT AUTHORITY CHIEF ENGINEER JOHN KYLE (LEFT), WEEHAWKEN MAYOR CHARLES KRAUSE, AND PORT AUTHORITY CHAIRMAN DONALD LOWE.

Bridge and Tunnel Stat-facts

BAYONNE BRIDGE

OPENED TO TRAFFIC	NOV. 15, 1931
TOTAL LENGTH OF BRIDGE	5,780 FEET
WIDTH OF BRIDGE	85 FEET
COST OF ORIGINAL STRUCTURE	$13 MILLION

GEORGE WASHINGTON

OPENED TO TRAFFIC	OCT. 25, 1931
TOTAL LENGTH OF BRIDGE	4,760 FEET
WIDTH OF BRIDGE	119 FEET
COST OF ORIGINAL STRUCTURE	$59 MILLION

HOLLAND TUNNEL

OPENED TO TRAFFIC	NOV. 13, 1927
LENGTH OF TUNNEL	
NORTH TUBE	8,558 FEET
SOUTH TUBE	8,371 FEET
COST OF ORIGINAL STRUCTURE	$48 MILLION

LINCOLN TUNNEL

OPENED TO TRAFFIC	
CENTER TUBE	DEC. 22, 1937
NORTH TUBE	FEB. 1, 1945
SOUTH TUBE	MAY 25, 1957
LENGTH OF TUNNEL	
CENTER TUBE	8,216 FEET
NORTH TUBE	7,482 FEET
SOUTH TUBE	8,006 FEET
COST OF ORIGINAL STRUCTURE	$75 MILLION

NEW YORK RESIDENT OMERO CATAN WAS THE FIRST PERSON TO DRIVE HIS CAR THROUGH THE LINCOLN TUNNEL AND PAY THE TOLL AT THE NEW JERSEY TOLL BOOTH.

LEFT, ABOVE: OPENING DAY TRAFFIC ON THE NEW JERSEY SIDE. EXECUTIVE DIRECTOR AUSTIN TOBIN RECALLED, "WHEN THE TUNNEL OPENED ON DECEMBER 22, 1937, IT WAS SOMETHING LESS THAN A SMASH HIT. IN THE FIRST YEAR OF OPERATION, ONLY 1.8 MILLION WELL-SPACED VEHICLES USED THE FACILITY. WE USED TO BET A DIME ON WHETHER WE'D PASS ONE, TWO, OR THREE VEHICLES WHILE DRIVING THROUGH THE TUNNEL!"

LEFT, BELOW: BEFORE LONG, HOWEVER, TRAFFIC AT THE TUNNEL GREW, AND THOSE UNCROWDED DAYS BECAME A MEMORY. HERE MOTORISTS BOUND FOR NEW YORK CONVERGE AT THE WEEHAWKEN PLAZA.

WHEN THE NEW PORT AUTHORITY BUILDING OPENED IN 1932 AT 111 EIGHTH AVENUE AT 15TH STREET, IT WAS CALLED THE COMMERCE BUILDING AND WAS REPORTEDLY THE SECOND LARGEST BUILDING IN THE WORLD.

GOVERNOR FRANKLIN D. ROOSEVELT AT THE GROUNDBREAKING FOR THE PORT AUTHORITY BUILDING, APRIL 30, 1931.

THE PORT AUTHORITY BUILDING—111 EIGHTH AVENUE

Before its prestigious World Trade Center address, the Port Authority was headquartered in one of the most massive buildings on earth. The monumental structure at 111 Eighth Avenue, in the Chelsea District of Manhattan (not far from Greenwich Village), was once ranked the world's second-largest building in square footage.

Initially called the Commerce Building, the structure's fifteen floors were designed as an industrial building, which would also provide space for Port Authority offices and for the Union Inland Freight Station No. One on the ground floor and in the basement. The Port Authority had moved its headquarters from 80 Eighth Avenue into the Commerce Building in 1933, some months after it was completed. Before long the structure became known as the Port Authority Building, remaining the agency's home office until 1973, when it relocated to the World Trade Center.

The original Port Authority Building occupied an entire city block between Eighth and Ninth Avenues and 15th and 16th Streets in Manhattan.

WELL-DRESSED PEOPLE OUTSIDE THE MAIN ENTRANCE TO THE NEW PORT AUTHORITY CORPORATE HEADQUARTERS.

The corridor on the executive floor ran the length of the building, and you could barely see one end from the other. Commercial tenants, attracted by the range of shipping facilities housed in the building, included nationally known business and light-manufacturing firms. One longtime tenant, a manufacturer of aromatic oils and essences, filled the stairwells on the Ninth Avenue side with the most delightful fragrances.

Freight elevators that could accommodate trucks and trailers connected the upper floors with the ground-floor terminal. (In the truck loading bays on Port Authority floors, hard-fought lunch-time handball games were played by many, including a youthful Executive Director Austin J. Tobin.) In rooftop laboratories, Port Authority technicians tested construction and maintenance materials for resistance to the elements.

From its helicopter pad, Port Authority helicopters flew to the agency's numerous facilities, to state offices in Albany and Trenton, and even to Washington, D.C.

The Port Authority Building was beautifully maintained. At the two avenue entrances, embedded in the lobby floors, were three-foot bronze castings of the seal of the Port Authority. The seal also adorned the bronze door-knobs in Port Authority offices.

After the agency relocated its headquarters to the World Trade Center, the Port Authority Building was sold to private interests. But not before one of the bronze seals was removed from the entrance floor and transformed into a coffee table, a farewell gift from employees for the soon-to-retire executive director of thirty years.

NATTILY UNIFORMED STARTERS AND OPERATORS MANNED THE ELEVATORS AT THE NEW PORT AUTHORITY BUILDING.

The War Years: Rolling Up Our Sleeves

NEW YORK AND NEW JERSEY DURING WORLD WAR II

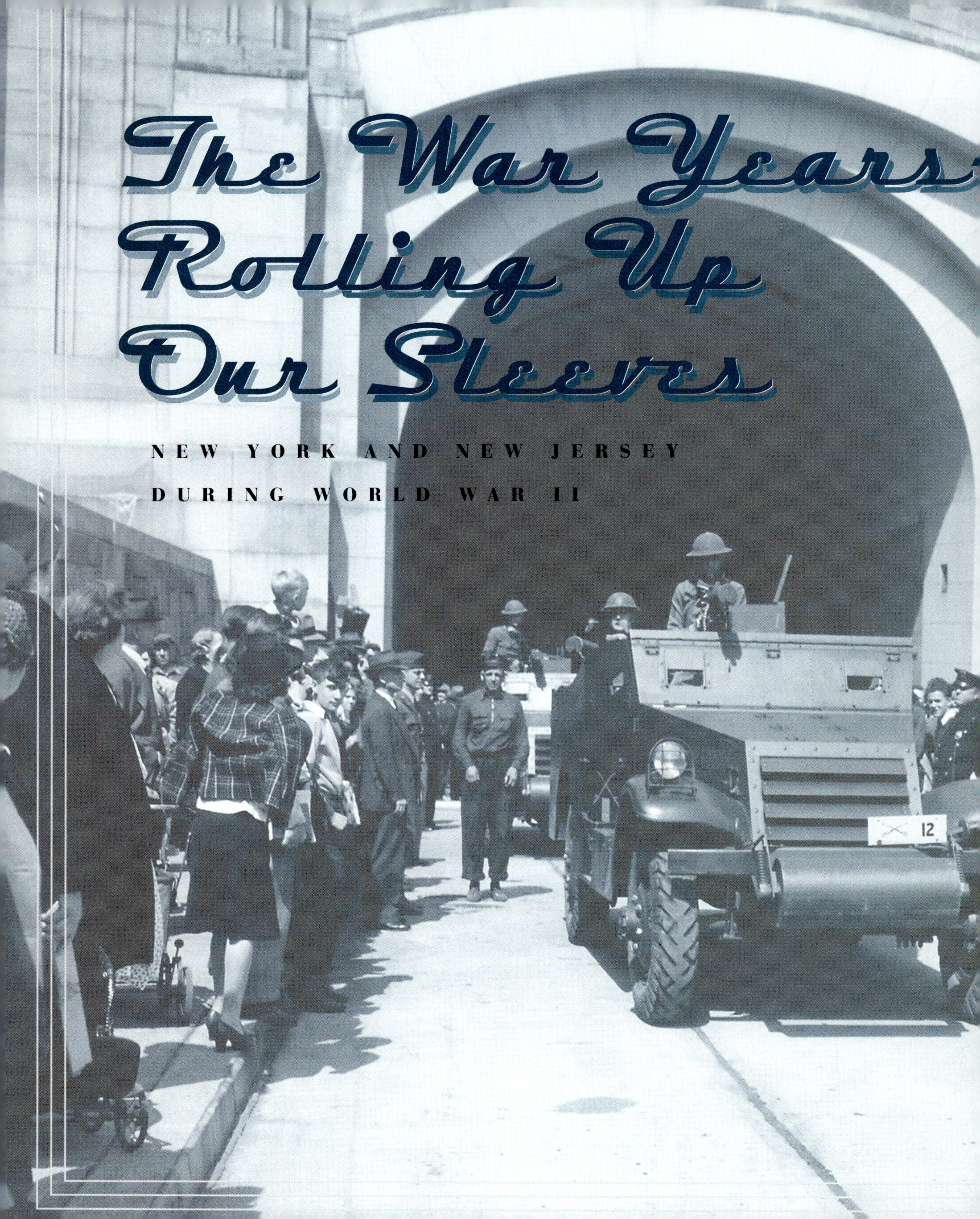

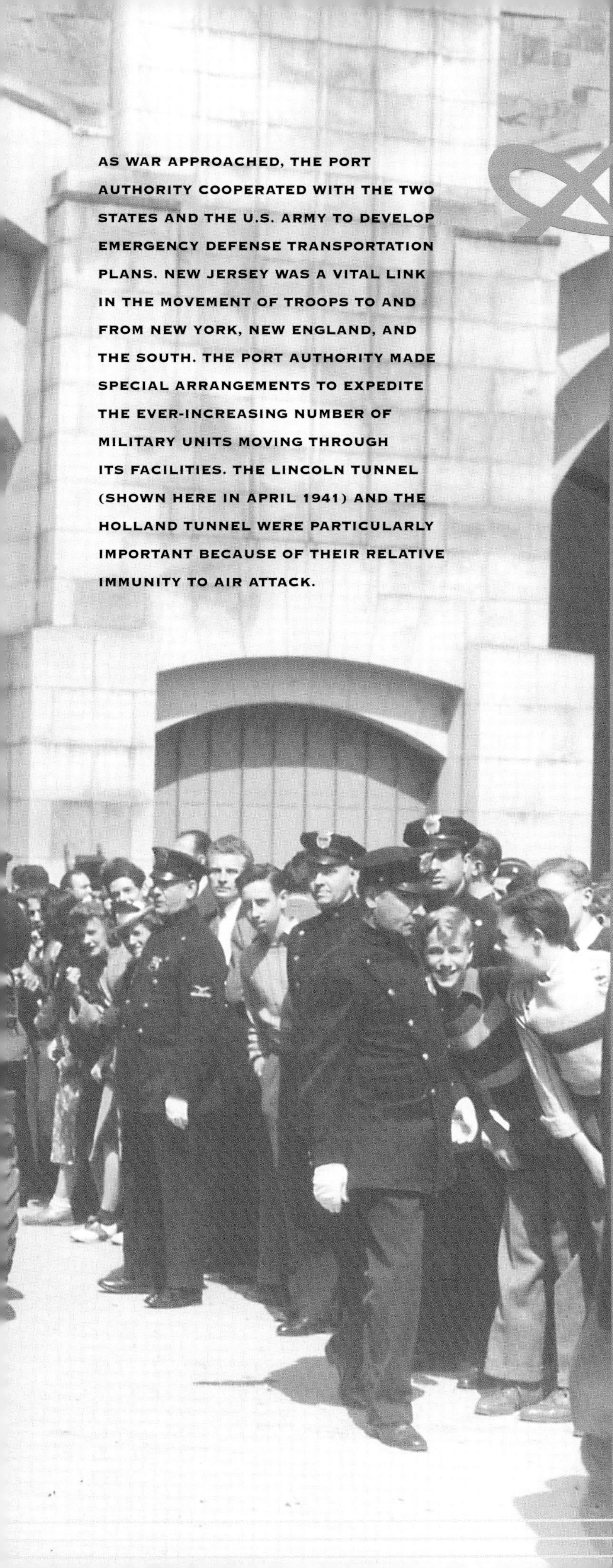

AS WAR APPROACHED, THE PORT AUTHORITY COOPERATED WITH THE TWO STATES AND THE U.S. ARMY TO DEVELOP EMERGENCY DEFENSE TRANSPORTATION PLANS. NEW JERSEY WAS A VITAL LINK IN THE MOVEMENT OF TROOPS TO AND FROM NEW YORK, NEW ENGLAND, AND THE SOUTH. THE PORT AUTHORITY MADE SPECIAL ARRANGEMENTS TO EXPEDITE THE EVER-INCREASING NUMBER OF MILITARY UNITS MOVING THROUGH ITS FACILITIES. THE LINCOLN TUNNEL (SHOWN HERE IN APRIL 1941) AND THE HOLLAND TUNNEL WERE PARTICULARLY IMPORTANT BECAUSE OF THEIR RELATIVE IMMUNITY TO AIR ATTACK.

As the futuristic 1939 World's Fair sputtered to a close, many Americans would have preferred to simply ignore the war raging in Europe. But the country's isolationism was tenuous, and industry was already providing the Allies with much-needed materiel.

American cities began to hear the air-raid sirens being routinely tested. Citizens practiced blackout exercises, marked the civil defense stations on their radio dials, and trained school children to duck under desks and cover their heads during an air raid. After the Japanese attack on Pearl Harbor in 1941, young Americans were drafted into the armed forces, and companies lost many of their workers. The ranks of the Port Authority Police were particularly affected, as able-bodied men were sought by the military. During the war, 10 to 15 percent of the agency's 1,200 employees were in the service.

Port Authority Servicemen

ALMOST 200 PORT AUTHORITY EMPLOYEES WENT OFF TO WAR, SERVING IN MOST BRANCHES OF THE MILITARY AND IN EVERY THEATER OF OPERATION. EXECUTIVE DIRECTOR AUSTIN TOBIN NOTED WITH PRIDE SHORTLY AFTER D-DAY THAT THE RANKS INCLUDED MANY COMMISSIONED AND NONCOMMISSIONED OFFICERS: "OF THE 187 PORT AUTHORITY MEN IN ACTIVE MILITARY SERVICE, 128 HAVE BEEN SELECTED FOR POSITIONS OF RESPONSIBILITY AND LEADERSHIP." TOBIN'S OFFICE KEPT IN TOUCH WITH ALL OF THEM THROUGH THE SEMIMONTHLY LETTER, "PORT AUTHORITY MAIL BOX."

The war effort demanded priorities for vital materials, and nationwide rationing began. Families were issued ration stamps for buying shoes, gasoline, tires, food, and other essentials. In 1942, automobile production was suspended; it would not resume until after the war. Even after the war, many of the new cars were merely modest remakes of 1942 models. There were long waiting lists of people wanting to buy cars, and dealers were bribed to move names to the top of the list. With all of the pent-up demand, prices jumped. It would be years before most of the dangerous old cars were removed from the road.

Major population shifts occurred during the war. Farm workers from the South and Southwest headed north to industrial centers like New York and New Jersey, which offered good jobs at decent wages. Big government contracts and a manpower shortage meant plenty of jobs were available. Industrial cities grew crowded, but housing was limited due to the rationing of construction materials.

On May 7, 1945, the Axis powers surrendered in Europe. The Japanese surrendered in August, after atomic bombs were dropped on Hiroshima and Nagasaki. The A-bomb was the culmination of the Manhattan Project, named to confuse spies (the experiments were never conducted in New York). The world had entered the nuclear age.

After the war, returning veterans settled down in new areas, far from their roots. Many wound up in the New York–New Jersey region, where so many of their immigrant forebears had arrived. Under the GI Bill, which paid tuition for college or technical training, vets found opportunities unheard of before the war.

THE PORT AUTHORITY IN WARTIME

In his memoirs, Port Authority general counsel Julius Henry Cohen recalled, "In 1917, when we got into World War I, there was chaos in the Port of New York." Things became so bad that chairman Eugenious Outerbridge lamented, "Good God, if this goes on we shall lose the war!" When World War II broke out, however, shipping at the port was organized almost immediately. In fact, more than a third of the tonnage for the war departed from the docks of the port, as did half of the troops that would later be sent overseas.

Gasoline and rubber rationing and restrictions on "pleasure driving" made the three and a half years of the war a trying period for the Port Authority. Bald and flat tires became a common sight at Port Authority bridges and tunnels. Aging cars, gasoline and parts shortages, and other wartime headaches caused frequent traffic tie-ups.

In the early days of the war, the U.S. Army got Port Authority permission to place light antiaircraft machine guns on the bridge structure of the Bayonne Bridge, but then changed plans. The Army decided that a battery of heavier guns was needed, and asked permission to use the old stone quarry at the Staten Island end of the Bayonne Bridge.

"The Army has indicated that this occupation of the bridge position will close a large gap now wide open in the defense of New York City, and will cut off an avenue of approach that exists for hostile aircraft right into the heart of the city," Port Authority executive director Austin J. Tobin reported to the commissioners. "The installation will include a battery of antiaircraft guns, together with necessary temporary-type buildings and utilities to house the personnel who will man the guns."

This was apparently as close as the war ever got to the Port of New York Authority, except for March 23, 1943. At 2:30 in the morning, Port Authority police may have actually engaged the enemy. Two men were noticed loitering around the New Jersey exit of the Holland Tunnel, peering over the parapet wall at the roadway, and looking suspicious. When they saw that they had been detected, they ran, with a Port Authority patrolman in hot pursuit. They escaped in a waiting taxicab, but not before Port Authority traffic officer Ruby shot four shots from his service revolver. The FBI, Army and Navy Intelligence, and the Jersey City Police Department were notified.

This was more than a seriocomic episode. For much of the war, and repeating a pattern they had set during World War I, German submarines prowled the waters off the port, sinking merchant marine ships.

HELP WANTED
Women Toll Collectors

$160 Monthly

Shift work at George Washington Bridge, Holland and Lincoln Tunnels
Height 5'2" minimum. Age 21 to 35.
Weight: 115 to 140 pounds
Bring references which will be carefully investigated. Change-making experience desirable but not essential. Good health requisite. Women employed in war work or essential industries will not be accepted without a certificate of availability. Applicants must be citizens and should bring a birth certificate. Apply daily except Saturdays 10 a.m. to 4 p.m.

Office of the Personnel Director
Room #1500
The Port of New York Authority
111 Eighth Avenue, New York City

IN EARLY 1944, THE ABOVE ADVERTISEMENT APPEARED IN THE CLASSIFIED SECTION OF NEW YORK METROPOLITAN NEWSPAPERS.

World War II and the Changing Workforce

World War II opened up opportunities for women in workplaces suddenly experiencing severe labor shortages. Such a change took place at the Port Authority in 1943, with the hiring of the first female toll collectors. On August 30, 20 women passed the test. The average age of these former housewives, saleswomen, cashiers, clerks, and machine operators was 27, and 15 were married. Their training course included intensive instruction in punctuality, regulations and obedience to orders, contact with the public, courtesy, toll rates, equipment operation, collection procedures, and military movements.

Austin J. Tobin

For 30 years, Austin J. Tobin presided over an agency that built some of the most enduring public works of the century. Recognizing the importance of international trade, aviation, and ports to the metropolitan region and to the nation after World War II, Tobin led the Port Authority through a dynamic period.

Tobin joined the Port of New York Authority as a law clerk in 1927, at age 24. The following year, he earned his law degree from Fordham Law School. From 1930 to 1935, he served as the agency's real estate lawyer, and in 1938 was named assistant general counsel. That year also marked the beginning of the successful seven-year battle against the federal government's attempts, in Congress and in the courts, to tax all state and municipal bonds, including the income from Port Authority obligations. Tobin, as executive secretary of the Conference on State Defense, organized the opposition, marshaled public opinion, directed strategy, and ultimately triumphed over the federal government's attempt to dominate the states through the taxing power. Tobin's leadership caught the eye of several commissioners and, in 1942, he became the agency's second chief executive officer.

When offered the position, the Brooklyn-born son of a court reporter and grandson of an immigrant dockworker from Tipperary, had to think about it. His son, Austin Tobin Jr., recalls, "He didn't want to be executive director. His dream was to be general counsel, and he asked my mother, 'Do you think if I turn this down, they will still let me be general counsel?'" Tobin took the job, and served in that position until his retirement 30 years later. At his peak he earned a salary of $70,000, making him the highest-paid public official except for the president of the United States.

As its longest-serving executive director, Tobin helped to establish the Port Authority's reputation. He helped build a professional, dedicated staff, and maintained its nonpolitical status throughout many political fights. During his career he saw the agency grow from little more than 300 employees in 1927 to more than 8,000.

Under Tobin's leadership, the Port Authority established nine Port of New York Trade Development Offices (five in the United States and four overseas), to provide services to shippers and others engaged in international trade. Tobin's expertise in transportation was sought by many public agencies and foreign governments. Active in an international port organization under the auspices of the UN Economic and Social Council, he organized other leaders of the world's developed ports in creating a voluntary program of technical consultation and assistance, which would be provided to ports in developing nations. Tobin received awards from prestigious civic, professional, and commercial bodies, and honorary degrees from five colleges. The Government of France presented him with the Cross of the Knight of the Legion of Honor and the rosette of Officer of that Order, and Italy conferred upon him its Order of Merit.

The Wall Street Journal *described Tobin as "a brilliant bulldog," who "ruled with dedication." In theory, of course, he reported to the commissioners, but in practice they seldom questioned his decisions. "He had absorbed the innuendos of politics," his son said recently,*

AUSTIN J. TOBIN, THE PORT AUTHORITY'S EXECUTIVE DIRECTOR FOR 30 YEARS (1942–1972), LED THE AGENCY DURING THE YEARS OF ITS MOST DYNAMIC GROWTH. HE WAS ONE OF THE MOST POWERFUL FIGURES IN THE CREATION OF THE MODERN NEW YORK–NEW JERSEY METROPOLITAN REGION.

"and wanted no part of it." Of necessity a fighter, Tobin wrote somewhat wearily to the commissioners in 1946, "The history of every Port Authority project is one of protracted effort, of temporary setbacks, of opposition that at the time seemed immovable."

Tobin was one of the most influential figures in the creation of the modern New York metropolitan region, arguably even more important than his contemporary—and frequent rival—Robert Moses. Much has been written about Moses, but there is no book-length biography of Tobin, and no volume of his collected works for municipal officials to study. Only the Austin J. Tobin Plaza at the World Trade Center commemorates his name.

Tobin did leave an extensive written record of the Port Authority in each "Weekly Report" he compiled every Saturday for the commissioners. The 10- to 40-page reports begin in 1942, a little stiff, a little uncertain, relying on legalese in spots, moving in fits and starts. By the 1950s, whatever uncertainty he once felt had disappeared, and the reports were confidently written and accompanied by charts, photographs, and press clips.

Tobin's sense of humor was evident in these missives. In one 1958 report he informed the commissioners that Perry Shoemaker, president of the Lackawanna Railroad, had proposed to the National Defense Transportation Association that the Port Authority take over the railroad's trans-Hudson ferries because it could run them without a loss by simply raising fees to break even, an option denied to the railroad. Puncturing the railroad president's reasoning, Tobin responded, "The picture of the Port Authority raising fees by about $5 million a year in order to break even, and thereby driving all the passengers into the Hudson Tubes so that we could get out of the ferry business as fast as we got into it, is really the neatest and nuttiest outline of how you run a railroad that I've been exposed to since I went to Coney Island as a boy and rode on Thompson's death-defying roller coaster."

Tobin frequently wrote letters to the editor pointing out sins of omission—and commission—in coverage of the Port Authority, keenly aware as he was of the power of the press.

The Port Authority's achievements during the first half of Tobin's tenure (1942–1957) include John F. Kennedy (originally called Idlewild) International Airport, Newark International Airport, LaGuardia and Teterboro Airports, and New York's first commercial heliports. The second and third tubes of the Lincoln Tunnel, a second level to the George Washington Bridge, and the Port Authority Bus Terminal were also built. Two and a half miles of the dilapidated Brooklyn waterfront were transformed into a modern marine terminal, the docks in Hoboken were reconstructed, Port Newark was redeveloped into a model seaport, and a 1,000-acre containership terminal was created out of marshland at Elizabeth.

The second half of Tobin's tenure (1957–1972) was marked by controversy. In 1959, plans to build a jetport in the Great Swamp of Morris County died due to community opposition. At the height of the controversy, House Judiciary Chairman Emmanuel Celler of Brooklyn opened an inquiry into the Port Authority, which resulted in Tobin being convicted of contempt of Congress for his refusal to respond to subpoenas for agency documents. He was sentenced to 30 days in jail and fined $100. The Court of Appeals overturned the verdict in 1962, and the Supreme Court refused to review it. Although the investigation did yield much media sympathy for the Port Authority at a time when it was under fire for being "too big," the battle had diverted the agency's energy, and damaged its morale.

After a prolonged battle, the Port Authority succeeded in getting the authorization to build the World Trade Center. But it also had to take on the H&M railroad, which the agency fought because the line was a money loser. Nonetheless, the Port Authority turned the antiquated railroad into PATH (Port Authority Trans-Hudson), the heavily used rapid transit system that brings thousands of commuters to and from Manhattan each day. Tobin's final legacy was the World Trade Center, whose construction he presided over but whose dedication ceremony he missed. When asked why, he told the New York Times *that he decided not to go because it was raining.*

Austin Tobin resigned in 1972, the year a new name—The Port Authority of New York and New Jersey—was given to the agency.

The Post-War Car

In 1945, Nathan Cherniack, the Port Authority's economist, looked into his crystal ball and predicted the shape of the car of the future. He knew it would be big, but he thought it would be efficient. Most of all, he believed it would be streamlined.

"Engineering ingenuity will get busy on the redesign-from-scratch of the transmission system, which is now only an apology for a scientifically designed system. Hydra-matic and other fluid transmissions waste too much gas, and low fuel consumption will be a postwar advantage. The future transmission system will lie somewhere between the conventional hand-operated gear system and the liquid automatic transmission, produced in a simple and inexpensive form.

"Postwar cars will be lighter by stripping cars of a lot of excess junk which is functionally useless, building into the cars standard equipment, heaters, defrosters, radios, and eliminating accident-generating projections, such as door handles, etc.

"Thus, the future car will be a lighter but not smaller car. The American public does not want small cars. They want roomy, five-passenger, comfortably seated cars with baggage room. They want noiseless, smooth riding, easy handling, attractive in appearance, mechanically designed, efficient cars, at lowest possible initial cost. The American public usually gets what it wants."

THE PORT AUTHORITY GRAIN TERMINAL, ON GOWANUS BAY, BROOKLYN. TRANSFERRED BY THE STATE OF NEW YORK TO THE AUTHORITY IN MAY 1944, THE TERMINAL INCLUDED A GRAIN ELEVATOR, A NEW GRAIN PIER, AND A GALLERY BUILT BY THE PORT AUTHORITY, AS WELL AS THE COLUMBIA STREET PIER AND A PUBLIC OPEN-STORAGE AREA. THE PORT AUTHORITY REHABILITATED THE ELEVATOR, PIERS, AND UPLAND AREA.

THE GRAIN TERMINAL

Built in 1922 by the State of New York as part of the barge canal system, the Gowanus Grain Terminal and Pier was transferred to the Port Authority on May 1, 1944. Located in Brooklyn, in one of the busiest waterfront areas, it was one of two marine terminals at the New York–New Jersey Port that could load grain directly from an elevator to a ship. The Port Authority was now directly involved in harbor operations. The transfer demonstrated the confidence of Governor Thomas E. Dewey and the New York State Legislature that the Port Authority could efficiently operate the facility in the public interest, and make it "available to all commercial and governmental agencies requiring grain storage and handling."

With room for almost two million bushels, the terminal represented half the grain handling capacity of the port. More than 10 million bushels had moved through the terminal in the past, but in recent years there had been a falling off of the port's grain trade. Port Authority executives believed that a rehabilitated grain terminal could reverse the decline, and perform an important service by speeding the flow of foodstuffs to a liberated but war-ravaged Europe.

Grain movement through the New York–New Jersey Port began to fall in the 1960s. The opening of the Saint Lawrence Seaway diverted large volumes of grain previously exported through ocean ports. Shipments of Canadian grain, which had constituted most of the grain exported through New York, fell with Canada's policy of encouraging use of its own ports. Increased labor costs for grain handling and higher rail rates compared with the ports of Baltimore, Philadelphia, and Norfolk also worked against New York. In September 1964 the Port Authority of New York and New Jersey left the grain business. But during its 21 years of operation, the port's grain terminal had handled almost 100 million bushels of grain. The agency sold the facility in 1997.

Port Authority Medal Awards

In 1944, the Port Authority started its Medal Awards program to acknowledge the contributions of dedicated long-term employees, and to reward heroism and other achievements by the staff.

Herman Jaeger and Charley Schaefer were perhaps the best-known employees of the Port Authority from the 1920s through the 1950s, although not everyone knew their names. They were Port Authority traffic officers, badges 548 and 337, whose duty was to direct traffic outside the entrances to the Lincoln and Holland Tunnels. Once, when Schaefer was taken ill and was absent from his post, the Port Authority received 1,000 letters from anxious fans. Another patron once said Jaeger was a better pick-me-up than a hot cup of coffee in the morning.

Schaefer started working for the Port in 1927, and told the Newark Evening News *in 1948 that he gave his job "everything I had. I did my work with a smile. Sometimes, it was hard because even the warmest kind of smile doesn't melt a line up of cars." He received the authority's first Distinguished Service Medal in 1944, in recognition of the "mountains of good will" he had brought to the Port Authority.*

The New York Herald Tribune *dispatched a reporter and a photographer in December 1947 to learn the secret of Officer Jaeger's "perpetual gleam," and found that things had not always been shiny and bright for him. In 1929, he had worked as a quotation-board clerk on Wall Street. "Sometimes it was hard to smile when I'd put up margin calls," he told the reporter. "No wonder they used to jump out of buildings." When pressed for an explanation of his positive attitude, Jaeger responded, "If you really want to know, it's my home life." Jaeger, who joined the force in 1937, won the Distinguished Service Medal in 1948. He accepted it with a smile.*

Joseph Lawless, who joined the Port Authority in 1937, received the first Port Authority Medal of Honor in June 1944, for acting "quickly, courageously, intelligently, and at great personal risk and with utter disregard for his own personal safety." His actions on the Christmas Eve of 1943, which saved the lives of 11 people, were described in Austin Tobin's Report to the Commissioners, December 31, 1943:

"At the tragic fire in the rooming house at 447 West 42nd Street, New York City, on the evening of December 24th, in which 19 people lost their lives, Traffic Officer Joseph Lawless of the Port Authority Traffic Force performed an outstanding public service in the face of grave personal danger. Except for his action and leadership in directing others on the scene in rescue work, the tragedy might well have been more calamitous.

"When the fire started, Traffic Officer Lawless, assigned to motorcycle duty at the Lincoln Tunnel, was standing at the corner of 36th Street and Dyer Avenue (the rooming house is on the north side of 42nd Street at the end of Dyer Avenue). He gave the alarm by telephone and then began his rescue work. Climbing the fire escape in front of the building, he made his way through the flame and smoke that was pouring from all the windows, and succeeded in guiding and carrying a number of persons who were severely burned and injured to the sidewalk. He also organized those who were first upon the scene, and directed them in similar efforts.

"The action of Traffic Officer Lawless has been carefully investigated by Inspector Cahalane, who has found that all those who witnessed his deeds felt that his work had been most outstanding. He had not only great control of himself but, by his leadership of those assisting him, showed complete command of the situation."

The Postwar Boom— The Port Authority From 1945 to 1960

THE POSTWAR YEARS

A FIELDSIDE VIEW OF THE CENTRAL TERMINAL BUILDING, 1949.

Like a gigantic New Year's Eve celebration, jubilant crowds danced in the streets. Drivers blew their car horns. Sailors and soldiers were hugged and kissed in the middle of Times Square. As radios broadcast the tremendous news, newsboys hit the pavement waving newspapers with huge headlines declaring what everyone had longed to hear—The War Is Over! Feelings of joy and pride mingled with tears of gratitude. Ticker tapes and confetti billowed out of the skyscrapers of Manhattan, and church bells rang from Brooklyn to Beverly Hills.

At Port Authority headquarters, Executive Director Austin J. Tobin dispatched the following telegram to agency employees in the military service: "Well done. Now we have another job for you here." His words affirmed the agency's commitment to retain the same or equivalent jobs for employees on military leave. Coworkers and a grateful nation welcomed them home. Out of 209 Port Authority employees who had gone to war, 101 returned to the agency, with 79 returning in 1945 alone. Three employees had been killed in the war: Daniel P. Donovan, Lewis Peale Elliott, and James J. Mahoney.

The Port Authority recognized the end of the war by turning on all 148 suspension-cable lights of the George Washington Bridge—the "double necklace" sparkled over the Hudson once again because it was no longer a potential target for enemy attack. Nighttime pictures of the glowing bridge were shown in newsreels and newspapers.

But winding down from the biggest war in history was as monumental and confusing a task as preparing for it. Initially there was a complete change in priorities—shipping personnel and materiel back to the United States instead of rushing them overseas. Tons of war supplies, much of it dangerous, had to be transported to where it would be mothballed, destroyed, recycled, or sold. Contracts for munitions and other supplies came to a close; retooling for peacetime forced manufacturers to ponder the question: Now what? The postwar years took enormous adjustment—a scramble for new business activities and figuring out what to do with all the new materials and technologies that had been developed during the war. Synthetics made it possible to replace everything from rubber to silk, plastics were replacing wood, leather, and porcelain, and by the late 1940s television began posing a threat to radio, movies, reading, and even socializing. The world had become a very different place.

The Port Authority had the same concerns as the private sector. With rationing ended, it too asked: Now what? Was it time to begin the commercial development of marine terminals, replacing military facilities with those that would bring commerce, trade, and jobs to the region? Was it time to expand and better organize airports, revamping passenger and cargo flights to better serve commercial markets? Was it time to increase the capacity of trans-Hudson crossings to compensate for a gigantic increase in traffic as cars became icons of power, style, and glamour? Was it time to build the world's greatest bus terminal, one befitting a great megalopolis and its suburbs?

The answer to all those questions was *yes*. During the postwar years, the Port Authority defined itself once again as a diverse organization, an authority on traffic and transportation management, and a prestigious agency that got things done. By the end of the 1950s, most citizens of New York and New Jersey couldn't imagine life without the tunnels, bridges, airports, and bus and marine terminals that had become so much a part of their world. People saw the Port Authority's name emblazoned on facilities that were huge, impressive, popular, and enduring.

THE PORT AUTHORITY TAKES OVER THE REGIONAL AIRPORTS

One of the first major projects for the Port Authority during the postwar era was taking responsibility for the region's three large airports—Newark, LaGuardia, and New York International. By 1948, the agency had added them to its portfolio of projects. Both the City of Newark and the City of New York had asked the Port Authority to take over the airports. Both cities were initially reluctant to turn over the airports; New York City, in fact, had toyed with the idea of setting up a city airport authority. But both New York and Newark came to realize that they had more than enough problems to solve without getting involved in aviation. The cities did not give away the airports; they leased them to the Port Authority. Since assuming operation of the three airports, the Port Authority has invested billions of dollars in capital improvements in each of them.

TEMPORARY BUILDINGS AND PARKING AREAS OF NEW YORK INTERNATIONAL AIRPORT TWO MONTHS AFTER ITS OFFICIAL OPENING.

THE 1,600-FOOT-LONG RUNWAY AT NEWARK AIRPORT, UNDER CONSTRUCTION IN 1928, WAS THE FIRST HARD-SURFACED STRIP OF ANY COMMERCIAL AIRPORT IN THE NATION. A SMALL FOUR-PASSENGER RYAN MONOPLANE FROM WASHINGTON, D.C., MADE THE FIRST LANDING ON A COMPLETED SECTION IN AUGUST OF THAT YEAR. (PHOTO COURTESY OF NEWARK EVENING NEWS)

READY TO BOARD A FORD TRIMOTOR BEING FUELED, PASSENGERS WEAR STYLISH CHESTERFIELD AND RACCOON COATS TO KEEP THEM WARM IN THE CHILLY PASSENGER CABINS ALOFT. NEWARK WAS THE WORLD'S BUSIEST COMMERCIAL AIRPORT BY LATE 1930, WITH PASSENGER TRAFFIC REACHING 90,177 IN 1931. THE AIRPORT COULD NOT YET AFFORD TO BUILD A TERMINAL, SO EACH AIRLINE SET UP ITS OWN PASSENGER FACILITY.

Newark's city-owned airfield had been the nation's busiest until New York City Mayor Fiorello LaGuardia built a new airport in Queens in 1939 and lured the airlines with below-cost leases. Such competition persuaded the Regional Plan Association to urge a unified system that would strengthen the region's prospects for developing aviation services. As air traffic grew, the terminals in both states became increasingly inadequate. In 1945, Newark's leaders asked the Port Authority to consider a takeover of its airport and an adjacent run-down marine terminal, which would eventually become the foundation for the agency's marine terminal program. During World War II, Newark Airport had been operated by the Army Air Corps, which oversaw priority flights that had played a key role in the war effort. The Port Authority assumed responsibility for airport operations and development in 1948, adding a new terminal building, a new control tower, and an air cargo center.

The opening of New York International Airport, better known as Idlewild because of its proximity to the Idlewild Golf Course, had been delayed because of its own problems: sandstorms. The airport's 4,900 acres, chief engineer John Evans told the *New Yorker*, consisted primarily of 65 million cubic yards of sand that had been pumped from the bottom of Jamaica Bay, "enough to cover every street in Manhattan to a depth of nine feet." Evans said that he was using beach grass, imported from Montauk and Cape Cod, to keep the airport from literally blowing away. New York International finally opened for business at

NEW YORK INTERNATIONAL AIRPORT IN 1947, THE YEAR THE PORT AUTHORITY ASSUMED RESPONSIBILITY FOR ITS DEVELOPMENT AND OPERATION. LOCATED JUST 14 MILES FROM TIMES SQUARE ON THE WEST END OF JAMAICA BAY, IT IS DIRECTLY OPPOSITE BROOKLYN'S FLOYD BENNETT FIELD. IN 1946, NEW YORK CITY MAYOR WILLIAM O'DWYER REQUESTED THAT THE PORT AUTHORITY MAKE A STUDY OF THE FIELD AT IDLEWILD AND SUBMIT A PROPOSAL FOR DEVELOPING THE SITE AS AN AIRPORT. ON JUNE 1, 1947, THE PORT AUTHORITY SIGNED A 50-YEAR LEASE WITH THE CITY TO FINANCE, DEVELOP, AND OPERATE NEW YORK INTERNATIONAL ON A SELF-SUPPORTING BASIS. AT THAT TIME, THE CINDER BLOCK BUILDING SHOWN HERE WAS THE ONLY PASSENGER TERMINAL AT THE AIRPORT. IT WAS SOON TO BE REPLACED BY THE 655-ACRE TERMINAL CITY.

12:01 A.M. on July 1, 1948, and the first unscheduled flight arrived at 1:00 in the afternoon. The plane turned out to be a single-engine Stinson Voyager piloted by Port Authority Commissioner Donald V. Lowe. Climbing out of the cockpit, Lowe looked around and said, "I would like to see some business coming in."

By 1951, air-passenger miles traveled in the U.S. had begun to exceed the total number of passenger miles traveled by Pullman railroad cars. But in early 1952, Newark Airport was closed for four months because of three airplane crashes in Elizabeth, New Jersey, that had killed 119 people. Many people believed that the nation's 60 airports should all be shut down until airplanes stopped inexplicably falling out of the sky. However, the *New York Times* supported commercial aviation in the editorial "The Airport Problem." "It is not possible to remove landing fields to entirely uninhabited areas. To do so would destroy the very value of air transport. It is not possible to dismiss aviation. The airplane is here to stay, and Lieutenant General James H. Doolittle, the World War II hero and chairman of President Harry S. Truman's Airport Commission, urged that Newark Field be allowed to reopen, saying, 'The Newark airport has had a most unusual accumulation of bad luck.'" By the 1960s, the Airport Problem would become one of traffic control, not safety. Air travel's popularity would far outstrip anything envisioned by the air pioneers and barnstormers of the 1920s.

MEMBERS OF AN AIRLINE'S FLIGHT CREW AT NEWARK AIRPORT IN 1953.

NEWARK AIRPORT, 1931.

NEWARK—AN AIRPORT OF MANY FIRSTS

On October 1, 1928, officials dedicated a new facility that would set the standard for airport design. Newark Airport quickly captured 25 percent of the world's commercial airline passenger traffic. It offered the first paved runways, an important improvement for smoother, safer landings and takeoffs. It was the first airport to provide nighttime runway lighting, which permitted round-the-clock flight operations. Newark built the first air traffic control tower in the United States, a structure that was later designated a national historic site. Newark had the first airport weather station, which analyzed weather conditions pertinent to air travel. And it established the first airport post office, a logical outgrowth of an important technological innovation—airmail.

AERIAL VIEWS OF NEWARK AIRPORT IN APRIL 1946 (ABOVE) AND JUNE 1951 (BELOW).

DURING WORLD WAR II, $15 MILLION WAS INVESTED BY THE U.S. GOVERNMENT WHILE THE AIRPORT WAS OPERATED BY THE ARMY AIR CORPS.

THE AIRPORT HAS SINCE BEEN ENHANCED BY $1.6 BILLION IN PORT AUTHORITY IMPROVEMENTS.

FIELD LIGHTS AT NEWARK AIRPORT IN 1929.

A BATTERY OF FLOODLIGHTS MOUNTED ON A WOODEN PLATFORM AND TRAINED ON THE RUNWAY WERE A CRUDE FIRST ATTEMPT AT NIGHT LIGHTING. THE GLARING LIGHTS ILLUMINATED ONLY A SMALL PORTION OF THE RUNWAY.

THE MAIN TERMINAL BUILDING AS IT LOOKED IN 1948, THE YEAR THE PORT AUTHORITY ASSUMED RESPONSIBILITY FOR NEWARK AIRPORT'S OPERATIONS AND DEVELOPMENT. THE PORT AUTHORITY WOULD SOON ADD A NEW TERMINAL BUILDING, A NEW CONTROL TOWER, AN AIR CARGO CENTER, AND OTHER FACILITIES.

Airmail service had exceeded airline passenger traffic during the '20s and '30s, when few people could afford to fly. The only other method of sending mail overseas then was by ship, which could take weeks. Airmail—which made virtually any point on the globe accessible in a few days—was as revolutionary then as E-mail is today.

Newark Airport had become a vanguard for the entire region's entry into the era of flight, establishing a preeminence that became the envy of every city on the East Coast. Throughout its first decade, Newark Airport welcomed such aviators as Charles Lindbergh, Amelia Earhart, Wiley Post, Howard Hughes, and Jimmy Doolittle.

Silver Anniversary of Powered Flight

Just five years after taking over the management of Newark Airport, the Port Authority dedicated a new passenger terminal building on July 29, 1953. That year marked the 25th anniversary of the airport as well as the 50th anniversary of powered flight.

At the dedication ceremony in Newark, General James H. Doolittle, an aviator who later became vice president of the Shell Oil Company, reminded people of the time when "aviation was still fighting to prove that it was not a fad or a fancy." During those early years Newark Airport had no terminal building and "hardly any runways." Doolittle recognized those who saw flight becoming "an important part of our military and economic strength." Just two years before the airport was established in 1928, he said, "All the airlines in the country put together had a total of only 28 planes. We knew, even then, that airports would soon be as indispensable to major cities as railroad stations and good roads. Aviation today is our first line of defense—and it is indispensable to our economy."

THE NEW CONTROL TOWER AT NEWARK AIRPORT IN 1960 WAS THE FOURTH IN THE HISTORY OF THE AIRPORT.

LAGUARDIA AIRPORT'S CENTRAL TERMINAL BUILDING, APRON, AND AIRCRAFT PARKING AREAS, LOOKING WEST TO FLUSHING BAY, 1953.

LaGUARDIA AIRPORT GETS NEW YORK OFF THE GROUND

By late 1930, Newark Airport had become the busiest commercial airport in the nation. Over in New York, Mayor Fiorello LaGuardia, not to be outdone by New Jersey, stepped up his campaign to bring the airport business to New York City. But strange as it may now seem, getting an airport to serve New York City wasn't easy. Initially, Manhattanites believed that this noisy, daredevil industry should be isolated in rural New Jersey or in the marshes of Brooklyn rather than near the skyscrapers of New York City.

Floyd Bennett Field on East Island in Jamaica Bay was chosen as the site for a New York City airport in 1927, but it wasn't accessible. The Shore Parkway had not yet been built, which left Flatbush Avenue, a street already choked with traffic, as the only link. Attempts to attract commercial aviation to New York became increasingly difficult as the Great Depression took hold.

Mayor LaGuardia used any means necessary to gain public support for a New York City airport. He often resorted to such publicity stunts as having aviation pioneers break time and distance records out of Floyd Bennett Field. LaGuardia's most outrageous act occurred in 1934 when he categorically refused to disembark from a TWA flight at Newark because his ticket said New York. There just happened to be a planeload of reporters onboard. Presumably as a goodwill gesture, all were flown to Floyd Bennett Field, where pictures were taken of the new administration building. But the field nonetheless languished commercially, and it was sold to the Navy in 1942 to aid the war effort.

The mayor's persistence in promoting a New York airport paid off in 1937 when President Franklin Delano Roosevelt authorized the construction of a new airport on Flushing Bay and Bowery Bay in Queens. Once occupied by the Gala Amusement Park at North Beach, the site was transformed in 1929 into a 105-acre airfield. It was enlarged with 357 acres of landfill through a joint effort between the federal Works Progress Administration and New York City.

INTERIOR OF THE CONTROL TOWER, CONSTRUCTED ATOP THE CENTRAL TERMINAL BUILDING.

THE NORTH BEACH SITE OF LaGUARDIA AIRPORT FORMERLY WAS OCCUPIED BY THE GALA AMUSEMENT PARK, SHOWN HERE IN 1892. IN 1929, THE PARK PROPERTY WAS PURCHASED BY GLENN H. CURTISS FOR USE AS A 105-ACRE PRIVATE FLYING FIELD.

NORTH BEACH AIRPORT BOASTED THREE HANGARS, A SEAPORT, AND A BLIMP DOCK. BECAUSE OF ITS PROXIMITY TO MANHATTAN AND THE ADJACENT WATER AREAS THAT COULD BE USED FOR FLYING-BOAT OPERATIONS, MAYOR FIORELLO LaGUARDIA ENVISIONED IT AS AN AIRPORT THAT WOULD SERVE NEW YORK. THE CITY ACQUIRED THE FIELD IN 1935.

A CROWD OF 325,000, THE LARGEST EVER TO VISIT AN AIRPORT IN A SINGLE DAY, TURNED OUT FOR THE DEDICATION OF NEW YORK MUNICIPAL AIRPORT ON OCTOBER 15, 1939. SEVENTEEN DAYS LATER, THE AIRPORT WAS RENAMED NEW YORK MUNICIPAL AIRPORT–LAGUARDIA FIELD. LAGUARDIA WAS THE FIRST AIRPORT TO PROVIDE A FLORIST SHOP, A DRUG STORE, A BANK, A HABERDASHERY, A JEWELRY SHOP, A BEAUTY SALON, AND A BROKERAGE OFFICE FOR AIR TRAVELERS. WHEN DEDICATED, THE AIRPORT WAS CALLED "THE WORLD'S GREATEST DEVELOPMENT IN CIVIL AVIATION SINCE LINDBERGH FLEW THE ATLANTIC." WITHIN A YEAR IT BECAME THE BUSIEST COMMERCIAL AIRPORT IN THE WORLD, A PREEMINENCE IT ENJOYED FOR MANY YEARS.

MAYOR LaGUARDIA GREETS A STEWARDESS AT THE ARRIVAL OF THE FIRST SCHEDULED FLIGHT, A TRANSCONTINENTAL AND WESTERN AIR (NOW TRANS WORLD AIRLINES) DC-3 FROM CHICAGO, WHICH LANDED JUST AFTER MIDNIGHT ON DECEMBER 2, 1939.

LaGuardia personally supervised much of the construction, making certain that the new terminal and aircraft hangars met his standards. The facility opened on October 15, 1939. Officially, it was called New York City Municipal Airport. But as the mayor started to address some 325,000 spectators gathered for the dedication, three planes carried a message across the sky: Name it LaGuardia Airport! The crowd roared its approval. The name was changed by the New York City Board of Estimate in November to honor the mayor's dogged determination to get New York its own airport.

On December 2, 1939, a TWA DC-3 from Chicago glided onto LaGuardia's pristine runway, the first scheduled flight to land there. American Airlines' Night Owl for Chicago claimed the first takeoff. By summer, more than 250 daily landings and takeoffs became routine. And in 1940, only a year after the airport opened, Pan American Airways (later renamed Pan American World Airways) made its first 26-hour New York to Europe flight. The Yankee Clipper carried 5,260 pounds of mail and nine passengers.

On June 1, 1947, the Port Authority leased LaGuardia Airport and began running it. Redeveloping the airport was an immense challenge. The old facility had become inadequate. Undaunted, the agency built a new terminal and control tower that greatly enhanced operations and expanded the airport's capacity.

THE DASHING MAYOR LaGUARDIA'S PHOTO OPPORTUNITY IN THIS TWA MAIL AIRCRAFT CALLS TO MIND HIS OWN FLYING CAREER. NO STRANGER TO THE COCKPIT, HE LEARNED TO FLY IN 1915 WITH PIONEER AIRCRAFT DESIGNER GIUSEPPE BELLANCA AT ROOSEVELT FIELD IN MINEOLA, NEW YORK. WHEN THE U.S. ENTERED WORLD WAR I, HE ENLISTED IN THE UNITED STATES AIR SERVICE AND SERVED ON THE ITALIAN FRONT IN COMMAND OF A BOMBER SQUADRON. HE WAS DECORATED SEVERAL TIMES.

WATCHING A CLIPPER LAUNCH: ON MARCH 30, 1940, PAN AMERICAN AIRWAYS INAUGURATED TRANSATLANTIC SERVICE FROM THE MARINE AIR TERMINAL WITH A 41-TON BOEING 314 "FLYING BOAT." IT WAS DESTINED FOR THE AZORES WITH NINE PASSENGERS ABOARD. THESE AIRCRAFT WERE NAMED CLIPPERS IN HONOR OF THE FAST AMERICAN SAILING SHIPS OF THE 19TH CENTURY.

BELOW: A CLIPPER LIFTING OFF.

THE FAMED CLIPPERS, ALWAYS AN ATTRACTION FOR VISITORS, WERE MAINTAINED IN THE HANGAR SHOWN IN THE UPPER RIGHT. THE HANGAR IS USED TODAY BY THE PORT AUTHORITY TO HOUSE LARGE AIRPORT MAINTENANCE VEHICLES.

WHEN CONSTRUCTED IN 1939, THE SIX LANDPLANE HANGARS AT LaGUARDIA FIELD WERE THE LARGEST IN THE WORLD. EACH WAS LARGER THAN MADISON SQUARE GARDEN, DWARFING EVEN THE TWIN-ENGINE DC-3 PLANES THAT WERE SERVICED AT LaGUARDIA. FOR TWO DECADES, THE DC-3 WAS THE BACKBONE OF AIRLINE FLEETS. THEY WERE SMALL ENOUGH TO BE MOVED BY AIRLINE GROUND PERSONNEL WHEN THEY GOT STUCK IN SNOW OR MUD.

MAYOR FIORELLO LaGUARDIA CUTS A GIANT BIRTHDAY CAKE TO CELEBRATE THE THIRD ANNIVERSARY OF THE OPENING OF NEW YORK MUNICIPAL AIRPORT–LaGUARDIA FIELD. THE AIRPORT WAS RENAMED LaGUARDIA AIRPORT BY THE PORT AUTHORITY IN 1947, AFTER THE AGENCY TOOK OVER OPERATIONS. THE CAKE WAS CROWNED WITH A "V FOR VICTORY," A POPULAR SYMBOL DURING WORLD WAR II. AT THE MAYOR'S RIGHT IS MRS. MARIE LaGUARDIA.

PRESIDENT EISENHOWER IS GREETED BY YOUNGSTERS AT LaGUARDIA AIRPORT FOLLOWING HIS ADDRESS TO THE GENERAL ASSEMBLY OF THE UNITED NATIONS, AUGUST 15, 1958.

THE "SHEEP RUN," FOREGROUND, WHICH SERVED AS AUXILIARY PASSENGER FACILITIES, 1951.

THE SKY WALK OBSERVATION DECK AT LaGUARDIA WAS A POPULAR ATTRACTION, ACCOMMODATING 5,000 SPECTATORS. ON A CLEAR WEEKEND, AS MANY AS 25,000 PEOPLE VISITED THE AIRPORT. BY 1947, MORE THAN A MILLION PEOPLE A YEAR CAME TO SEE THE BUSY FACILITY. EVEN IN THE 1950s, THOUSANDS OF PEOPLE STILL PAID 10 CENTS APIECE TO WATCH THE HUSTLE AND BUSTLE ON THE FIELD AND THE EXCITEMENT IN THE SKIES OVERHEAD.

THE LANDPLANE ADMINISTRATION BUILDING, LATER CALLED THE CENTRAL TERMINAL BUILDING, SERVED AIR TRAVELERS FOR NEARLY A QUARTER OF A CENTURY. A STAINLESS STEEL EAGLE SOARED ABOVE THE MARQUEE AND FRONT ENTRANCE. ALL AIR TRAFFIC IN THE NORTHEAST WAS HANDLED FROM THE CIVIL AERONAUTICS AUTHORITY (NOW THE FEDERAL AVIATION ADMINISTRATION) OFFICES IN THIS BUILDING. IN THE 1960s THE PORT AUTHORITY REPLACED THE BUILDING WITH A MODERN TERMINAL SEVEN TIMES AS LARGE. THE EAGLE NOW ADORNS THE ADMINISTRATION BUILDING, HANGAR 7.

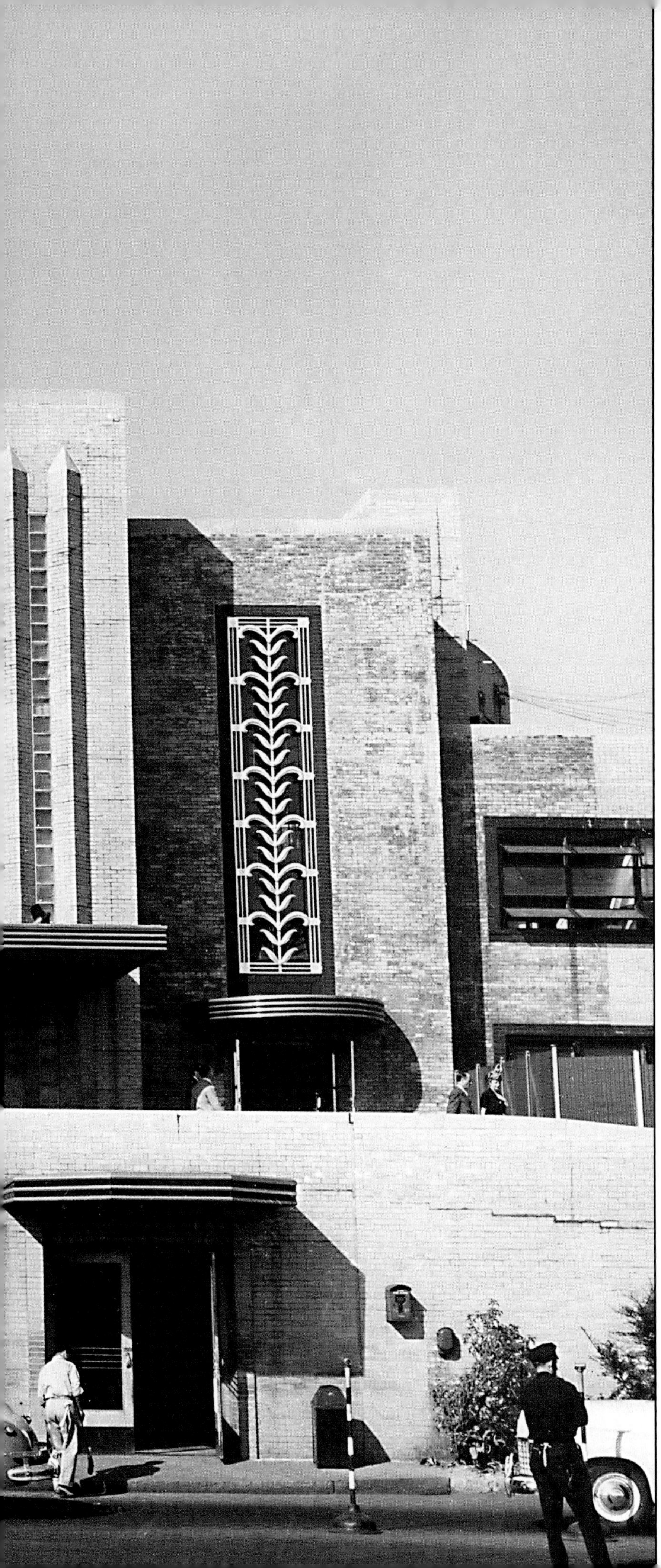

THE CENTRAL TERMINAL BUILDING SHOWING THE TICKET COUNTERS IN THE MAIN FLOOR ROTUNDA, 1948.

SAILORS AND CIVILIANS AWAIT FLIGHTS IN THE CENTRAL TERMINAL BUILDING PASSENGER WAITING AREA. AFTER WORLD WAR II, LaGUARDIA AIRPORT RETURNED TO A CIVILIAN ROLE. RETURNING VETERANS AND A BOOMING PEACETIME ECONOMY FUELED A RAPID GROWTH OF THE AIRLINE INDUSTRY.

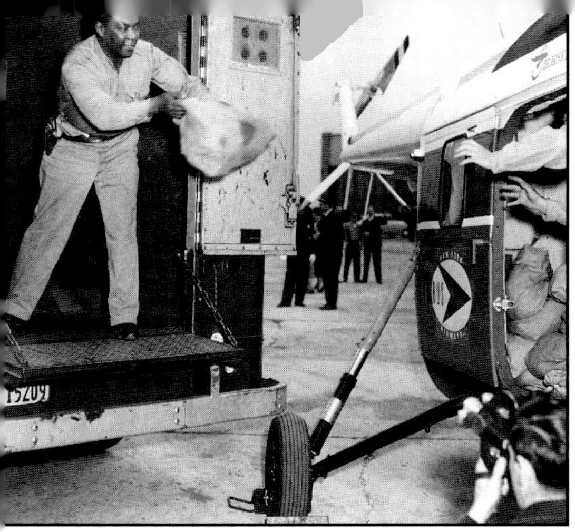

ABOVE: REGULAR HELICOPTER SERVICE BEGAN IN THE PORT DISTRICT ON OCTOBER 15, 1952, WHEN NEW YORK AIRWAYS INITIATED A REGULAR MAIL RUN WITH S-55 HELICOPTERS BETWEEN LAGUARDIA, NEWARK, AND NEW YORK INTERNATIONAL (NOW JFK). BY THE END OF 1953, NEW YORK AIRWAYS CARRIED PASSENGERS AND CARGO ON THE SAME ROUTES.

TOP: FOR A NICKEL YOU COULD LOOK AT EVENTS CLOSE-UP.

CENTER: THE COMINGS AND GOINGS OF THE RICH AND FAMOUS MADE THE NEWS. IN THIS 1949 *DAILY MIRROR* PHOTO, THE MEDIA AS WELL AS THE FANS WELCOMED THE BROOKLYN DODGERS BACK FROM A TRIUMPH OVER ST. LOUIS.

BOTTOM: PURCHASING SNACKS AT LAGUARDIA'S SKY BAR.

A MECHANIC STARTS UP AN EXACT REPLICA OF THE SPIRIT OF ST. LOUIS AT LAGUARDIA BY TURNING ITS PROPELLER. THE AIRCRAFT WAS USED IN THE 1957 MOVIE *THE SPIRIT OF ST. LOUIS*, WHICH STARRED JIMMY STEWART AS FAMED AVIATOR CHARLES LINDBERGH ON HIS EPIC 1927 SOLO FLIGHT ACROSS THE ATLANTIC FROM NEW YORK TO PARIS. BUTLER AVIATION CORP. FACILITIES AT LAGUARDIA WERE USED TO OVERHAUL AND CHECK THE PLANE BEFORE ITS DEPARTURE FOR THE NEXT FILMING LOCATION.

THE AIRPORT IN THE LATE 1950s, ON THE EVE OF MAJOR REDEVELOPMENT. ITS PROXIMITY TO MANHATTAN, WHOSE TOWERS RUN ACROSS THE CENTER TOP OF THE PHOTO, ILLUSTRATES MAYOR LaGUARDIA'S REALIZED DREAM OF A CLOSE-IN AIRPORT.

The Birth of the Shuttle at LaGuardia Airport

On Sunday, April 30, 1961, The New York Times carried the following article: "Eastern Airlines' six-month experiment in operating a no-frills airline shuttle operation between New York and Washington and New York and Boston will begin today. Eastern's approach is probably about as close as any airline has yet come to reducing air transportation to its basic job of moving passengers and goods from point A to point B. How much demand there is for minimum fuss rides at cheaper fares will be tested to a considerable degree. The answers will be of interest to Eastern and every other carrier."

Eastern offered eight flights a day to each city from LaGuardia Airport on 95-seat Super C Constellations; fare was $14 one-way to Washington and $12 to Boston. By comparison, rail fare from New York to Washington was $10.65 and to Boston $11.58.

By the end of the first week, Eastern reported that 6,147 passengers had booked a no-frills shuttle flight. The shuttle, now operated by USAirways, and another shuttle service now operated by Delta, currently serve nearly 64,000 passengers every week.

Fieldside at LaGuardia Airport, overlooking the lagoon in front of the Central Terminal Building. The need for space and the need to control flooding at the airport ultimately claimed the lagoon, which was fed by water from Flushing Bay, Jackson Creek, and a large storm sewer. Starting in 1958, sand from the ocean floor off Coney Island was used to fill the lagoon and provide a foundation for paving. The redevelopment was the first major overhaul at LaGuardia since its completion in 1939.

F-BAZL

NEW YORK INTERNATIONAL AIRPORT

A persistent champion of aviation, Mayor LaGuardia proclaimed, "the greatest airport in the world is rising from the meadows at Idlewild in New York City" as concrete was being poured for the main runway in 1945. "It will cost $71 million." The mayor predicted that the new airport would bring in millions of dollars in commerce, business, and traffic each month, and that 30,000 passengers would go through its gates daily. "The airport is a costly undertaking, yet it will be one of the best investments the city ever made. It will pay its way," he said. The mayor died in 1947, a year before the airport opened, but The Little Flower, as he had been called, was right—the New York–New Jersey region would become the center of the aviation world.

MOTORISTS PASS UNDER TAXIWAY AS AIRPLANE HEADS TO RUNWAY AT NEW YORK INTERNATIONAL AIRPORT IN 1948.

DEDICATED ON JULY 31, 1948, AS NEW YORK INTERNATIONAL AIRPORT, THE FACILITY WAS COMMONLY REFERRED TO AS IDLEWILD UNTIL IT WAS RENAMED JOHN F. KENNEDY INTERNATIONAL AIRPORT IN 1963. IDLEWILD WAS THE NAME OF THE GOLF COURSE THAT HAD PREVIOUSLY OCCUPIED PART OF THE HUGE, MOSTLY MARSHLAND PROPERTY. PORT AUTHORITY LORE HAS IT THAT WHEN AN AGENCY STAFF MEMBER REFERRED TO THE FACILITY BY ITS NICKNAME, RATHER THAN BY ITS PROPER NAME, EXECUTIVE DIRECTOR AUSTIN TOBIN WOULD ADMONISH, "IT'S NEITHER IDLE, NOR WILD!"

LaGuardia had been wrong about one thing—the investment of $71 million covered only the cost of preparing the runway. Another $100 million would be needed to build the entire facility. In 1945, neither the city nor the airlines could afford that kind of investment. Plans for the airport were almost scrapped for an industrial park or a low-cost housing project. Ultimately, LaGuardia's successor, Mayor William O'Dwyer, requested the Port Authority to make a study of both Idlewild and LaGuardia fields and consider taking over their development and operation. The agency completed the study and submitted a proposal to the city. On June 1, 1947, the Port Authority signed a 50-year lease with the city to finance, develop, and operate the two airports on a self-supporting basis.

NEW YORK INTERNATIONAL'S APRON, TOWER, AND TERMINAL IN 1953. TODAY, THIS MAMMOTH AIRPORT, ALMOST TEN TIMES BIGGER THAN LAGUARDIA, ENCOMPASSES 5,000 ACRES, EMPLOYS OVER 37,000 PEOPLE, AND GENERATES $20.4 BILLION OF ECONOMIC ACTIVITY.

THE AMERICAN AIRLINES TERMINAL IN 1961. A PRINCIPAL OBJECTIVE OF THE MASTER PLAN FOR THE DESIGN OF THE AIRPORT WAS TO KEEP AIRPLANES SUFFICIENTLY FAR APART TO ELIMINATE CROSS TRAFFIC. THE MAJOR AIRLINE BUILDINGS WERE PLACED ALONG THE OUTER OVAL OF TERMINAL CITY—UNITED'S AND EASTERN'S PASSENGER TERMINALS IN 1959, AMERICAN'S AND PAN AMERICAN'S IN 1960, AND TWA'S AND NORTHWEST ORIENT'S IN 1962. ALL WERE CONSIDERED BELLWETHERS OF MODERN DESIGN AND PASSENGER CONVENIENCE. EACH AIRLINE ATTEMPTED TO OUTDO THE OTHERS.

New York International Airport was dedicated on July 31, 1948, with the opening of a nine-day international air exposition. The ceremonies were attended by more than 200,000 people, including President Harry S. Truman and his Republican challenger, New York Governor Thomas E. Dewey.

A mile and a half of aviation history exhibits were displayed, from a model of the Wright brothers' plane to the latest innovations in radar and jet engines. Overhead, 1,400 combat planes roared by in an impressive formation, in one of the greatest aerial reviews ever staged.

THE DESIGN OF PAN AMERICAN'S TERMINAL, WHICH OPENED IN 1962, FEATURED MILTON HEBALD'S 12-PIECE SIGNS OF THE ZODIAC, ONE OF THE LARGEST BRONZE GROUPINGS EVER EXECUTED. THE LOUNGE IN THE TERMINAL CONVEYED AN "OUTER SPACE" AMBIANCE WITH ITS FUTURISTIC MOTIF AND ULTRAMODERN LUCITE CHAIRS.

WHEN TWA DEDICATED ITS $15 MILLION TERMINAL ON MAY 26, 1962, IT BECAME AN INSTANTLY RECOGNIZABLE ICON FOR AIR TRAVELERS. NOTED ARCHITECT EERO SAARINEN'S SOARING, GULL-WINGED DESIGN WAS HAILED AS AN EXPRESSION OF THE DRAMA AND WONDER OF AIR TRAVEL. THE QUEENS CHAMBER OF COMMERCE AWARDED THE TERMINAL A SPECIAL BRONZE PLAQUE IN 1962 AS "A MOST OUTSTANDING STRUCTURE." IN 1994, IT WAS DESIGNATED A NEW YORK CITY LANDMARK.

On July 9, 1948, the first passenger arrived at New York International Airport. Four-year-old Donna Moore disembarked from the first regularly scheduled airliner, a Peruvian International Airlines DC-4 arriving from Santiago, Chile. A decade later, a master plan for expanding New York International Airport was unveiled and construction was begun on Terminal City—a mile-long oval of passenger terminals, one for each major U.S. carrier. The centerpiece was the International Arrivals Building, with a massive sweeping arch that dwarfed even the 40-foot Alexander Calder mobile hung from the ceiling. Adjoining the IAB, foreign air carriers designed and built their own separate passenger service facilities. Called by the *New York Times* "an authentic wonder of the world," the IAB was dedicated with a lavish ceremony on July 31, 1957.

THE 11-STORY AIR TRAFFIC CONTROL TOWER, A 40 FT. X 65 FT. STEEL FRAMEWORK STRUCTURE, AT ITS COMPLETION IN 1952. ON THE TOP FLOOR IS THE OCTAGONAL CONTROL CAB. OPERATED BY THE FEDERAL AVIATION ADMINISTRATION, THE TOWER WAS LOCATED IN THE CENTER OF THE AIRPORT ADJACENT TO THE INTERNATIONAL ARRIVALS BUILDING, BUILT AFTER THIS PHOTO WAS TAKEN.

NEW YORK INTERNATIONAL AIRPORT CARGO FACILITY

To accommodate the exploding growth in air cargo, the Port Authority opened a huge air cargo facility on June 27, 1956, at New York International Airport. Cargo City consisted of five buildings in which 27 airlines rented space. The complex included the Cargo Service Building, which housed common services such as federal inspection, freight forwarders, customhouse brokers, warehousing, and pickup and delivery companies.

The cargo business had grown from just over 9 million pounds in 1949 to more than 106 million pounds in 1955. Over the next 10 years domestic air cargo tripled and international cargo rose by 10 percent annually. New York International Airport became the cargo center of the region.

ALMOST AS SOON AS IT OPENED, CARGO BEGAN SPEEDING THROUGH NEW YORK INTERNATIONAL. DURING THE FIRST YEAR, 1,600 TONS OF FREIGHT WERE HANDLED IN THE EARLY MAKESHIFT OPERATION. BY 1952, THAT FIGURE HAD RISEN TO 50,000 TONS. IN THIS 1953 PHOTO, A SLICK AIRWAY'S C-47 LOADS UP. NOTWITHSTANDING THE COMPANY'S TRENDY NAME, ITS AIRCRAFT CARRIED THE NAMES OF HISTORICALLY RENOWNED SAILING SHIPS, SUCH AS *MAYFLOWER* AND *CONSTITUTION*.

Arriving Passengers
Do Not Enter
Do Not Enter
Restricted
Area

THE INTERNATIONAL ARRIVALS BUILDING, DEDICATED IN 1957, FEATURED AN EFFICIENTLY LAID-OUT CUSTOMS AREA. BAGGAGE INSPECTIONS WERE MADE AT SUPERMARKET-STYLE CHECKOUT LANES. ALEXANDER CALDER'S MOBILE, *FLIGHT* (TOP RIGHT), NOT ONLY BEAUTIFIED, BUT HELPED TO HUMANIZE THE VAST SCALE OF THE MAIN HALL.

THIS MONUMENTAL MURAL, HIDDEN FOR 27 YEARS UNDER LAYERS OF WALL PAINT, WAS FULLY RESTORED AT LaGUARDIA AIRPORT'S MARINE AIR TERMINAL IN 1980. SPANNING THE 12-FOOT HIGH, 235-FOOT LONG ARC OF THE TERMINAL ROTUNDA, THE MURAL IS WPA ARTIST JAMES BROOKS' PORTRAYAL OF MAN'S STRUGGLE TO FLY, FROM DAEDALUS THROUGH DA VINCI TO THE WRIGHT BROTHERS AND MODERN TECHNOLOGY. FIRST UNVEILED IN 1942, THE MURAL TOOK THREE YEARS TO COMPLETE AND 10 MONTHS TO RESTORE. IT WAS THE LARGEST AND LAST OF THE MURALS COMMISSIONED BY THE WPA.

WPA Murals at the Airports

BROOKS "FLIGHT" AT LaGUARDIA AIRPORT'S MARINE AIR TERMINAL

James Brooks unveiled an extraordinary mural in the rotunda of LaGuardia Airport's Marine Air Terminal in 1942. The larger-than-life-sized work, named *Flight*, depicts the history of aeronautical aspirations. The first section shows the legendary flight of Daedalus and his son, Icarus, who fell from the sky after his wax wings were melted by the sun. The second and the third sections depict Leonardo da Vinci's flying devices, the Wright brothers flight at Kitty Hawk, and a Pan American Clipper.

Brooks created the mural as part of the federal government's Works Progress Administration, which employed thousands of artists throughout the United States during the Great Depression. For the first time in American history, artists were paid to create murals, mosaics, and sculptures on the walls of public buildings.

REPRESENTATION OF HEROIC MAN AND WOMAN FROM THE "FLIGHT ACCOMPLISHED" PANEL OF JAMES BROOKS' MURAL "FLIGHT," IN THE ROTUNDA OF THE MARINE AIR TERMINAL, LAGUARDIA AIRPORT.

IN THIS DETAIL, JAMES BROOKS DEPICTS THE ARRIVAL OF THE PAN AM CLIPPER.

The *Flight* mural at LaGuardia was painted over in the 1950s, and was hidden from public view for more than 20 years. In the 1970s, painting conservator Alan Farancz was commissioned to oversee the mural's restoration. The project took more than a year to complete. Fourteen layers of paint had to be painstakingly removed without damaging the original mural.

The decision to resurrect *Flight* was prompted by Dorothy M. Miller, a member of the Port Authority's Committee on Art. The restoration was financed by such notables as Laurance Rockefeller and De Witt Wallace, the founder of *Reader's Digest*.

THIS DETAIL DEPICTS BUILDINGS AND TOWERS, SYMBOLS OF MAN'S TIRELESS ATTEMPT TO CLIMB.

THE FLIGHT OF ICARUS IN THE "RELEASE" PANEL BRINGS TO LIFE A PART OF GREEK MYTHOLOGY.

WILBUR AND ORVILLE WRIGHT'S FIRST POWERED FLIGHT AT KITTY HAWK.

WPA ARTIST ARSHILE GORKY IN 1936, WORKING ON *THE ACTIVITIES ON THE FIELD* PANEL OF HIS MONUMENTAL 10-PANEL, 1,530-SQUARE-FOOT MURAL *AVIATION: EVOLUTION OF FORMS UNDER AERODYNAMIC LIMITATIONS.* THE MURAL WOULD ENHANCE THE ADMINISTRATION BUILDING BEING CONSTRUCTED BY THE FEDERAL GOVERNMENT UNDER ITS DEPRESSION-ERA PUBLIC WORKS PROGRAM. THE NEW ADMINISTRATION BUILDING, COMPLETED IN 1935 IN ART DECO STYLE, DISPLAYED SUCH FEATURES AS PLASTER WINGS ON THE CAPITALS OF COLUMNS AND ON THE GRILLES. POLISHED MARBLE WALL FACINGS AND GRACEFUL ALUMINUM STAIR RAILS EMBELLISHED THE GROUND FLOOR PUBLIC AREAS. THIS PANEL WAS INTENDED FOR THE NORTH WALL OF THE SECOND FLOOR. PAINTED OVER DURING WORLD WAR II, THE MURAL WAS RECLAIMED FROM DARKNESS IN THE 1970s.

GORKY'S *AVIATION* AT NEWARK AIRPORT

Arshile Gorky's *Aviation: Evolution of Forms under Aerodynamic Limitations: Aerial Map (1936–37)* are oils on canvas now housed in the administration building at Newark International Airport. They were created as part of a mural program at Newark Airport, but only two of the 10 mural panels survive. Gorky, born in Turkish Armenia in 1904, came to the United States in 1920, living first in Providence and Boston, then moving to New York about 1925. Like so many others, he was living in extreme poverty during the Depression, despite having achieved recognition soon after arriving in New York. He studied and taught at the Grand Central School of Art, and in 1935 joined the Federal Art Project. A year later he began painting the Newark Airport murals.

As with James Brooks' *Flight* mural at LaGuardia's Marine Air Terminal, Arshile Gorky's work at Newark Airport was born of the Great Depression era's Works Progress Administration. Both murals were painted over years later, when WPA artworks were no longer popular. Gorky's work had been painted over by the Army Air Corps when it took command of Newark Airport during World War II. But because Brooks' and Gorky's murals were two of the major undertakings of the WPA Art Project, both were restored in the 1970s through the efforts of the Port Authority's Committee on Art.

HISTORIC TETERBORO AIRPORT

ABOVE: TETERBORO AIRPORT, THE OLDEST AIRPORT IN THE REGION, 1947.

The Port Authority purchased Teterboro Airport on April 1, 1949. The oldest airfield in the region, it was built on land acquired by Walter C. Teter in Bergen County, New Jersey, in 1917. When it opened, it handled primarily training flights and cargo planes. During World War I, it was used as an aircraft manufacturing site by the North American Aviation Company. After the war the airport served as a base of operations for aircraft designer Anthony Fokker. The airport was taken over by the Army Air Corps during World War II.

RIGHT: LOCATED IN NORTHERN NEW JERSEY, TETERBORO WAS PURCHASED BY THE PORT AUTHORITY IN ANTICIPATION OF NEEDING ANOTHER AIRPORT IN THE REGION AS AIR TRAFFIC INCREASED.

THE PRIME MINISTER OF NORTHERN NIGERIA AND HIS DELEGATION ON THE PORT AUTHORITY BUILDING'S 16TH FLOOR HELIPAD AFTER INSPECTING AGENCY FACILITIES FROM THE AIR IN JULY 1960.

THE WEST 30TH STREET HELIPORT

Visionaries have often drawn futuristic cityscapes with skywalks, rocket pads, monorails, and, of course, helicopters hopping from roof to roof. A staple in every sci-fi fantasy from Flash Gordon to the Jetsons, the whirlybird has been Tomorrowland's answer to fast local travel.

Manhattan's first commercial heliport opened on September 16, 1956, at the foot of West 30th Street. It was the first of several planned for the region as part of a coordinated heliport system. Built by the Port Authority under a lease with the City of New York, the convenient midtown site began with mail and cargo service only, but quickly captured corporate and commercial passengers who sought the helicopter's speed, convenience, and ability to land almost anywhere. The first operator was New York Airways.

THE WEST 30TH STREET HELIPORT DEDICATION CEREMONY FEATURED THE FIRST FLIGHT OF MAIL FROM THE HELIPORT TO LaGUARDIA AIRPORT. WHEN SOLD BY THE PORT AUTHORITY IN 1996, THE HELIPORT WAS HANDLING MORE THAN 22,000 HELICOPTER FLIGHTS PER YEAR. THE HELIPORT CLOSED IN 1997.

The Jetport That Was Never Built

Of all the Port Authority projects that might have been, perhaps none proved as divisive as the fourth jetport. Opposition to building the airport led to a state investigation of the Port Authority as well as to a congressional inquiry, which led to a contempt citation for Port Authority executive director Austin Tobin when he refused to turn over agency documents to a committee chaired by Brooklyn Congressman Emmanuel Celler. The case advanced all the way to the U.S. Supreme Court, where the Port Authority prevailed.

The fourth jetport was announced in December of 1959 as the Port Authority's next great public works project. Forecasting a 350 percent increase in air traffic by 1975, the agency outlined plans for a $220 million jet airport to be located in the Great Swamp in Morris County, New Jersey, 25 miles west of Manhattan. Planned for completion by 1970, the airport would be twice the size of Idlewild and would feature four 10,000-foot runways.

But news of the airport site had already leaked out well before the agency made the announcement. The New Jersey newspapers picked up the story and wrote about "an explosion of violent proportion" that was simmering in Morris County, one of New Jersey's finest residential areas.

The Port Authority underestimated the opposition to its plan. Interviewed on WCBS radio's long-running program "Let's Find Out," Tobin elaborated on what he called the inevitability of the project: "I fully believe that if there's not a major airport for this area built there, there'll never be one built." He said that in his more than 30 years with the Port Authority, each of its projects had been strongly opposed.

Shortly after the Port Authority recommended Morris County as the "inevitable" site of the fourth jetport, the New Jersey congressional delegation prevailed upon Congressman Celler to have his Committee on the Judiciary launch a detailed probe of the agency.

The fourth jetport was only part of the reason for the House inquiry. The other was the Port Authority's long-standing refusal to take over the Hudson and Manhattan Railroad, which it contended would never be self-sustaining. The congressional inquiry went on for three years, during which time Celler unsuccessfully introduced legislation that would have resulted in the Port Authority reporting to Congress.

The fourth jetport idea was abandoned in 1969, when the agency announced that henceforth it would concentrate on expanding existing facilities to maximize their capacity.

AFTER THE ABANDONMENT OF THE FOURTH AIRPORT PLAN, TETERBORO WAS DESIGNATED AS A RELIEVER AIRSTRIP FOR CORPORATE AND PRIVATE OPERATORS, AS PART OF THE NATIONAL PLAN OF INTEGRATED AIRPORT SYSTEMS. JOHNSON CONTROLS NOW OPERATES THE 827-ACRE AIRPORT'S TWO RUNWAYS FOR THE PORT AUTHORITY AROUND-THE-CLOCK. TETERBORO HAS AN ADMINISTRATION BUILDING, A PASSENGER OPERATIONS TERMINAL, AND 18 HANGARS (10 OF THEM CONSTRUCTED AFTER 1969). THE FEDERAL AVIATION ADMINISTRATION'S 80-FOOT CONTROL TOWER HOUSES AN AERONAUTICAL MUSEUM, THE NEW JERSEY AVIATION HALL OF FAME.

THE DOWNTOWN MANHATTAN HELIPORT PROVIDED QUICK AND EASY ACCESS FROM THE FINANCIAL DISTRICT TO THE REGION'S THREE MAJOR AIRPORTS.

THE DOWNTOWN MANHATTAN HELIPORT

The Port Authority Downtown Manhattan Heliport was opened on December 8, 1960—the first heliport in the U.S. to be certified for scheduled passenger service. Situated close to the Financial District and less than 10 minutes flying time from the three regional airports, it quickly became a key component in the regional air travel system.

Port Authority Investment in the Regional Airports

After taking over Newark Airport, the Port Authority enlarged it, constructed a $9 million runway in 1952, and completed an $8.5 million passenger terminal in 1953 that housed elegant shops and a popular restaurant, The Newarker.

Port Authority investment in Newark Airport exceeded $39 million by the end of 1960. Both passenger and air cargo activity continued to grow, the cargo being spurred by a modern four-building Air Cargo Center that had opened the previous December. A new 150-foot-high control tower, located between the two active runways, was opened by the FAA in 1960 to handle the rapidly growing number of plane movements, which approached 160,000 in 1959 alone. By the Port Authority's 75th anniversary, the agency had invested more than $1.6 billion in Newark Airport.

In 1958, New York International (now John F. Kennedy) Airport, the most rapidly expanding air terminal in the region, became the leading passenger terminal for the first time. It served most of the region's 2 million overseas air travelers, who accounted for more than 15 percent of the region's total air passengers. The airport continued to expand, and by the end of the 1950s the Port Authority had invested $263 million in the airport.

The International Arrivals and Airline Wing Buildings, the first great structures to be completed in the 655-acre Terminal City, began operating in 1958. The International Arrivals Building housed Customs, Public Health, and Immigration facilities as well as restaurants, retail shops, public services, and observation areas. Plans for a new three-faith Chapel Plaza in Terminal City's International Park were approved in 1960. Chapel Plaza, to be constructed by the Catholic, Jewish, and Protestant faiths, would replace the existing chapels. Port Authority investments at John F. Kennedy Airport now total more than $2 billion.

LaGuardia Airport handled more domestic air traffic than either New York International or Newark. A reconstruction and improvement program begun in 1957 included a much larger, three-story terminal building out of which the six major airlines serving LaGuardia would operate, along with a new control tower, a new southeast-northwest runway, a two-level terminal roadway, and an enlarged parking area next to the new terminal. In 1959, the Port Authority added $2.25 million to its investment in the airport, which reached $16.4 million by the end of the year.

Did You Know?

- IN 1926, ALL THE AIRLINES IN THE UNITED STATES COMBINED REPRESENTED A FLEET OF ONLY 28 PLANES. IF ALL THOSE PLANES WERE IN THE AIR AND FULLY BOOKED, JUST 112 PEOPLE WOULD HAVE BEEN IN FLIGHT.
- IN THE EARLY DAYS OF AVIATION MOST PILOTS WERE MILITARY AVIATORS WHO HAD LEARNED THEIR SKILLS IN WORLD WAR I.
- BEFORE 1927, 90 PERCENT OF ALL AVIATION ACTIVITY IN THE UNITED STATES TOOK PLACE IN THE NEW YORK–NEW JERSEY REGION. MOST OF IT WAS MAIL CARGO.
- UNTIL 1948, WHEN IDLEWILD AIRPORT (NOW JFK) WAS OPENED, ALL OVERSEAS FLIGHTS WERE ROUTED THROUGH LAGUARDIA AIRPORT'S MARINE AIR TERMINAL.
- NEWARK AIRPORT IS THE HOME OF THE WORLD'S FIRST PAVED RUNWAY AND THE FIRST AIR TRAFFIC CONTROL CENTER. THE BUILDING THAT HOUSED THE ORIGINAL CONTROL CENTER IS STILL THERE.

PORT NEWARK WAS CARVED OUT OF AN AREA THAT HAD BEEN LARGELY MARSHLAND. IT OPENED ON OCTOBER 20, 1915, WITH A DOCK NEARLY A MILE LONG AND A CHANNEL DEPTH OF 20 FEET WHERE A SHALLOW CREEK HAD FLOWED BEFORE. WORLD WAR I ALL BUT MONOPOLIZED PORT NEWARK. COMMERCIAL DEVELOPMENT LANGUISHED IN THE ENSUING YEARS AND DURING THE GREAT DEPRESSION. THE SEAPORT WOULD AGAIN BE "DRAFTED" INTO MILITARY SERVICE FOR WORLD WAR II, BUZZING FURIOUSLY WITH THE FLOW OF WAR SUPPLIES CRUCIAL TO THE ALLIED VICTORY.

THE PORT AUTHORITY AND THE PORTS

For years, Brooklyn's waterfront was renowned for shipbuilding. During the Civil War, the ironclad Monitor was launched from Brooklyn's shipyards, and scores of clippers, yachts, battleships, and destroyers originated there. The shipyards were particularly busy during World War II, when ships could not be built fast enough to replace those destroyed at Pearl Harbor and by the war being waged on the oceans.

After World War II, a booming U.S. economy was fueled by the pent-up demand for consumer products that had been unavailable or rationed during the war. Military personnel brought many U.S. products with them overseas and brought many foreign products back home. This exchange of cultures and products made the world seem like a smaller place.

Returning military personnel triggered an enormous demand for housing, products and services, as they spawned the largest generation in history—the baby boomers. Demand for residential and commercial properties soared to accommodate the population growth, and "inflation" became the new buzzword that described the economy. Stevedore operations, warehouses, and other shipping services found it difficult to find sufficient space in urban areas to handle, store, and distribute the growing flow of goods, particularly in and around Manhattan.

The Port Authority was charged with facilitating the monumental transition from the eclectic urban wharves of Manhattan, Brooklyn, Hoboken, Jersey City, and other port towns to the specialized marine terminal facilities at Port Newark, Elizabeth, Red Hook, and Howland Hook. During the postwar years, the design and operation of such specialized terminals would be duplicated in virtually every major port in the world.

THE DAWN OF THE MODERN SHIPPING ERA

Like airports, modern marine terminals required a lot of space. Ships had grown larger, their cargo loads were greater, and the resulting economies of scale needed to be handled by expanded dockside services. The turnaround time for a ship was also important. The longer it took to unload and reload, the less profitable the operation. And getting those cargoes efficiently distributed inland was important to both truckers and the railroads.

AN EASTWARD VIEW OVERLOOKING NEWARK CHANNEL ACROSS TO NEWARK BAY AND THE CITY OF BAYONNE, NEW JERSEY, BEYOND, IN 1951. NOTE THE DREDGING TAKING PLACE ALONG THE WHARF AT THE FOOT OF THE CHANNEL (FOREGROUND).

All of these concerns led to the introduction of containerization, which is to shipping what mass production is to manufacturing. This innovation was introduced at Port Newark on April 26, 1956, a date that many in the shipping industry hail as the dawn of the modern maritime era.

The Ideal X, a converted World War II tanker, was rigged for an experiment to use standardized cargo containers, which could be uniformly stacked and secured on ships and later unloaded to a compatible truck or rail chassis. Pioneered by the McLean Trucking Company at the Port Authority's marine terminal at Port Newark, these "snap-on boxes" made it possible to move cargo safely and securely in a fraction of the time it previously took. Modern steel containers are weatherproof and lockable, which reduces damage and theft and simplifies inventory tracking. They can also be refrigerated to protect perishable goods.

Within a few years containerization revolutionized the shipping industry, triggering a redesign of trucks, ships, rail cars, cranes, and other equipment used to transport goods. On August 15, 1962, the Port Authority opened the Elizabeth–Port Authority Marine Terminal, the world's first all-container port facility, a prototype that other modern ports would copy. At Elizabeth the Pan-Atlantic Steamship Company, predecessor of Sea-Land Service, Inc., pioneered a full-scale effort to perfect containerization; Elizabeth became known as America's Container Capital.

THE ONE DENT IN THE CONTAINER PLAN

Because containerization could greatly reduce costs, the shipping companies agreed to a Guaranteed Annual Income (GAI) until retirement for longshoremen whose services would no longer be needed. The thinking of the time was that the GAI payments were small compared to the enormous amount of money saved through the efficient new cargo handling processes. The payments were deemed a cost-effective compromise. Indeed, without such an agreement, local unions might easily have blocked the plan altogether to save jobs.

With the passage of time, however, all major ports embraced containerization, and the competitive edge initially held by the Port of New York and New Jersey was eventually eroded. Many other ports also had to sign similar GAI agreements, but their workforces were smaller so their payments

FACING PAGE:
PORT NEWARK, LOOKING WEST OVER NEWARK CHANNEL TO NEWARK AIRPORT. IN MARCH 1948 THE PORT AUTHORITY ASSUMED RESPONSIBILITY UNDER A 50-YEAR LEASE WITH THE CITY OF NEWARK TO FINANCE, DEVELOP, AND OPERATE PORT NEWARK. THERE WERE THEN ONLY 14 USABLE DEEP-SEA BERTHS, AND THE ROADWAYS, RAIL SYSTEMS, TRANSIT SHEDS, AND CARGO BUILDINGS GREATLY NEEDED REPAIR OR REPLACEMENT. BY 1951, PORT NEWARK HAD BECOME A MODERN TERMINAL, WITH 21 BERTHS AND A DEEPENED 35-FOOT CHANNEL ABLE TO ACCOMMODATE THE LARGEST CARGO SHIPS AFLOAT. TODAY, AFTER MORE THAN $400 MILLION IN PORT AUTHORITY IMPROVEMENTS, PORT NEWARK ENCOMPASSES 930 ACRES, MORE THAN TRIPLE ITS ORIGINAL LAND AREA, WITH 38 DEEPWATER BERTHS.

DREDGING BERTHS AT PORT NEWARK IN 1950 TO ACCOMODATE THE LARGEST MODERN CARGO VESSELS.

THE CARGO HANDLED AT PORT NEWARK COULD INCLUDE FROZEN HAWAIIAN PINEAPPLE, PUERTO RICAN SUGAR, AFRICAN CROCIDOLITE, ARGENTINE WOOL, SPANISH OLIVES, BRAZILIAN CARNAUBA WAX, ITALIAN CHERRIES IN BRINE, ICELANDIC SALTED COD, PORTUGUESE BALED CORK, CALIFORNIA WINE, BUSES FOR EXPORT TO COLOMBIA, AND VERMONT MARBLE AS WELL AS SWEDISH GRANITE BLOCKS, BASKETS, CHRISTMAS TREE ORNAMENTS, FEATHERS, FROZEN FISH, AND EVER-INCREASING AMOUNTS OF LUMBER AND SCANDINAVIAN WOOD PULP.

were not as high as those incurred by the Port Authority of New York and New Jersey.

Deregulation of the shipping and transportation industries over the next few decades fostered a return of stiff competition that made it difficult for the port to pass along the cost of the GAI to its customers. By the 1980s, traffic was gravitating to cheaper ports, and shippers, the unions, and the Port Authority needed to find a way to preserve the port industry and the thousands of jobs it provided. Incentives to longshoremen to retire proved the most cost-effective way to reduce the GAI, a move that brought cargo handling costs down and made the New York–New Jersey Port more competitive with other world ports.

CEREMONIES ABOARD THE *U.S.S. CORREGIDOR*, BERTHED AT PORT NEWARK IN JULY 1951.

PORT NEWARK HANDLED A RECORD TONNAGE OF CARGO IN THE EARLY 1950s AS THE PORT AUTHORITY'S IMPROVEMENT PROGRAM LED TO INCREASINGLY HIGHER RATES OF EMPLOYMENT, TENANT OCCUPANCY, AND NEW BUSINESS DEVELOPMENT.

JERSEY CITY TOLL PLAZA, 1956.

VEHICULAR TUNNELS

THE NORTH TUBE OF THE LINCOLN TUNNEL IS BUILT

It did not take long for postwar traffic to test the limits of the trans-Hudson crossings. By early 1945, the Port Authority contemplated building another tunnel to supplement the Holland and Lincoln, one that would stretch from Hoboken to 14th Street in Manhattan. By 1952 the press reported that the agency believed this new tunnel would cost about $200 million. In addition to the cost, the impact on local traffic and the problem of building access roads in a densely populated area led the Port Authority to scrap the idea. The agency instead added a third tube to the Lincoln Tunnel; it opened in 1957, at a cost of $100 million.

The Lincoln Tunnel's second tube, the North Tube, opened to traffic as a two-lane, westbound roadway between midtown Manhattan and Weehawken, New Jersey, at noon on February 1, 1945. The opening of the North Tube permitted the South Tube, which had been carrying both eastbound and westbound traffic, to be converted to a one-way, two-lane eastbound roadway between Weehawken, New Jersey, and Manhattan. Together with the Holland Tunnel, there were now eight lanes of underwater crossings operated by the Port Authority between New York and New Jersey.

Ground was broken for the North Tube in February 1937. But the Port Authority suspended construction of the 7,500-foot roadway after it was holed-through in May 1938 because there was not enough traffic to justify its completion. During the next three years, however, traffic in the single South Tube more than doubled, and in June 1941, construction of the North Tube resumed.

Most civilian construction was constrained during the early 1940s because of the war. Because of the urgent need for an additional trans-Hudson artery to expedite the movement of military personnel and materiel, the War Production Board awarded priorities to the Port Authority to obtain the critical materials necessary to complete the connection.

When the war ended in 1945, both tubes of the Lincoln Tunnel carried the increased traffic caused by the lifting of gasoline restrictions. In its first year of operation the North Tube alone accommodated more than 3 million vehicles.

HOLLAND TUNNEL'S MANHATTAN TOLL PLAZA IN 1957. CARS ARE HEADED FOR JERSEY CITY, NEW JERSEY.

Snowbirds

The Lincoln Tunnel was opened to pedestrian traffic twice due to blizzards. On December 26, 1947, after 25.5 inches of snow fell, about 600 New Yorkers were permitted to walk through the South Tube after their buses had stalled on the New Jersey approaches. On December 12, 1960, the same tube was opened to pedestrians after a similar storm; it remained open throughout the day. Edward J. Silberfarb, a reporter for the Herald Tribune, *made the trek and reported on the grand march in the next day's paper: "The sound of the Marine Hymn, tramping feet, and rattling boot buckles echoed through the tube." About 2,000 commuters made the walk.*

THE NEW YORK UNION MOTOR TRUCK TERMINAL OPENED IN NOVEMBER 1949. IT OCCUPIED A FOUR-BLOCK AREA NEAR THE HOLLAND TUNNEL. THE HUGE BUILDING WAS A TRANSFER STATION FOR FREIGHT HEADING FOR LOCAL SITES. THE TERMINAL WAS CONVENIENTLY LOCATED TO PROVIDE ACCESS TO STEAMSHIP PIERS AND RETAIL STORES BELOW 59TH STREET.

VEHICULAR TERMINALS

THE UNION MOTOR TRUCK TERMINALS

With new bridges and tunnels across the Hudson, and an improved regional highway system, cars and trucks poured into Manhattan's already crowded streets. Vast numbers of heavy trucks crawled along to markets, warehouses, piers, and small terminals inadequate to the task of accommodating them.

In response to the urgent need for well-located terminals, the Port Authority opened the New York Union Motor Truck terminal in 1949, and the Newark Union Motor Truck Terminal in March 1951.

Heavy tractor-trailer units transporting freight into and out of the Port District could now efficiently exchange loads with local fleets of light trucks. Delivered to the terminal, the contents of the heavy over-the-roaders were sorted and classified for local destinations, then picked up and delivered in efficiently routed, consolidated loads by the light trucking fleet. Outbound freight was handled similarly: collected from shippers by light trucks, delivered to the terminals, consolidated into full-truckload consignments, and loaded for over-the-road shipment.

Trucking companies began to set up their own terminals and satellite stations in many locations in the region more accessible to their customers, making the concept of a central receiving point for the handling of long-distance shipments less desirable.

The impact of these changes affected the Newark Truck Terminal first. By 1960 its lease with a consortium of over-the-road carriers expired and various individual truck operators took over truck dock space. The extensive office space, however, remained largely vacant despite continuing attempts to rent it, and the future of the building as a Port Authority facility now looked doubtful. It was not until 1980, however, that the Port Authority could close the book on the building with the announcement of its sale to a local mineral and chemical concern.

The New York Truck Terminal fared somewhat better with respect to its original purpose. United Parcel Service leased the building in 1973 and operated it as a cargo consolidation and distribution center handling local and worldwide distribution of packages, many of which were associated with New York City's garment and financial districts. UPS, with an eye to buying the facility, expanded its workforce there and made plans to reconstruct and modernize it and to connect it with an additional structure to be built across the street.

In 1992, 43 years after adding truck terminal operations to its activities, the Port Authority sold the New York Union Motor Truck Terminal to UPS and left the business.

An interesting sidebar to the truck terminal story is that in 1979, during a period of declining activity at the terminal, the Port Authority invited various not-for-profit arts organizations to occupy space in the building at below-market rates until the space was once again needed. When UPS renegotiated its lease 10 years later, the Port Authority and the New York State Council on the Arts enlisted the cooperation of the company to minimize the hardship of relocation for these arts groups by assisting them with finding other suitable and affordable space. To their credit, UPS pursued this venture with sensitivity to the needs of the arts groups and earned the praise of the New York governor for its efforts.

HEAVY TRACTOR TRAILERS IN THE TRUCK BAYS AT THE NEW YORK UNION MOTOR TRUCK TERMINAL.

Growing the Transportation Network

As the region grew in the 1950s, so did traffic, and the federal government launched the Interstate Highway Program. On January 11, 1955, the Triborough Bridge and Tunnel Authority and the Port Authority agreed on a $1.2 million plan to construct a second deck on the George Washington Bridge; a new regional expressway system; a new bridge at Throgs Neck; the world's longest single-span suspension bridge across the entrance to New York Harbor, the Verrazano Narrows Bridge; and miles of new roads and bridge approaches.

The Port Authority of the 1950s was involved not only with bridges and tunnels, but also with expanding three major airports, building heliports, renovating the Brooklyn piers, constructing Port Newark and Elizabeth, dredging New York Harbor and its approaches, and creating international shipping and truck terminals. The agency also facilitated mass transit by building a consolidated bus terminal.

IN 1954, A 50-MAN CREW BEGAN THE TWO-YEAR SAGA OF PAINTING THE MILE-LONG GEORGE WASHINGTON BRIDGE. RUST SPOTS WERE SCRAPED OFF AND A PROTECTIVE COATING WAS APPLIED. NEXT, ALL OF THE STEELWORK WAS PAINTED—THE TOWERS AND CABLES THE FIRST YEAR, AND THE STEEL UNDER THE ROADWAY THE FOLLOWING YEAR. MORE THAN 20,000 GALLONS OF PAINT WERE USED. ON SOME PARTS OF THE BRIDGE PAINTERS WORKED AT HEIGHTS MORE THAN 600 FEET ABOVE THE HUDSON RIVER.

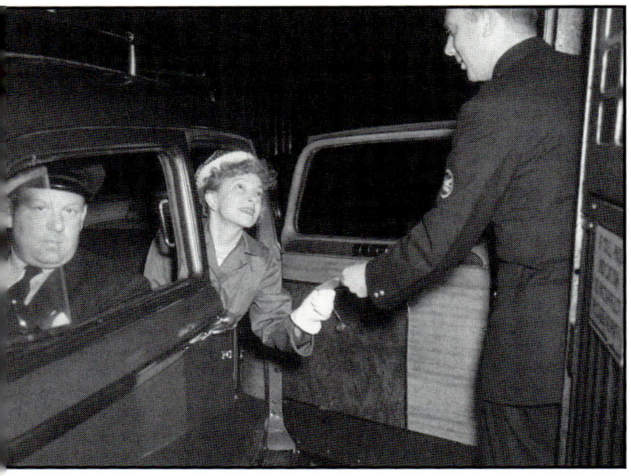

ACTRESS HELEN HAYES CROSSED OVER THE GEORGE WASHINGTON BRIDGE AT MIDNIGHT ON JUNE 15, 1950. SHE WAS AMONG THE FIRST TO USE THE NEW TICKET SYSTEM INSTALLED AT THE THREE HUDSON RIVER CROSSINGS. THE SYSTEM BECAME AN INSTANT HIT WITH COMMUTERS, WITH NEARLY 10,000 40-TRIP TICKETS SOLD IN ADVANCE.

THE BATTLE FOR A CONSOLIDATED BUS STATION IN MANHATTAN

The Port Authority Bus Terminal, the largest bus facility ever built in New York, and, indeed, in the U.S., consolidated several smaller bus stations into one facility. Its opening in 1950 was the culmination of efforts begun more than a decade before by the fiery and effervescent Mayor Fiorello LaGuardia. According to Princeton political scientist Jameson Doig, the evolution of the terminal from concept to reality exemplifies "the mixture of rational planning and adroit political maneuvering that became the Port Authority's hallmark during Executive Director Austin Tobin's era."

The story below calls on Doig's extensive research on the planning and politics of the bus terminal project. In the early 1930s, motorbuses heading to midtown Manhattan from New Jersey crossed the Hudson either via the Holland Tunnel downtown or the George Washington Bridge uptown. After the first tube of the Lincoln Tunnel was completed in 1937, bus travel to midtown became more popular, and 2,000 buses soon made the trip each day. By 1939, trans-Hudson bus trips reached 1,520,000 a year—approximately double the 1930 level.

But the growing interstate bus traffic was causing chaos in midtown. Almost every bus company operated its own facility—eight separate terminals were used in less than one square mile. Traffic congestion was further aggravated by buses driving to and from the private terminals scattered throughout midtown. Little or no shelter was provided for passengers, and the buses had to cross the city sidewalks to get into or out of the terminals. Official concern grew, and Mayor LaGuardia appointed Manhattan Borough President Stanley Isaacs chairman of a committee of city officials that would study interstate bus operations and their impact on midtown traffic.

The committee recommended that all bus terminals be situated west of Eighth Avenue, and bus improvements be banned east of Eighth Avenue between 32nd and 52nd streets. The bus companies successfully challenged the restrictions, so the mayor asked the Port Authority to study the idea of consolidating the small bus stations into one large terminal.

The Port Authority agreed to build a consolidated station, but under certain conditions. Those conditions put the agency into a 20-year battle with the Greyhound Bus Company and its ally, the powerful Robert Moses, who was, in addition being chairman of the Triborough Bridge and Tunnel Authority, a member of the City Planning Commission.

By June 1944, the Port Authority had sketched out plans for a large bus station between Eighth and Ninth Avenues, with ramps and bridges over four streets that would connect it to the Lincoln Tunnel. The design permitted most interstate buses to go directly to the terminal without crossing city streets, thereby reducing traffic congestion. The system would be the equivalent of adding two or three crosstown thoroughfares.

To persuade the bus companies to move into the new terminal, the Port Authority wanted the city to agree that no other bus terminals could be built or expanded in midtown. Unless this were done, the agency argued, bus companies would fear that their competitors would build or enlarge other more centrally located terminals. The restriction would also ensure that the terminal would have enough passengers to generate rental and concession income needed to make the huge project self-supporting.

Most of the bus companies were willing to move into the consolidated terminal. But the nation's largest bus company, Greyhound, insisted that it be allowed to retain and possibly expand its 34th Street terminal between Seventh and Eighth Avenues. Despite the potential loss of income to the new terminal, Port Authority executive director Austin Tobin did not object as long as Greyhound agreed that it would not encourage other bus companies to use its station. Greyhound opposed this restriction.

Until the spring of 1945, Robert Moses had been a supporter of the Port Authority's plans. But in early May he changed his stance and used his position as a member of the City Planning Commission to support Greyhound. Moses then engaged in maneuvers that threatened to destroy the entire bus terminal project. The reasons for his about-face are not entirely clear to this day.

The Port Authority faced a battle. The director of public relations, Lee Jaffe, worried that the agency would not prevail over the powerful Robert Moses, but nonetheless launched a strategy to defeat him. The Port Authority would compile information on midtown traffic and present it during meetings with reporters and their editorial boards. The results of Mrs. Jaffe's strategy began to pay off in the early weeks of 1946, when the *Herald Tribune*, the *New York Times* and the *Sun* endorsed the Port Authority's plan; the *Bergen Evening Record* soon did the same.

Unfortunately, for the Port Authority however, Mayor LaGuardia, a strong supporter of the new bus terminal, left office in December 1945. His successor, William O'Dwyer, dragged his feet on the bus-terminal legislation. The agency marshaled support from business groups and the two governors, however, and eventually the New York and New Jersey bills were passed and signed into law.

The Port Authority would begin building the new terminal as soon as the prohibition against further building or expansion of bus stations was approved. But Mayor O'Dwyer postponed action, and the City Planning Commission voted down the bus-terminals exclusion measure. In fact, a report commissioned by Moses endorsed the Greyhound plan, saying that it might actually reduce congestion in midtown. Greyhound reaffirmed its plans to spend $10 million to modernize and expand its 34th Street terminal. "Moses Wins, We Lose," proclaimed the *New York Post* on May 2, 1946.

Port Authority Chairman Howard Cullman announced that the agency would return the state planning funds, stating, "Evidently, O'Dwyer does not seem to want a bus terminal." Former Mayor LaGuardia joined the attack, calling the decision of Moses and his fellow commissioners a "betrayal of the public interest." The Regional Plan Association and other civic and business groups joined in the criticism of Moses and the city administration. The newspapers accused O'Dwyer of not being in charge, and called Moses "the Super Mayor of New York City." It was even suggested that Greyhound's power and influence be the subject of a special investigation.

DIGGING IN AT THE GROUNDBREAKING CEREMONIES FOR THE PORT AUTHORITY BUS TERMINAL ON JANUARY 27, 1949, ARE (LEFT TO RIGHT) PORT AUTHORITY COMMISSIONER DONALD V. LOWE, NEW JERSEY STATE SENATOR DAVID VAN ALSTYNE, JR., NEW YORK CITY MAYOR WILLIAM O'DWYER, NEW YORK GOVERNOR THOMAS E. DEWEY, AND PORT AUTHORITY CHAIRMAN HOWARD CULLMAN.

BY SEPTEMBER 1949, EXCAVATION FOR THE FOUNDATION OF THE PORT AUTHORITY BUS TERMINAL WAS UNDER WAY. THE HUGE STRUCTURE WOULD RISE ON AN ENTIRE CITY BLOCK, BETWEEN EIGHTH AND NINTH AVENUES AND 41ST AND 42ND STREETS.

IN DECEMBER 1950, THE NEW $24 MILLION PORT AUTHORITY BUS TERMINAL WAS OFFICIALLY OPENED. COMMUTERS WERE AWED BY ITS ART DECO DESIGN WITH ITS SEMICIRCULAR FACADE SET OFF WITH AN IMPRESSIVE CLOCK, ITS GLEAMING STAINLESS STEEL TRIM, AND MIRRORLIKE FLOORS OF POLISHED STONE.

THE TERMINAL WAS A MAJOR LINK IN THE REGIONAL CHAIN OF TRANSPORTATION FACILITIES. IT OFFERED A CENTRAL LOCATION FOR BOTH LONG- AND SHORT-HAUL BUSES IN AND OUT OF NEW YORK CITY.

By the summer of 1946, O'Dwyer's faith in Moses had waned. He announced that he was ready to champion a resolution prohibiting bus terminal expansion in midtown. Early the next year, he introduced a resolution that would block future Greyhound expansion and any other bus-terminal construction east of Eighth Avenue. The resolution was passed without dissent.

But the battle was not over. According to Jameson Doig, Moses "suffered defeat as much as he suffered fools, which was not gladly." Even as the Port Authority relocated tenants, demolished structures on the site, floated bonds for financing, built the terminal, and began operating it, Moses and his allies sought ways to defeat the Port Authority and win approval for Greyhound to double the size of its 34th Street bus station.

Early in 1950, Moses drafted a bill to create a New York City Parking Authority, which would have the power to build any kind of terminal; its projects would be exempted from zoning laws and review by the Board of Estimate. Tobin and his aides knew that the bill could be used to achieve the Moses-Greyhound goal. Greyhound could sell its 34th Street property to the new agency, which would lease it back to the company, and Greyhound could build a parking garage for cars and buses. Tobin went into action with the newspapers, and he and his commissioners appealed to Governor Dewey and their legislative allies in Albany. Before it was passed, the Parking Authority bill was amended, requiring that its projects conform to the 1947 bus-restriction resolution.

In 1951, Moses tried to insert wording in the parking authority law that would lift the bus restriction, claiming that a public agency could apply for permission to build a terminal in a restricted area. Tobin and Commissioner Bayard Pope spoke with O'Dwyer, who disavowed the proposal. The measure was dropped after the newspapers attacked it.

Throughout the 1950s, Greyhound tried to persuade city elected officials to let it expand its bus station. But each time the issue was raised, newspaper editorials and Manhattan business groups would attack, and the bus exclusion would be reaffirmed. Finally, in 1963, Greyhound agreed to abandon its 34th Street and 50th Street bus stations and begin operating at the Port Authority Bus Terminal. The 20-year battle was over.

BUS COMMUTERS GET A BREAK

In the early 1960s, in response to the growth of bus and automobile traffic, the Port Authority Bus Terminal was expanded vertically. The bus operating level was moved to the roof of the original terminal, and three levels of parking were erected over the existing structure that provided space for more than 1,000 cars.

Connected by direct ramps to the Lincoln Tunnel, the North Wing was added in 1981. This project extended the terminal north to 42nd Street, between the former McGraw-Hill Building and Eighth Avenue. Fifty-two new bus gates and space for 26 more were added. The South Wing of the terminal was modernized. Twenty-four open-island platforms were enclosed, with separate heating and air conditioning systems. A new ticket plaza was opened, storefronts were modernized, and public concourses were upgraded.

THE ORIGINAL FACADE OF THE PORT AUTHORITY BUS TERMINAL, AS SEEN FROM THIS AERIAL VIEW, EVOKED AN ALMOST NAUTICAL IMAGE, PERHAPS INSPIRED BY THE NAME PORT AUTHORITY. MAJOR RENOVATIONS WERE SOON TO DRAMATICALLY CHANGE THIS LOOK.

LOOKING EAST OVER THE BUS RAMPS LEADING DIRECTLY FROM THE LINCOLN TUNNEL INTO THE PORT AUTHORITY BUS TERMINAL. THE PRIME BENEFIT OF CONSTRUCTING THE TERMINAL WAS RELIEF FROM THE INTOLERABLE STREET CONGESTION OF THE CURBSIDE BUS LINES THAT HAD MULTIPLIED RAPIDLY TO SERVE THE INCREASING SUBURBAN POPULATION OF THE POSTWAR ERA.

Two Decades of Expansion

THE TWA TERMINAL INTERIOR IN 1963. TWA WAS THE ONLY CARRIER OPERATING BOTH DOMESTIC AND INTERNATIONAL FLIGHTS. THIS LEVEL OF SERVICE EARNED TWA THE CHOICE SITE FOR ITS NEW TERMINAL IMMEDIATELY NEXT TO THE INTERNATIONAL ARRIVALS BUILDING.

Screaming fans greeted the Beatles when they landed at John F. Kennedy Airport in February 1964. They were part of the so-called "British Invasion" of rock groups and movie stars that influenced everything from musical tastes to haircuts and the way people dressed.

Even in the most conservative corporate and governmental cultures, such as the Port Authority, the winds of change were evident, as the population experimented with rising hemlines, longer hairdos, Nehru jackets, and flared slacks—a collection of eclectic styles that would mark the era as a time of colorful innovation.

THOUSANDS ASSEMBLE NEAR JFK'S INTERNATIONAL ARRIVALS BUILDING, HOPING TO GET A GLIMPSE OF THE BEATLES.

THE BEATLES WAVE TO ADORING FANS AS THEY DEPART FROM JFK IN 1964.

A "HAPPENING" IN GREENWICH VILLAGE'S WASHINGTON SQUARE PARK.

EVERYONE WAS PROTESTING SOMETHING, IT SEEMED, AND THEY OFTEN DID SO AT THE PORT AUTHORITY'S TRANSPORTATION TERMINALS. TOURISTS VISITING NEW YORK VIA PATH, BUSES, AND THE AIRPORTS WERE OFTEN GREETED BY "FLOWER CHILDREN" AND DEMONSTRATORS.

GRAFFITI BECAME A MODE OF EXPRESSION FOR YOUNG PEOPLE, AND THE PORT AUTHORITY CONDUCTED A CONSTANT VIGIL TO KEEP IT OUT OF ITS FACILITIES. PATH TRAINS AND STATIONS WERE RELATIVELY GRAFFITI-FREE.

By the time the hippie movement took off in the late '60s, concern over clothing styles seemed trivial, compared to such national preoccupations as civil rights, the environment, and the Vietnam War.

In the '70s, America's bubble was about to burst again. An energy crisis generated by OPEC would shake up a country that had banked on stable oil and gas prices. Shock waves were sent throughout the economy, with prices of petroleum-dependent products going through the roof.

Fuel prices skyrocketed. Lines formed at gas stations, with many cars running out of gas as they waited to get a $3 ration before the pumps ran dry. Cars frequently ran out of gas in tunnels and on bridges.

American auto sales plummeted, as consumers eschewed gas-guzzling models with eight-cylinder engines, and sought smaller, fuel-efficient foreign cars, many of which sported price tags higher than those found on American luxury models.

The Port Authority promoted the use of mass transit. Drivers were wooed out of their single-occupancy vehicles and into buses, PATH trains, and carpools. Accommodations for bicycles were made at several agency facilities.

The economy began to decline. New York City was having its own problems, with the flight of both the middle class and industry. Since the 1960s, the New York City budget was coming up short each year, and officials taxed and borrowed to temporarily meet the budget. By 1975, the city faced a fiscal crisis. The Municipal Assistance Corporation and, later, the Emergency Financial Control Board were formed to oversee the city's finances as New York teetered near bankruptcy and sought federal aid.

The World Trade Center, opened in the early 1970s, became a beacon of hope for a city beset with financial problems. Serving as both a tourist attraction and a stimulus to international and domestic business, it became the core of one of the city's biggest urban-renewal plans. The World Financial Center, Battery Park, office buildings, apartments, condos, and hotels joined the World Trade Center in revitalizing lower Manhattan.

THE DAYS OF THE GAS GUZZLER WERE NUMBERED AS FUEL PRICES SHOT THROUGH THE ROOF WITH THE OPEC CRISIS, AND SHORTAGES LEFT MANY A PUMP DRY.

THE PORT AUTHORITY AND THE FIGHT OVER MASS TRANSIT

The railroads, dominant throughout the first half of the twentieth century, were losing money by the 1950s, especially in passenger service. Among the factors combining to destroy the passenger railroads were mismanagement, overregulation, and the rise in popularity of the automobile. Although no one realized it at the time, what was about to happen was the takeover of metropolitan mass transit by the public sector.

The Port Authority had long refused to tackle the problem of mass transportation. It opposed taking on mass transit because the agency had no taxing powers, and was dependent upon the credit markets for capital, and upon the success of its completed projects for revenues. The agency had to be selective in what it undertook because each project had to be self-sustaining—the project had to pay for itself over a projected number of years. Commuter rail transit was not self-sustaining from the farebox. Even when the private sector ran such lines, more often than not they were offset by highly profitable freight operations. As the *New York Times* stated in a 1959 story on "The Commuter Problem," "The delivery of 210,000 commuters from 17 surrounding counties in three states in a three-hour span in the morning and then their return at night within an equal span of time is not going to be economic. Too much high-priced equipment and manpower stand idle the other eighteen hours."

On the other hand, few methods of transportation can match the payload efficiency of a train. One bus can carry as many passengers as 36 automobiles. But a single train can transport as many people as a dozen buses. As early as 1954, the *Jersey Journal* and *Jersey Observer* editorialized: "All of the metropolitan area appreciates that there is a severe problem of commuter transportation and that to attempt solving it in terms of the automobile would involve a tremendous congestion in city streets.... All the studies boil down to the harsh fact that a proper interstate rapid transit system would cost from one-quarter to one-half a billion dollars and that such a system would operate at a deficit of from $5 million to $15 million a year."

Hardly a week went by in the late 1950s without some article in the press about the "commuter problem" and the "commuter crisis." But nobody in state or local government wanted to use tax dollars to subsidize commuter railroads. And at that time, the idea of state agencies buying commuter railroads outright was unheard of. But many believed that the Port Authority, with its reputation for "efficient construction and tidy finance," could solve the commuter problem at little cost. Some even contended that the rescue of the commuter railroads was the duty of the Port Authority because its trans-Hudson tunnels and bridges had contributed to their decline.

Things really heated up in 1958, when the Federal Transportation Act permitted railroads to discontinue unprofitable services. The Interstate Commerce Commission argued in federal court that the New York Central and Erie railroads be allowed to discontinue their trans-Hudson ferry services. The ICC even implied that it would consider allowing the railroads to eventually abandon passenger traffic because of the "chronic deficit" it caused. But, the trans-Hudson ferry service had already been abandoned, with 8,000 former commuters taking to cars, buses, or the Hudson & Manhattan Railroad.

The New Jersey Assembly met throughout the year to discuss the commuter problem. It even introduced legislation that would require the Port Authority to take on commuter rail service. But the agency argued that acquiring such a losing operation would violate its contractual obligations with bondholders and lower its credit rating. Port Authority executive director Austin Tobin reported to the commissioners, "Once again, as we have seen on innumerable occasions during the past 25 years, we are faced with another attempt to saddle the Port Authority with the deficit operations of the H&M."

By 1960, the H&M announced that it was seeking a buyer for its 52-year-old Hudson Tubes. At the same time, Chase Manhattan's David Rockefeller and other business leaders pressed for a new World Trade Center at the east end of Wall Street that would revitalize the financial district. The Port Authority was interested in the project, but New Jersey would not consent unless the agency also took over the H&M Railroad. The World Trade Center development was now linked to the commuter rail issue.

On May 5, 1960, the *Newark Evening News* carried a story headlined "Trade Center May Bring PA Into Commuter Picture." Reporter Guy Savino quoted Austin Tobin, who had told a luncheon meeting of the Society of Foreign Consuls, "One of the most important ingredients for the success of such a center, of course, is accessibility, and a study is now under way to analyze and suggest possible improvements in transportation to the proposed site." Savino speculated: "The center would be built at the foot of Wall Street on the East River, in an area that, because of collapsing train and ferry service, is becoming increasingly more difficult to reach from New Jersey....The state sends about 40,000 now into the financial district, of which the proposed center would be the capital. The Hudson & Manhattan Railroad is one of the principal means of reaching the district."

On September 27, 1960, after six months of study, the Port Authority offered to buy the H&M for $20.5 million. Calling the railroad line itself "valueless," the agency used most of the money to acquire the property at 30 and 50 Church Street on which the H&M buildings stood. Renovating the railroad would cost another $50 million, putting the total cost of the deal at about $70 million. "After reviewing the legal and financial commitments of the Port Authority and the need for maintaining its sound credit," Tobin reported to the commissioners, "I stated that the core of the problem was whether or not the two states could build a statutory fence around the H&M by guaranteeing the investors that the Authority would not and could not become involved in the large and increasing deficits of the New York and New Jersey commuter railroads." The Port Authority would acquire the Hudson Tubes, but be excused from any larger involvement in the commuter problem.

The Port Authority's takeover of the H&M was widely hailed, although H&M trustee Herman Stichman called the bid too low, saying it should be more than doubled, to between $40 million and $50 million. Tobin noted, "There's only one issue left after all this talk, and that's how much." The exact amount was decided by the courts.

In September 1962, at long last, the Port Authority took over operation of the H&M, and called the system Port Authority Trans-Hudson, or PATH. As it turned out, the total cost of the takeover was about what Tobin had predicted: $72.6 million.

The takeover agreement was embodied in bistate legislation which also contained a covenant between the two states and Port Authority bondholders to preclude further Port Authority involvement in deficit rail mass transportation projects. This covenant has had many critics. In fact, in the early 1970s political support for the repeal of the covenant was widespread. Labor attorney Theodore Kheel filed suit in federal court, challenging the agreement as unconstitutional, and organized citizens' committees to support improved mass transit. The two states enacted legislation in 1972 to prospectively repeal the covenant. In 1973, Governors Brendan Byrne of New Jersey and Malcolm Wilson of New York signed retroactive repeal legislation, but in 1977 the courts declared the retroactive repeal unconstitutional. The last series of Port Authority bonds to which the covenant applies is scheduled to be retired in February 2007.

While the H&M railroad deal was being hammered out, the World Trade Center project was being planned. In January 1960, the Downtown–Lower Manhattan Association asked the Port Authority to study how the project would be financed and operated. The *Herald Tribune* editorialized: "The idea of such a trade center is to provide within a concentrated, easily accessible area all the services and facilities needed for the development of international trade.... As everyone knows, the Port Authority has a tremendously successful record in planning and developing big public projects.... Meanwhile, the Downtown–Lower Manhattan Association is to be congratulated for getting things started. Civic leadership, we are delighted to see, is very much alive in New York." The *New York Times* called the proposed project "an exciting, stimulating prospect."

In March 1961, the Port Authority released its study of the World Trade Center. The project would still be located on the East River, but its cost was estimated at $355 million. If construction began in 1962, the complex could open by 1968.

To proceed with the plan, however, legislation allowing the Port Authority to undertake the project had to be approved by the New York and New Jersey legislatures. On March 20, 1961, executive director Tobin wrote: "In New York, the bill, which apparently will be sponsored by the Governor's office, would be in the form of one legislative package covering both the World Trade Center and the H&M acquisition. The purpose of this package, as we have been advised over the past three weeks or so, is to compel New Jersey to accept and approve Port Authority development of the World Trade Center as New York's price for the Port Authority acquisition of the H&M."

The World Trade Center was conceived as a latter-day version of the Tontine Coffee House, site of the New York Stock Exchange in the 1790s. The Coffee House was located at the corner of Wall and Water Streets, and the World Trade Center almost was, too. The original site of the project, as announced by the Downtown–Lower Manhattan Association on January 26, 1960, extended from Old Slip to Fulton Street, between Water and South Street, where the South Street Seaport is today.

But in December 1961 the Port Authority announced that the World Trade Center project was being moved to the opposite side of lower Manhattan: "The Port Authority is undertaking a study of the possibility of developing a World Trade Center on the west side of Manhattan and of combining this facility with a new modern terminal for the Hudson & Manhattan Railroad to replace the antiquated terminal facilities in the same area which are now used by New Jersey and New York commuters....The combined facility would occupy a nine-block area bounded by Church Street on the east, Cortlandt Street on the south, West Street on the west, and Vesey Street on the north. The obsolete H&M buildings at 30 and 50 Church Street would be removed to make way for the new development." The same bistate legislation that authorized the takeover of the H&M also authorized the Port Authority to effectuate the World Trade Center.

THE SITE OF THE WORLD TRADE CENTER PRIOR TO CONSTRUCTION, WITH THE HUDSON TERMINAL TOWERS SEEN CENTER RIGHT.

DOWNTOWN—BEFORE THE WORLD TRADE CENTER

Downtown Manhattan in the early 1960s was a rather eclectic neighborhood, a patchwork of brokerage firms, banks, insurance companies, and employment agencies mingled with block after block of electronics, hardware, and junk shops selling parts for almost anything imaginable. The streets surrounding Hudson Terminal were called Radio Row, a place for tinkerers and would-be inventors to shop for electronic widgets and whatnots.

Although amateur electronics were all the rage in the 1950s, the era of vacuum tubes and wired kits came to a close with the introduction of transistors and printed circuits. Indeed, by 1965 solid-state equipment became so inexpensive that it no longer paid to buy kits or repair radios. A new transistor radio cost only $10, less than the price of old parts. Radio Row was thus on the verge of technological extinction when the World Trade Center was proposed for the site. Its demise seemed inevitable, for few such stores survived elsewhere in the city.

The 22-story Hudson Terminals building was the largest office complex in New York when built by the Hudson & Manhattan Railroad between 1907 and 1909. A ponderous building, its walls rose unbroken by the "setback" mandates later imposed on New York towers to permit natural light to reach the sidewalks. Consequently, the streets surrounding Hudson Terminal were bleak and dark, with narrow sidewalks and tunnel-like perspectives. The financial woes of the H&M even precluded cleaning of the soot-covered building, which further added to the neighborhood's Gothic gloom.

THE ELEVATED WESTSIDE HIGHWAY AND DERELICT DOCKS ARE STILL STANDING IN THIS 1967 VIEW. ALSO SEEN IS THE HUDSON TERMINAL (CENTER) AND SEVERAL SMALLER STRUCTURES THAT WOULD BE RAZED TO MAKE WAY FOR THE ENORMOUS WORLD TRADE CENTER COMPLEX.

EXCAVATION OF THE WORLD TRADE CENTER'S FOUNDATION IS WELL UNDER WAY IN THIS 1968 VIEW, WHICH SHOWS THE EXPOSED PATH TUBES LEADING TO HUDSON TERMINAL. SERVICE ON PATH AND SUBWAYS WAS MAINTAINED DURING THE CONSTRUCTION OF THE WORLD TRADE CENTER.

HOW THE TWIN TOWERS WERE BUILT

Construction of the World Trade Center began in 1965. The foundation was sunk into Manhattan bedrock, 70 feet below the strata of rubble, silt, sand, gravel, and boulders. Building the foundation required relocating a maze of utility installations; telephone and electrical cables; fire-alarm wires; pneumatic tubes; and gas, steam, and water lines. Debris and landfill were moved across West Street, to create more than 23 acres of new land (now the site of the World Financial Center and Battery Park City). The excavation turned up anchors, pieces of ships, bottles, old shoes, and various coins, including an "almost perfect" 1749 British half-penny.

Another construction challenge was that PATH, with a station underneath the old Hudson and Manhattan structures, had to continue to operate normally until the new terminal was completed in 1971. During excavation, PATH actually operated with its tubes under Fulton and Cortlandt Streets exposed.

The construction of the World Trade Center provided a fascinating event for thousands of spectators. Work started first on the North Tower, followed by the South Tower and the low-rise buildings encircling the plaza. More than 200,000 tons of steel were used. Enough concrete was used to lay a 5-foot- wide sidewalk to Washington, D.C. The electrical wire used could stretch to Mexico. At the peak of construction, some 5,000 workers swarmed over the site.

Concrete footings were formed and poured into the bedrock to support the steel for the towers and the plaza. Grillages, the steel beams on which the core columns rest, were then laid on the footings. Next came the building of the core, the rectangular elevator-service area within each tower building, where the interior columns are located.

The placement of the load-bearing outer columns kept pace with the core columns. Each 22-ton prefabricated panel, with vertical columns welded to the beams, was spliced onto the next. As the columns and walls rose, the floor systems were installed in preassembled single-unit sections. Next came the skin of aluminum with stainless steel trim that enclosed the structural steel. The 22-inch spaces between the columns formed the windows, which were made of bronze-tinted heat-reflective glass.

Kangaroo cranes lifting tons of steel up the sides of the towers was a spectacular sight that could be seen for miles around. When the building walls rose to the height of the cranes, the kangaroo equipment was heaved a dozen feet to a new position straddling the construction. When the job was done, the cranes were dismantled and lowered by a neighboring crane. The last crane left on each building was taken apart by a guy derrick, which was itself dismantled, its parts taken through a roof hatch and brought down by freight elevator.

The Design of the Twin Towers

The design for the World Trade Center was unveiled in January 1964—twin 110-story towers designed by Minoru Yamasaki. At 1,350 feet high, the towers would be the tallest buildings in the world.

Designed with load-bearing steel walls rather than a conventional steel skeleton, the buildings would contain a vertical railway of 99 local and express elevators in each tower. The only interior columns would be in the core, which would contain the elevators. This design provided for column-free interior floor spaces. In effect, the builders would erect a huge four-sided lattice, bound together for great strength.

The twin towers were to rise above a spacious sun-drenched plaza with an enormous globelike fountain at the center. Silver columns would ascend in contrast to the inset windows, accentuating the height of the towers. Functionally pure, but not without pattern or symmetry, the twin towers possessed a simple elegance which enabled them to maintain their modernity to the present day. When one considers that most skyscrapers built in 1930 lost their contemporary look by 1950, this was no small achievement.

Yamasaki, a Seattle native, said when the design was revealed, "The World Trade Center should be imbued with the feelings of man's belief in both his greatness and his humanity." He also advised the New York Times that the building's full-length windows would be 22 inches wide, adding, "People are not afraid of height when the width of the window is not much more than their shoulders."

Ada Louise Huxtable, the noted architecture critic of the New York Times, said of the design: "Esthetics and engineering are mutually dependent.... Here the delicate verticality of the handsome twin towers is no curtain wall paste-over; these slender ribs are visible metal-sheathed supporting steel columns that form a wall-supporting truss....From the design aspect this is not only the biggest but the best new building project that New York has seen in a long time. It represents a level of taste and thought that has been distressingly rare in the city's mass of nondescript post-war commercial construction." The newspaper itself editorialized, "No project has been more promising for New York."

MINORU YAMASAKI HAD THE OPPORTUNITY TO CREATE A PROJECT THAT MOST ARCHITECTS MIGHT ONLY DREAM ABOUT.

FROM TOP LEFT: KANGAROO CRANES WAVE THEIR BUSY ARMS AS THEY HOIST THE STEEL THAT WILL BUILD A PATH INTO THE SKY. TOWER ONE ROSE SOME 20 FLOORS AHEAD OF ITS TWIN IN THIS 1970 VIEW, AND ALREADY EXCEEDED THE HEIGHT OF NEIGHBORING SKYSCRAPERS ON LIBERTY STREET.

THE ALUMINUM AND STAINLESS STEEL SKIN MOVES UP THE SUPERSTRUCTURE OF THE TOWERS.

CONSTRUCTION OF TOWER ONE OF THE WORLD TRADE CENTER AT ABOUT THE HALFWAY MARK.

THE WORLD TRADE CENTER COMPLEX TODAY

Because of its scale and diverse use of space, the World Trade Center is not just two office towers. Essentially a city within a city for some 50,000 occupants, it contains banks, shops, restaurants, an observation deck, a plaza, law offices, medical facilities, a day-care facility, and rapid transit stations. The World Trade Center opened in 1970, but the final building was not opened until 1987.

The complex occupies some 16 acres. The twin towers soar above a five-acre parklike plaza the size of four football fields. Nestled around the towers are four low-rise buildings—the U.S. Customhouse, the Southeast Plaza Building, the Northeast Plaza Building, and the World Trade Center Marriott Hotel (formerly the Vista). A seventh building, on the north side of Vesey Street, is connected to the complex by a pedestrian bridge of stainless steel. A larger pedestrian bridge connects the World Trade Center with the Winter Garden atrium of the World Financial Center.

STILL UNDER CONSTRUCTION, THE HUGE LOBBIES OF THE TWIN TOWERS RISE APPROXIMATELY FOUR STORIES HIGH, WITH LANCET WINDOWS AND A MEZZANINE THAT OVERLOOKS THE LOBBY.

International Aesthetics at the World Trade Center

Sculptures, tapestries, and architectural enhancements are an integral part of the public areas of the World Trade Center. In keeping with the theme of world trade, the complex incorporates designs by people from all over the globe. These include works by such famous artists as Alexander Calder, Louise Nevelson, Joan Miró, Fritz Koenig, James Rosati, and Masayuki Nagare. Landscaping and floral arrangements on the plaza, in the mall, and in public areas provide colorful touches to a bustling environment.

SET IN AUSTIN J. TOBIN PLAZA, NAMED FOR THE PORT AUTHORITY'S EXECUTIVE DIRECTOR FROM 1942–1972, IS JAMES ROSATI'S STAINLESS STEEL CONSTRUCTIVIST *IDEOGRAM* (1974).

MADE OF BLACK SWEDISH GRANITE, MASAYUKI NAGARE'S *WORLD TRADE CENTER PLAZA* IS SUGGESTIVE OF THE GREAT PYRAMIDS.

ALEXANDER CALDER'S RED WORLD TRADE CENTER STABILE WAS ONCE LOCATED ON THE CORNER OF VESEY AND CHURCH STREETS, BUT WITH THE COMPLETION OF SEVEN WORLD TRADE CENTER, IT WAS MOVED TO BECOME THE CENTERPIECE OF THE NEW SKYSCRAPER'S ELEVATED PLAZA CONNECTION TO AUSTIN J. TOBIN PLAZA OVER VESEY STREET.

SPHERE FOR THE PLAZA FOUNTAIN (1969), DESIGNED BY GERMAN SCULPTOR FRITZ KOENIG. THE 25-FOOT-HIGH WORK IS BRONZE ON A BLACK-GRANITE BASE.

THE MEZZANINE OF TOWER TWO HOUSES JOAN MIRÓ'S WORLD TRADE CENTER TAPESTRY. FABRICATED OF WOOL AND HEMP, IT IS 20 FT. X 35 FT.

KING KONG MEETS HIS DEMISE ON THE NORTHEAST PLAZA OF THE WORLD TRADE CENTER IN THE 1976 REMAKE OF THE 1933 FILM CLASSIC. THE TWIN TOWERS REPLACED THE EMPIRE STATE BUILDING OF THE ORIGINAL FILM AS THE DRAMATIC BACKDROP FOR THE TRAGIC DEATH OF THE GIGANTIC APE BROUGHT TO NEW YORK FROM A MYSTERIOUS, UNEXPLORED TROPICAL ISLE TO BECOME A SIDESHOW SPECTACLE. THIS WAS THE ONLY SEQUENCE SHOT IN NEW YORK.

A Daredevil's Delight

The tallest buildings in the world were too tempting for daredevils to ignore. In its first years, the World Trade Center towers attracted a number of thrill-seekers bent on being the first in their class.

Aerialist Philippe Petit, the first to take up the challenge, completed two crossings between the twin towers on Wednesday, August 7, 1974. A street artist and acrobat, Petit even balanced upside down on his heels. Afterwards, he quipped to reporters, "When I see three oranges, I have to juggle. And if I see two towers, I have to walk."

Petit had planned his stunt for weeks, making numerous visits to the towers, including a tour of the observation deck. Over several days prior to the walk, he and four accomplices, all disguised as construction workers, smuggled a crossbow, arrows, balancing pole, and coil of heavy steel wire into the building. In a nod to his incredible moxie, instead of throwing the book at him, New York City officials let him off with a mere trespassing charge. He was then ordered, as restitution, to repeat the performance for the children of the city, this time at a much lower elevation—between two office buildings across Central Park's Belvedere Lake.

...and there were other feats of derring-do at the World Trade Center:

- *When asked why they climbed the mountain, climbers usually say, "because it was there." That's how Daniel Goodwin explained his climb up the 110-story North Tower on May 30, 1983. He also called it the "state of the art in climbing buildings." His feat was an encore to a climb two years earlier at Chicago's Sears Tower, where he was dubbed Spiderman.*

- *Others who met the challenge of the World Trade Center were toy designer George Willig, who walked up the face of the South Tower on May 26, 1977; John Quinn, who parachuted to the ground from the North Tower in 1975; and John Carta, who parachuted from a light plane from about 10,000 feet onto the roof of the South Tower in 1980.*

Did You Know?

1. THE TWIN 110-STORY WORLD TRADE CENTER TOWERS WERE THE TWO TALLEST BUILDINGS IN THE WORLD WHEN THEY WERE COMPLETED IN THE EARLY 1970s. THE JOHN HANCOCK BUILDING AND THE SEARS TOWER IN CHICAGO CLAIMED THE TITLE OF WORLD'S TALLEST A FEW YEARS LATER, BUT WHEN A TV BROADCAST ANTENNA WAS ADDED TO TOWER ONE IN 1979, THE WORLD TRADE CENTER ONCE AGAIN RULED THE SKIES AT 1,730 FEET.
2. MORE THAN 240 ELEVATORS SERVE THE WORLD TRADE CENTER COMPLEX, 99 IN EACH OF THE TWIN TOWERS. THE WTC CONTAINS SOME 12 MILLION SQUARE FEET OF OFFICE SPACE. EACH TOWER FLOOR IS APPROXIMATELY ONE ACRE IN SIZE. THE COMPLEX HOUSES ABOUT 350 ORGANIZATIONS AND ORGANIZATIONS EMPLOYING A WORKDAY POPULATION OF SOME 50,000 PEOPLE. AN ADDITIONAL 70,000 PEOPLE VISIT THE COMPLEX EACH DAY.
3. THE WORLD TRADE CENTER NOT ONLY HAS SKY-LOBBIES FOR ELEVATOR TRANSFERS BUT ALSO SKY-BASEMENTS. EACH TOWER IS BUILT LIKE THREE BUILDINGS STACKED ON TOP OF EACH OTHER, WITH BREAKS ABOUT EVERY 30 FLOORS FOR WATER PUMPS AND OTHER UTILITIES. THE SIZE AND STRENGTH OF THE WATER PIPES WOULD HAVE TO BE ENORMOUS TO SUPPORT PRESSURE OVER THE ENTIRE 110 FLOORS, SO THEY WERE BROKEN UP INTO SECTIONS.

A "PATH" TO THE FUTURE

When the Port Authority acquired the "Cinderella" H&M railway on September 1, 1962, in many ways it became its fairy godmother. First came a scouring of all public facilities and numerous cosmetic improvements. The agency tackled the enormous task of learning how to run a railroad. Engineers pored over the system, formulating hundreds of needed improvements. By 1965, the first fleet of 157 gleaming new PA-1 cars hit the tracks. Air-conditioned, bright, comfortable, and roomy, these ultramodern, stylish trains wooed patrons back to rapid transit. Improvements to power, signal, and track systems boosted the reliability and timeliness of PATH trains. Station improvements included new turnstiles and brighter lighting. The PA-1 cars were succeeded by 44 PA-2 cars and 46 PA-3s, which brought the entire fleet into the modern era.

With the completion of the World Trade Center in lower Manhattan and the Journal Square Transportation Center in Jersey City in the early 1970s, the PATH system was carrying larger passenger loads. This was partially caused by New Jersey's Aldene Plan, which funneled Central New Jersey Railroad (CNJ) passengers commuting from Somerville, Plainfield, Westfield, and the New Jersey shore into Newark's Penn Station, where they then boarded PATH for the ride into Manhattan. This arrangement proved to be cost-effective for the CNJ, which was suffering from high operating deficits, while boosting patronage on PATH, which needed more passengers. PATH assumed full responsibility for the right-of-way between Journal Square and Newark, a rail corridor that had long been jointly operated by the H&M and the Pennsylvania Railroad.

PATH ridership had increased so much that its entire 248-car fleet had to be rebuilt and new cars needed to be purchased to provide more reliable and frequent service. Additional escalators were installed at the World Trade Center to speed patrons on and off the platforms.

During the 1980s construction boom on Jersey City's Gold Coast, the stations at Exchange Place, Grove Street, and Newport Center were revamped to complement the new office towers, luxury apartments, and shopping malls springing up along the Hudson River. Passenger traffic now ran in both directions, as workers and shoppers took advantage of PATH's fare.

THE JOURNAL SQUARE TRANSPORTATION CENTER

Journal Square is to Jersey City what Times Square is to Manhattan. Once known only as the Summit Avenue Station on the H&M Railroad, it was renamed Journal Square in the '20s, when the area blossomed with new attractions—the Orpheum, State, Loew's, and Stanley theaters, along with elegant restaurants, nightclubs, hotels, and fashionable stores. At the time the Stanley was the fourth-largest theater in the world, and the entire district was a tourist attraction. A sports arena akin to Madison Square Garden had been planned for Journal Square, but the Great Depression hit Jersey City hard.

Journal Square is actually a huge bridge that stretches across railroad yards and the PATH station below. It was at one time, in fact, listed as one of the widest bridges in the world. Many of the buildings bordering the square are built over the tracks, as is the Journal Square Transportation Center (JSTC).

Dedicated in October 1975, JSTC was designed to house not only the PATH station, but a large bus terminal—the first comprehensive transportation center for Jersey City. Before it was built, the buses serving the city and the surrounding towns collected and discharged passengers on the unsheltered pavement of the square. Long lines of people waited unprotected in the snow or rain, or in the hot sun, waiting for their buses. A crisscross traffic pattern made negotiating the square a hazard for both pedestrians and vehicles. JSTC was designed with the same ideas that had worked so well at the Port Authority Bus Terminal during the 1950s.

THE JOURNAL SQUARE TRANSPORTATION CENTER BROUGHT A MODERN TOUCH TO JERSEY CITY'S SKYLINE AND CONSOLIDATED BUS AND PATH CONNECTIONS FOR COMMUTERS.

Over the past few decades, the lights dimmed on the marquees of its movie palaces, and Journal Square was transformed into an eclectic office complex. This process slowed to a halt after stock-market plunges in the late 1980s. Journal Square was also competing with the Gold Coast businesses on the Hudson River, which were closer to Manhattan. This was an odd twist in the changing fortunes of commercial life, for Journal Square's businesses had pulled commerce away from that very district during the 1920s.

Today, JSTC serves as the administrative headquarters of the PATH Corporation, and remains a striking example of modern architecture. It is now part of a plan to renovate and restore Journal Square. Offices, stores, banks, and restaurants serve crowds who are frequently entertained by cultural events held in the parklike plaza.

ANTHONY PADOVANO'S *SPHERICAL DIVISION*, A STAINLESS STEEL SCULPTURE, GRACES THE JOURNAL SQUARE TRANSPORTATION CENTER IN JERSEY CITY, NEW JERSEY. IT WAS ACQUIRED WITH FUNDS PROVIDED IN PART BY THE U.S. DEPARTMENT OF TRANSPORTATION.

THE GEORGE WASHINGTON BRIDGE BUS STATION IS BUILT

A bus station to serve the needs of commuters with an award-winning design that delights the eye? That's what the George Washington Bridge Bus Station provided to metropolitan area travelers when it opened in 1963. With a direct link to the upper level of the bridge, the station offered off-street bus loading primarily for commuter passengers from Northern New Jersey and Rockland County. It featured a barber shop, dental and optician services, and a greeting card and stationery store not only for commuters but for the surrounding community. The station was a gathering place where community groups could showcase their art and music and hold special events.

The creation of Pier Luigi Nervi, the renowned Italian engineer and architect who designed the 1960 Olympic Stadium in Rome, the bus station won the Concrete Industry Board's 1963 award for best design in concept, originality, and applicability of concrete. The building has a concrete roof made of 26 triangular sections that simulate the wings of butterflies when seen from above. The interior's blue-and-white color scheme is carried out in mosaic tile that covers the walls and columns. The floor is made of polished Venetian terrazzo.

THE $14 MILLION GEORGE WASHINGTON BRIDGE BUS STATION, OPENED IN 1963, WAS BUILT AS AN INTEGRAL PART OF THE BRIDGE'S LOWER-LEVEL EXPANSION. ITALIAN ARCHITECT PIER LUIGI NERVI DESIGNED THE ARTISTIC FARFALLA (BUTTERFLY) ROOF. THE PRESS DUBBED HIM THE WIZARD OF CONCRETE FOR HIS SCULPTURAL USE OF THE MATERIAL. TODAY, THE BUS STATION SERVES MORE THAN 4 MILLION PASSENGERS A YEAR.

A DISPATCHER DIRECTS A BUS FROM THE GEORGE WASHINGTON BRIDGE BUS STATION TO THE 1964 WORLD'S FAIR, WHERE THE PORT AUTHORITY'S TRANSPORTATION BUILDING WITH ROOFTOP HELIPAD WAS BILLED AS THE "AERIAL GATEWAY TO THE FAIR."

THE LINCOLN TUNNEL ACCOMMODATED 19 ELEPHANTS AND HALF OF NOAH'S ARK WHEN THE BARNUM & BAILEY CIRCUS CAME TO TOWN IN 1971. AND YES, THEY HAD TO PAY A TOLL.

The Elephants

The circus is coming to town" was the cry on the night of May 17, 1971, when 19 elephants, a pony, a zebra, and a llama took an unscheduled march through the Lincoln Tunnel. Stranded by a nationwide rail strike, officials of the Ringling Brothers Barnum and Bailey Circus decided to take an unorthodox route to get to their New York engagement on time. So how much do you charge an elephant? The Port Authority decided on $9.50 per pachyderm, with the circus wagons, llama, pony, zebra, horse and baby elephant, Karen, going through toll-free.

Irate letters poured into the Lincoln Tunnel management office from a class in Iselin, New Jersey, schoolchildren protesting not the fact that the elephants walked through the tunnel, but that the agency charged them a toll. One schoolgirl wrote, "I don't think you were very fair to charge the elephants money. Who is going to get all of it? They came when the traffic was slow and didn't do any harm...You're mean." A Port Authority police officer made a goodwill visit to the school to explain the agency's toll system. The children were eventually satisfied that the toll charged was fair, since the circus charged people to see the elephants.

THE PASSENGER SHIP TERMINAL

ILYA BOLOTOWSKY'S 1979 CERAMIC TILE MURAL AT THE PASSENGER SHIP TERMINAL WAS ACQUIRED WITH FUNDS PROVIDED IN PART BY THE NATIONAL ENDOWMENT FOR THE ARTS.

Designed as a modern gateway for thousands of ocean travelers, the New York City Passenger Ship Terminal was constructed at a cost of $40 million by the Port Authority on Manhattan's Hudson River waterfront between 48th and 52nd Streets. At the request of the city, three obsolete piers were rebuilt and refurbished to provide temperature-controlled passenger lounges, improved customs and baggage-handling facilities, rooftop parking for 1,000 cars, and an elevated roadway system. The terminal, which the Port Authority operated under a lease with New York City, was formally dedicated on November 23, 1974.

Consisting of six berths shared by passenger ships using the Port of New York and New Jersey, the Passenger Ship Terminal is the region's cruise ship center. The halls are used for trade shows, conventions, and special events such as antique shows, banquets, and fund-raisers.

On January 1, 1997, the terminal reverted to the city.

EXPO '64

The Port of New York Authority heralded the 1964 World's Fair (Expo '64) six months prior to its official opening by unveiling its own exhibit building on October 16, 1963. The structure, in the shape of a "T" for transportation, was the world's first building designed primarily for use as a heliport. It was billed as "the aerial gateway to the fair." Linking Expo '64 with Manhattan and LaGuardia, New York International (now John F. Kennedy), and Newark International Airports, it provided scheduled helicopter service from November 1963 to October 1965. The inaugural flight hosted New York Governor Nelson A. Rockefeller, New Jersey Governor Richard J. Hughes, and New York City

Council President Paul R. Screvane. The building also housed a glass-enclosed twin-level dining facility and cocktail lounge, and a theater-in-the-round exhibit featuring the history of the Port of New York and New Jersey.

OPPOSITE: THE PORT AUTHORITY'S 1964 WORLD'S FAIR EXHIBIT BUILDING

The heliport was the centerpiece of the fair's transportation section, designed and managed by the Port Authority, which featured the latest modes of transportation for the mid-20th century as well as prototypes for future vehicles.

What's in a Name?

In 1946, Frederick G. Reinecke, commissioner of the New York City Department of Marine and Aviation, told an audience, "The Port Authority has nothing to do with the Port of New York and has no authority in it." Oddly enough, he was right. Despite its name, the Port Authority had almost nothing to do with docks and marine terminals for almost the first 25 years of its operation.

Howard Cullman, then chairman, responded to the sardonic observation in a letter to the New York Times*: "It is obvious that the commissioner of docks is totally unaware of the statutory obligations and functions of the Port of New York Authority." Cullman pointed out that the agency was obliged to complete those projects assigned to it by the two states via the Port Compact.*

While the Port Authority had conducted port studies during those early years, it was never given the job of actually running and rehabilitating the 200-plus municipal piers around the harbor. Eventually, however, it did acquire port projects, albeit in a piecemeal fashion: The Grain Terminal in 1944; Port Newark after World War II; the Hoboken piers, the Elizabeth waterfront, and a large chunk of the Brooklyn docks in the 1950s; and the New York City Passenger Ship Terminal in 1971—a destiny belatedly realized.

PORT AUTHORITY

LEFT: A LONG VIEW OF THE PORT AUTHORITY'S BROOKLYN WATERFRONT PROPERTIES, WITH ERIE BASIN AND COLUMBIA STREET PIER IN THE FOREGROUND. THE SITE OF THE RED HOOK CONTAINERPORT IS AT LEFT CENTER, OPPOSITE THE NORTHERN END OF GOVERNORS ISLAND. CONTINUING NORTHWARD FROM THERE, ALONG THE SHORE OF THE EAST RIVER FOR SOME TWO MILES, IS THE BROOKLYN PORT AUTHORITY MARINE TERMINAL, WHICH INCLUDES 118 ACRES OF UPLAND AREA AND WAREHOUSE SPACE.

CARGO OPERATIONS AT BROOKLYN–PORT AUTHORITY MARINE TERMINAL WERE AT A PEAK IN THE LATE-1970s.

BACKGROUND: A SEA OF IMPORTED CARS IN THE UPLAND AREA OF PORT NEWARK.

TOP: MAJOR GORDON COOPER, ONE OF THE FIRST SEVEN U.S. ASTRONAUTS, DEPARTS FROM NEWARK INTERNATIONAL AIRPORT ON MAY 23, 1963. AFTER RUSSIA'S YURI GAGARIN BECAME THE FIRST MAN IN SPACE IN OCTOBER 1959, PRESIDENT DWIGHT D. EISENHOWER ANNOUNCED THE MERCURY PROGRAM TO PUT AN AMERICAN INTO SPACE.

PAN AMERICAN WORLD AIRWAYS' $100 MILLION SIXFOLD EXPANSION OF ITS PASSENGER TERMINAL AT JFK INTERNATIONAL AIRPORT, COMPLETED IN 1973, MADE IT THE NATION'S LARGEST PASSENGER TERMINAL OPERATED BY A SINGLE AIRLINE.

PAN AMERICAN

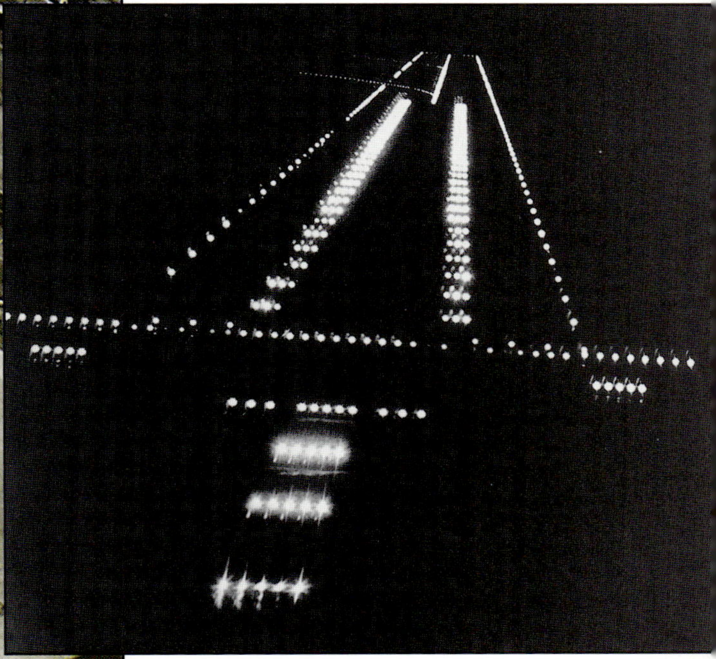

LEFT: THE TWA FLIGHT CENTER AT JFK IN THE MID-1960s.

TOP RIGHT: THE FIRST COMMERCIAL INSTRUMENT RUNWAY IN THE WORLD TO HAVE FLUSH CENTERLINE LIGHTING WAS OPERATIONAL AT NEW YORK INTERNATIONAL IN 1960.

BOTTOM RIGHT: PLANES WAITING TO TAKE OFF AT JFK ON A TYPICALLY BUSY DAY IN 1969.

A REPLICA OF THE WRIGHT BROTHERS' PLANE, COMMEMORATED IN JFK'S INTERNATIONAL ARRIVALS BUILDING. THE ORIGINAL COULD HAVE FLOWN THE ENTIRE DISTANCE OF ITS FIRST FLIGHT AT KITTY HAWK WITHIN THE CONFINES OF THE TERMINAL ITSELF.

buses to other airlines →

THE NEW CENTRAL TERMINAL BUILDING AT LaGUARDIA AIRPORT, NEARLY SEVEN TIMES THE SIZE OF ITS PREDECESSOR, UNDER CONSTRUCTION IN 1963.

MARINE CORPS LIEUTENANT COLONEL JOHN H. GLENN, THE FIRST AMERICAN ASTRONAUT TO GO INTO ORBIT, AND VICE PRESIDENT LYNDON B. JOHNSON ARE WELCOMED AT LaGUARDIA AIRPORT IN MARCH 1962, THREE WEEKS AFTER GLENN'S HISTORIC SPACE FLIGHT. GLENN LATER BECAME A U.S. SENATOR.

A NEW BOEING 727 THREE-ENGINE JET, DESIGNED FOR SHORT-RANGE TRAVEL TO AND FROM SMALL AIRPORTS, MAKES ITS FIRST FLIGHT OUT OF LaGUARDIA, ON SEPTEMBER 15, 1963, AS PART OF A WORLDWIDE TOUR TO DEMONSTRATE THE AIRCRAFT'S REDUCED SOUND LEVEL. A REDEVELOPMENT PROGRAM TRANSFORMED LaGUARDIA INTO A FACILITY FULLY EQUIPPED FOR THE JET AGE. THESE WERE THE FIRST ENGINES TO INCORPORATE THE LATEST ADVANCES IN NOISE REDUCTION TECHNOLOGY. ITS AIRFRAME ALSO INCORPORATED SIGNIFICANT AERODYNAMIC IMPROVEMENTS, WHICH CONTRIBUTED TO ITS ABILITY TO OPERATE AT ACCEPTABLE NOISE LEVELS.

ABOVE: THE PRINCIPAL STRUCTURES OF THE "NEW" LaGUARDIA AIRPORT, THE $36 MILLION, 1,300-FOOT-LONG PASSENGER TERMINAL (CURVED BUILDING AT CENTER IN THIS SOUTHWEST VIEW) AND THE $1.6 MILLION, 150-FOOT-HIGH CONTROL TOWER (LOWER RIGHT), SEVERAL WEEKS BEFORE THE OFFICIAL DEDICATION CEREMONIES OF APRIL 16, 1964. THAT DAY WOULD ALSO MARK THE AIRPORT'S 25TH ANNIVERSARY.

RIGHT: FIORELLO PARK, WITH A FOUNTAIN, POOL, AND FLOWERING PLANTS, FRONTS THE CENTRAL SECTIONS OF LaGUARDIA'S NEW PASSENGER TERMINAL. THE DESIGN OF THE TERMINAL, SERVED BY A BI-LEVEL ROADWAY, PROVIDES FOR THE SEPARATION OF ARRIVING AND DEPARTING PASSENGERS.

WITH 650,000 SQUARE FEET OF FLOOR SPACE (EQUIVALENT TO SIX CITY BLOCKS), THE CENTRAL TERMINAL BUILDING INCORPORATED A FOUR-STORY CENTRAL SECTION, THREE-STORY EAST AND WEST WINGS, AND FOUR BI-LEVEL ARCADES LEADING TO 36 AIRCRAFT GATES. ONE YEAR AFTER THE TERMINAL OPENED, THE AIRPORT'S REDEVELOPMENT PROGRAM WAS IN ITS FINAL STAGES. THE RUNWAY EXTENSION PROJECT, TO BE COMPLETED IN 1967, IS SEEN AT THE EXTREME TOP LEFT.

LAGUARDIA'S TWO RUNWAYS WERE LENGTHENED TO 7,000 FEET OVER A 50-ACRE, L-SHAPED PIER BUILT INTO RIKERS ISLAND CHANNEL. OTHER AIRCRAFT IMPROVEMENTS WOULD INCLUDE EXPANDED APRON AND WARM-UP AREAS, AND NEW TAXIWAYS AND HELICOPTER LANDING PADS. ABOVE LEFT: CONSTRUCTION OF AIRPORT RUNWAY EXTENSION 22. RIGHT: THE COMPLETED EXTENSION.

LEFT: A 1971 VIEW OF NEWARK INTERNATIONAL AIRPORT. IN ADDITION TO NEW TERMINALS, THE AIRPORT REDEVELOPMENT OF THE EARLY 1970s INCLUDED THE PORT AUTHORITY ADMINISTRATION BUILDING, A CENTRAL HEATING AND REFRIGERATION BUILDING, A FUEL STORAGE TANK FARM, AND TAXIWAYS AND ROADWAYS.

BELOW: NEWARK INTERNATIONAL AIRPORT WITH THE NEW YORK SKYLINE IN THE BACKGROUND.

The 1980s—A Decade of Economic Development

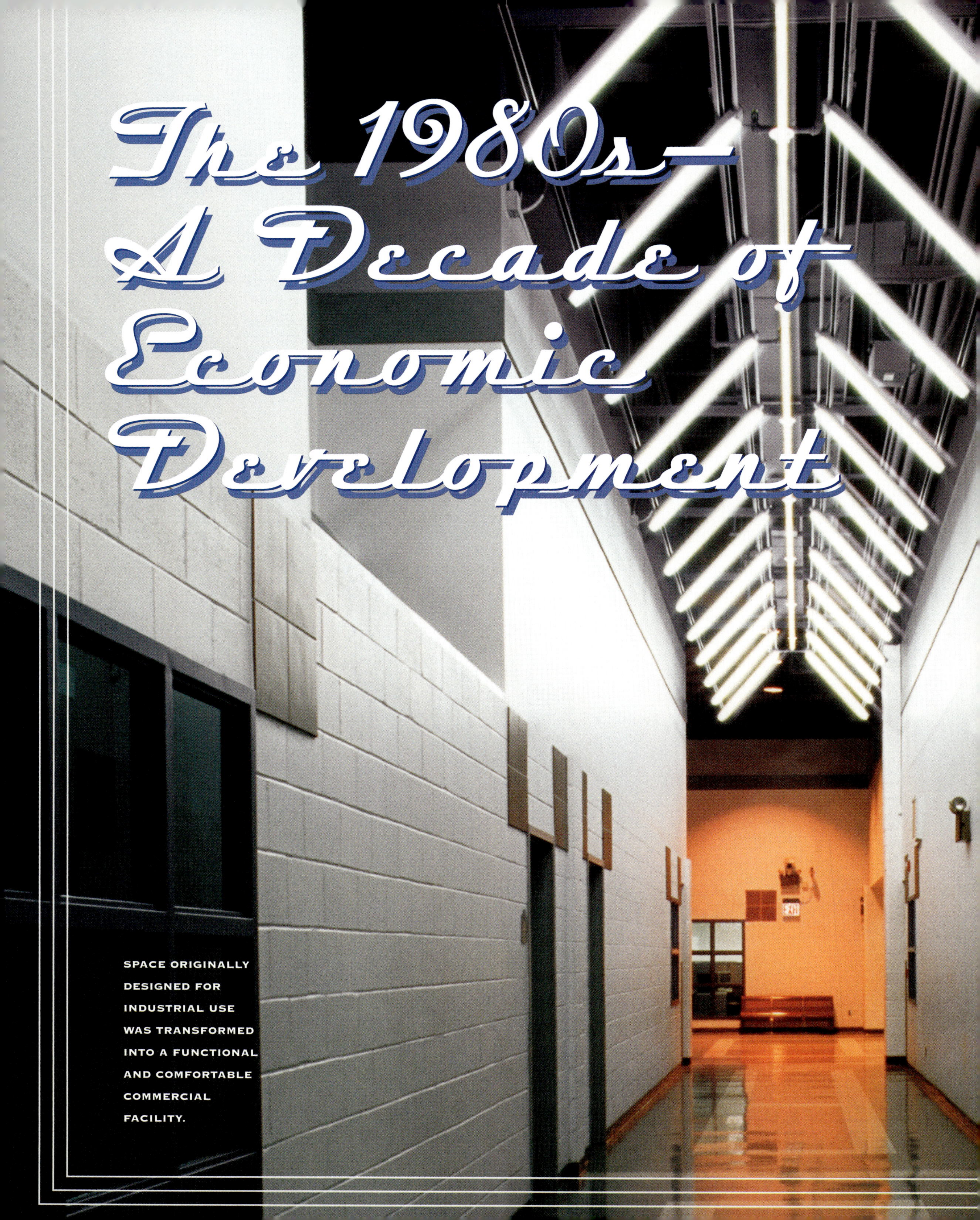

SPACE ORIGINALLY DESIGNED FOR INDUSTRIAL USE WAS TRANSFORMED INTO A FUNCTIONAL AND COMFORTABLE COMMERCIAL FACILITY.

Perhaps it was the baby boomers coming into their prime as the largest group of consumers in history; maybe it was pent-up demand from the late-1970s, a time of reduced expectations; or perhaps it was a new economic bubble inflated by the growing national deficit—whatever the cause, the boom of the 1980s in many ways mirrored the "buy now, pay later" attitude of the 1920s.

During the 1980s, many joined the ranks of young urban professionals, dubbed "yuppies." Part of a growing population with access to college education and professional careers, they plunked their discretionary income into a booming economy, one fanned by the expectation that the high inflation of the 1970s and early 1980s would continue unabated. Since an entire generation had known nothing but escalating rates of inflation, many believed today's extravagance would prove to be tomorrow's bargain.

AREA YOUTH WERE ON HAND AT THE GROUNDBREAKING FOR BATHGATE INDUSTRIAL PARK IN 1982.

Suddenly, everyone was building, particularly in the New York–New Jersey area. Old buildings were turned into luxury condos, rotting riverfront properties were converted to massive Gold Coast developments, and shopping malls were sprouting up like mushrooms. Thanks to easy credit—albeit at extremely high interest rates—the region, like the country, built, bought, and borrowed at unprecedented levels.

Unemployment was so low that many help-wanted ads begged people to come out of retirement. Real estate agents, although busy, were perplexed by the surge in mortgage rates. First-time home buyers were being priced out of the market as even the worst properties suddenly became "hot." Even the depressed urban core was experiencing unprecedented speculative investment and redevelopment.

It was, therefore, not surprising that regional redevelopment became the vogue. This was the time to refurbish dying neighborhoods, breathe new life into cities, restore the infrastructure, and create more jobs and prosperity.

By the late '70s, still smarting from the post-OPEC recession, the New York–New Jersey region suffered an erosion of its industrial base. Manufacturers were packing up and heading south for better tax and wage deals, which created hardships for those just entering the workforce, particularly unskilled and semiskilled laborers. In 1978 New York and New Jersey, with congressional consent, passed legislation authorizing the Port Authority to begin a program of industrial development. The agency launched various projects: a resource recovery plant, export trading initiatives, a fish processing terminal, a telecommunications center, an office building for lawyers in Newark, and industrial parks in the Bronx; Yonkers, New York; and Elizabeth, New Jersey.

Although many people questioned whether the agency should be in the business of running industrial parks and buildings, the agency fulfilled its new mandate to retain many of the manufacturing firms—and jobs—in the region. The agency acted as a catalyst for development by acquiring land and building new structures or renovating old ones. It provided loans when necessary, managed properties, and even helped companies acquire new business.

By the mid-1980s, regional prosperity and shifting commuting patterns had stretched the Port Authority's transportation and trade facilities to the limit. In addition, other regions of the country were aggressively capturing shares of New York's aviation and shipping, both the domain of the Port Authority.

Governors Mario Cuomo of New York and Thomas Kean of New Jersey recognized that it was time for a massive investment in the region's transportation infrastructure. In March 1987, the board of commissioners committed the Port Authority to a five-year, $5.8 billion capital program, the largest in its history. The funds would be used to modernize and expand the airports, improve air cargo and shipping services, increase the capacity of interstate bridges and tunnels to reduce congestion, and make major fleet and facility improvements at PATH.

BATHGATE INDUSTRIAL PARK PRIOR TO DEVELOPMENT IN 1982.

DEVELOPMENT AT BATHGATE INDUSTRIAL PARK IN 1985.

BATHGATE HAS ITS OWN POSTAL STATION THAT SERVES BOTH THE INDUSTRIAL PARK AND THE SURROUNDING COMMUNITY. THE POST OFFICE SHARES ITS BUILDING WITH A CATERING SERVICE AND THE BRONX EDUCATIONAL OPPORTUNITY CENTER.

TIM ROLLINS AND HIS *KIDS OF SURVIVAL,* THE WINNERS OF THE PORT AUTHORITY'S PUBLIC ART FUND COMPETITION IN 1988, STAND BEFORE THEIR MURAL, WHICH ADORNS THE SIDE OF THEIR SCHOOL, COMMUNITY ELEMENTARY SCHOOL NO. 4, ADJACENT TO BATHGATE INDUSTRIAL PARK. THE YOUNGSTERS ARE MEMBERS OF ROLLINS' WORKSHOP FOR STUDENTS, TEACHERS, AND STAFF. THE MURAL, INSPIRED BY FRANZ KAFKA'S *AMERIKA*, DEPICTS MUSICAL INSTRUMENTS PLAYING SONGS OF FREEDOM, DIGNITY, AND HOPE TO THE WORLD.

BATHGATE INDUSTRIAL PARK

The first Port Authority industrial park was located in the South Bronx, a neighborhood in distress. The Port Authority, the City of New York (owner of the land), and the city's Economic Development Corporation developed Bathgate to attract small manufacturing firms. The 21.5-acre park's 10 tenants include a generic drug manufacturer, a packager of consumer products, a distribution center for a national baked goods chain, an academic and vocational training center, and a child care facility. A company that operates a local chain of dry cleaning establishments is adding its central processing plant to the park. The surrounding neighborhood has shown great improvement since Bathgate opened—some 1,500 people, mostly local residents, have jobs there.

THE INDUSTRIAL PARK AT ELIZABETH

This project presented the Port Authority with a tough challenge in 1981, because it was to be built on a landfill that required a massive cleanup. But despite its environmental problems, the 71-acre parcel of land was ideally located between Newark International Airport and the Port Newark/Elizabeth Marine Terminals. The Port Authority made the land suitable for building, and the new industrial park attracted warehouses, freight forwarding firms, and retail stores. In 1989, the Swedish home furnishings company IKEA purchased 21 acres for its flagship U.S. retail operation. IKEA later purchased additional acreage and developed a retail shopping center.

THE INDUSTRIAL PARK AT YONKERS

The Industrial Park at Yonkers is situated on a site abandoned in the early 1980s by the Otis Elevator Company, which eliminated 1,500 jobs. The Port Authority acquired the 21 acres of waterfront property in 1985 and secured the Union Rail Car Partnership, now called Kawasaki Rail Car, as a major tenant. The firm provided hundreds of jobs building and refurbishing rail cars for PATH. The park also became home to several small- to medium-sized manufacturers. In the mid-1990s, the rail-car company landed a $179.5-million contract to provide cars for the Long Island Railroad. In the 1990s the Port Authority decided that the seven-building facility should be privatized, and several buildings were sold.

THE ELIZABETH INDUSTRIAL PARK BEFORE DEVELOPMENT.

THE ELIZABETH INDUSTRIAL PARK UNDER DEVELOPMENT.

IKEA, THE SWEDISH FURNISHINGS RETAILER, PURCHASED 46 ACRES FROM THE PORT AUTHORITY FOR ITS U.S. FLAGSHIP STORE AND SHOPPING CENTER.

DANGER
HIGH

PATH RAIL CARS WERE THE FIRST CONTRACT LANDED BY KAWASAKI RAIL CAR INC. WHEN IT MOVED INTO YONKERS INDUSTRIAL PARK IN 1986.

THE COMPANY CURRENTLY HOLDS A FIVE-YEAR CONTRACT WITH THE METROPOLITAN TRANSPORTATION AUTHORITY TO BUILD CARS FOR THE LONG ISLAND RAILROAD.

THE YONKERS INDUSTRIAL PARK, ADJACENT TO AN INTERSTATE HIGHWAY SYSTEM, RAIL LINES, AND ACCESSIBLE TO FOUR AREA AIRPORTS (INCLUDING WESTCHESTER COUNTY AIRPORT), WAS WELL SITUATED TO CONNECT MANUFACTURERS WITH RAIL AND TRUCK TRANSFERS.

THE ESSEX COUNTY RESOURCE RECOVERY FACILITY IS A STATE-OF-THE-ART WASTE-TO-ENERGY PLANT.

THE ESSEX COUNTY RESOURCE RECOVERY FACILITY

In an era of growing concern about conservation and the need to dispose of waste in an environmentally responsible manner, the federal government passed legislation in 1978 that funded waste-to-energy facilities. The Port Authority, under agreements with Essex County, New Jersey, and the private company American Ref-Fuel, constructed the Essex County Resource Recovery Facility, New Jersey's largest waste-to-energy plant. The facility provided jobs for local residents, a valuable by-product in the form of electricity, as well as revenue to the City of Newark. The plant is now operated by American Ref-Fuel.

THE TELEPORT

The Port Authority supported the "information superhighway" as early as 1986 with the opening of the Teleport on Staten Island. The Teleport was one of the world's first high-tech business park and communications center. It is the hub of the region's primary fiber-optic network, which is linked to

THE FIRST HIGH-TECH OFFICE PARK IN THE UNITED STATES HOUSES AN ARRAY OF SATELLITE DISHES.

a state-of-the-art satellite transmission system. Major business centers found the network to be of high speed, and the system's high-quality voice, data, and video transmissions vital to their operations. The 100-acre business park and satellite communications center houses major financial, insurance, and communications firms. The $70 million invested by the Port Authority in the Teleport has generated more than 1,500 jobs and $450 million in additional private investment.

THE NEWARK LEGAL AND COMMUNICATIONS CENTER

The effort to revitalize Newark's downtown business district got a boost when the Port Authority built a "Class A" office building to stem the flow of law firms leaving the city. The Newark Legal Center, opened in 1989, boasts an impressive list of major law firms. The blue-tinted glass tower offers fiber-optic telecommunications service linked to the Teleport on Staten Island. Not even the most optimistic projections could have anticipated the dramatic renaissance that the 20-story building would spark for the business district. It inspired private developers to erect four high-rise office buildings nearby. The Legal Center is part of a downtown transportation and business complex called Gateway Center, which links Newark's Penn Station, PATH, and bus connections to Newark Airport.

THE NEWARK LEGAL CENTER'S STRIKING DESIGN IS SEEN AGAINST THE NEWARK SKYLINE. THE PATH COMMUTER RAILROAD IS IN THE FOREGROUND.

A CONTAINERSHIP DOCKED AT PORT NEWARK/ELIZABETH.

MARITIME DEVELOPMENT

PORT NEWARK/ELIZABETH

Containerization was in full swing by the 1960s. Port Newark/Elizabeth had been transformed from a vacant expanse of land to thriving container and break-bulk facilities for ocean shipping.

In the '80s, expansion was needed to handle new markets, particularly for the import and export of motor vehicles. On the Jersey City/Bayonne waterfront, the Port Authority developed a new terminal to provide direct access to ocean-going vessels and offer superior connections for transporting vehicles via rail and truck. The facility also provided on-site auto preparation services needed by dealers in the region.

Opened in 1989, the terminal helped position the region to capture the newest growth markets for the U.S.—the Far East and Southeast Asia. During the '90s it became the site of auto preparation for some of the leading car importers, including BMW, Nissan, Toyota, and Hyundai, which placed the Port of New York and New Jersey among the top three ports in America for auto imports and exports.

CONTAINERS ARE UNLOADED BY CRANE AT PORT NEWARK/ELIZABETH.

OPERATION SAIL, HELD ON THE FOURTH OF JULY, 1986, WAS A HUGE INTERNATIONAL PARADE OF TALL-MASTED SAILING SHIPS THAT GRACED NEW YORK HARBOR TO MARK THE CENTENNIAL OF THE NEWLY RESTORED STATUE OF LIBERTY.

PETER GOLDMARK JR., EXECUTIVE DIRECTOR, 1977–1985.

STEPHEN BERGER, EXECUTIVE DIRECTOR, 1985–1990.

Two Executive Directors—Peter Goldmark and Stephen Berger

Economic development and planning for the end of the century were the hallmarks of Peter Goldmark's years as executive director of the Port Authority. The former director of the budget for the State of New York led the agency out of the uncertain years following Austin Tobin's resignation into the growth years of the '80s. From 1977 to 1985, he guided the Port Authority into an era of long-term planning that would see growth in Newark International Airport, the building of a containerport in Brooklyn, and a partnership with the states and municipalities to develop industrial parks. Those parks restored neglected areas of the region to profitable commercial use. Goldmark's Committee on the Future identified transportation trends for the coming decades and offered ways in which the Port Authority could help to meet those needs. Seeing the explosive growth in passenger traffic, he initiated the modernization of the Port Authority Bus Terminal in 1978.

After Goldmark left the agency in 1985, investment banker Stephen Berger was appointed executive director. Berger, a former member of the board of the New York State Metropolitan Transportation Authority and chairman of its Finance Committee, had served as executive director of the New York State Emergency Financial Control Board for the City of New York (the group that helped New York reenter the credit markets) from 1976 to 1977.

Berger engaged the agency in self-examination that enabled it to function more efficiently. He increased emphasis on providing quality services to patrons and tenants. During his tenure, the Port Authority made major improvements at its three airports, developed new international air-traffic facilities at Newark International Airport, instituted trans-Hudson ferry service, and improved the automated cargo system at Port Newark.

Concerned that deregulation of the airline, trucking, and shipping industries would create a fiercely competitive environment for the Port Authority, Berger enhanced the agency's role in marketing the region and the Port Authority overseas, and strove to introduce regionally manufactured products into the international market.

DURING MAJOR RENOVATION OF THE ORIGINAL HELIPORT SITE AT THE FOOT OF WALL STREET ON THE EAST RIVER, THE PORT AUTHORITY–DOWNTOWN MANHATTAN HELIPORT TEMPORARILY LOCATED ITS OPERATIONS ON THE HUDSON RIVER, WHERE BATTERY PARK CITY IS TODAY. THE WALL STREET FACILITY WAS REOPENED IN 1987.

Careers for Women at the Port Authority

During the 1980s, women were encouraged to train for—and succeed in—nontraditional jobs. They were also moving into the management ranks. The Women in Maintenance Program graduated its first seven students in 1981. Although women had previously been hired in jobs such as general maintainers, trades helpers, auto mechanics, and electrical and utility systems maintainers, this was the first time that the Port Authority recruited women to pursue careers in maintenance and technical areas.

Already experienced in some form of maintenance work, the women attended a three-week course in carpentry, plumbing, rigging, and driving heavy-duty vehicles for the jobs they would fill at the Holland Tunnel, George Washington Bridge, and the three airports. They would subsequently be trained as electricians.

The agency also increasingly hired women as engineers, economists, managers, lawyers, and analysts. Efforts begun in the mid-1970s to recruit women for management posts were beginning to pay off by the 1980s, when women were filling department director slots and serving on the Board of Commissioners.

Commuter Aesthetics at the Port Authority Bus Terminal

To many New Yorkers and New Jerseyans, the Port Authority is synonymous with the Port Authority Bus Terminal on midtown Manhattan's West Side. For years, it was the world's largest bus terminal, serving 60 million passengers annually.

The terminal was remodeled in the early 1980s. The bus, concourse, and roof levels along Eighth Avenue and across to 42nd Street were expanded, a roadway underpass and a four-story ventilation building were constructed, and the terminal concourses, bus platforms, and heating and air-conditioning systems were modernized. To enhance these dramatic renovations, the agency commissioned several equally dramatic art acquisitions.

GEORGE SEGAL'S LIFE-SIZE WORK IN THE SOUTH WING WAITING ROOM DEPICTS THREE TRAVELERS IN LINE AT A BOARDING GATE. THE SCULPTURE WAS SELECTED IN AN INTERNATIONAL COMPETITION THAT DREW MORE THAN 100 ENTRANTS.

AMERICAN SCULPTOR GEORGE RHOADS'S KINETIC SCULPTURE IS LOCATED IN THE TERMINAL'S NORTH WING. THIS "RUBE GOLDBERG"—LIKE CONTRAPTION, ENCLOSED IN A 96" GLASS CUBE, CONTINUALLY FASCINATES VIEWERS.

ACCENTING THE EXPANSE OF THE MAIN LOBBY OF THE PORT AUTHORITY BUS TERMINAL IS RICHARD ANUSZKIEWICZ'S SERIES OF 12 SILKSCREEN DOUBLE-FACED BANNERS, EACH 12 FT. X 4 FT.

The Early 1990s

REORGANIZING FOR A CHANGING WORLD

NEW RESTAURANTS AND RETAIL STORES MADE THE PORT AUTHORITY BUS TERMINAL A MORE COMFORTABLE PLACE FOR COMMUTERS IN THE 1990s.

As many impressive office buildings and residential developments blossomed to take advantage of the boom started in the 1980s, American industry was "getting lean," not only to compete better in the world economy, but to boost shareholder returns. By the early 1990s, possibly as the aftermath of two stock-market plunges, escalating debt, and tighter credit markets, a prolonged recession set in.

While there was a loss of only 1 percent of the wage and salary jobs in the nation as a whole, one estimate indicates the New York–New Jersey region lost some 650,000 jobs, approximately 8.5 percent of its job base. Unlike most recessions, this one struck the white-collar sector, as well as manufacturing.

The Port Authority responded to increasing financial pressures in the 1990s. The agency slashed operating costs, made efficiency improvements, reorganized its management, and reduced total staff by 10 percent. "Back to basics" was an evolving philosophy adopted by the new administration, as tighter reigns were being placed on the $5 billion capital program launched in 1986.

PATH CARRIES OVER 200,000 RIDERS DAILY TO AND FROM MANHATTAN.

A WHALE OF A WALL, A 450-FOOT PAINTING BY WYLAND, DOMINATES THE PORT AUTHORITY BUS TERMINAL'S WALL ON 41ST STREET BETWEEN EIGHTH AND NINTH AVENUES. THE ARTIST PAINTED IT DURING A 17-CITY TOUR IN WHICH HE CREATED A MURAL IN EACH CITY.

The capital plan for core transportation improvement projects went forward, however, including extensive airport redevelopment, a new toll plaza at the Holland Tunnel, refurbishment of the Lincoln Tunnel's interior tile and lighting, and numerous infrastructural and operating enhancements at marine terminals.

Round-trip tunnel and bridge tolls went from $3 to $4 in 1991, but efficiency efforts permitted PATH's $1 fare to remain frozen at 1987 rates, a measure meant to encourage the use of mass transit.

Several programs were aimed at making the facilities easier to use. Better signs and better traffic control were helping to smooth commuting at bridges and tunnels. Programs were launched to cut down on crime and quality-of-life problems, and customer service improvement programs stressed responsiveness and courtesy.

With safer, cleaner, more attractive retail space now available at the airports, the bus terminals, and the World Trade Center, the agency was able to attract a diverse mix of shops and restaurants, and all of these measures helped give travelers an improved image of the region.

Outreach measures included customer surveys and focus groups to solicit ideas for improving services. The agency also worked to reduce air-traffic noise on impacted communities and to soundproof schools in such areas.

Amid the flurry of these and many other activities, the agency and its employees would endure the bombing of the World Trade Center on February 26, 1993, and take on the heroic task of its swift reconstruction.

SINCE THE 1976 BICENTENNIAL, WHICH FEATURED A MASSIVE GATHERING OF INTERNATIONAL NAVY SHIPS, TALL-MASTED SAILING VESSELS, AND THOUSANDS OF SMALL CRAFT, AN ANNUAL MARITIME CELEBRATION HAS BEEN HELD IN THE HARBOR. IT EVOLVED INTO TODAY'S FLEET WEEK FESTIVITIES IN 1987, WHEN U.S. AND FOREIGN NAVIES WERE FORMALLY INVITED TO SCHEDULE SHIP VISITS IN CONJUNCTION WITH NEW YORK CITY'S MEMORIAL DAY WEEKEND OBSERVANCES. A FAVORITE VISITOR WAS *U.S.S. WISCONSIN*, A LEGENDARY BATTLESHIP BUILT IN WORLD WAR II. MODERNIZED AND RESTORED TO DUTY IN 1988, *WISCONSIN* SERVED HONORABLY IN DESERT STORM. IN 1991, IT WAS REMOVED FROM THE ROLL OF ACTIVE SHIPS AND RETIRED.

STOP
STOP
STOP
STOP
STOP
PAY TOLL
4
8

THE LINCOLN TUNNEL'S EXCLUSIVE BUS LANE (LEFT) IS THE MOST HEAVILY TRAVELED SUCH LANE IN THE WORLD. THE 2.5-MILE STRETCH, WHICH RUNS FROM THE NEW JERSEY TURNPIKE TO THE CENTER TUBE OF THE LINCOLN TUNNEL, SAVES COMMUTERS 10 TO 25 MINUTES ON THEIR TRIP INTO MANHATTAN. MORE THAN 1,600 BUSES NOW USE IT DURING THE MORNING RUSH HOUR.

COMPLETION OF THE NEW USAIR TERMINAL AT LAGUARDIA IN 1992 WAS A KEY ELEMENT IN THE OVERALL REDEVELOPMENT AND MODERNIZATION OF THE AIRPORT. IN THE REDEVELOPMENT PHASE, BEGUN IN 1987, THE PORT AUTHORITY JOINED WITH ITS AIRLINE TENANTS TO INVEST MORE THAN $800 MILLION TO REBUILD THE INTERNAL ROADWAY SYSTEM, PROVIDE NEW ACCESS ROADS, EXPAND THE CENTRAL TERMINAL BUILDING, IMPROVE ACCESS TO THE PARKING GARAGES, AND CENTRALIZE PASSENGER TRAFFIC.

USAIR'S NEW TERMINAL IS A STRIKING PIECE OF MODERN ARCHITECTURE, WITH SLOPED WINDOWS AND BRIGHT INTERIORS.

FLYING TO 2000

During the 1980s, when business was booming, the Port Authority had drawn up plans to revamp the airports. The John F. Kennedy International Airport redevelopment program, and similar plans for Newark and LaGuardia Airports, were designed to mark not just the turn of a new century but a new era in air travel services and convenience.

The recession of the early 1990s hit just as these plans were getting off the ground. Beset with generally poor financial conditions in the aviation industry, most major airlines had to retrench, with some going out of business. Nonetheless, the Port Authority recognized the need to proceed with major capital improvements. The agency went forward with revised plans that were appropriate to the financial constraints of the time.

LaGuardia's redevelopment included a new passenger terminal and a revamped roadway network. A $100 million, 12-gate USAir Terminal opened in 1992, part of the Port Authority's master plan for decentralizing the terminals to relieve congestion. It was deemed so attractive that USAir also modernized its shuttle terminal next door to make it aesthetically compatible.

Work also began on the expansion and modernization of LGA's Central Terminal Building, a project encompassing enlarged baggage claim areas; more passenger service counters; better accommodations for people with

LAGUARDIA'S CONTROL TOWER IS A SCULPTURAL LANDMARK COMPOSED OF CIRCULAR FORMS.

disabilities; and myriad upgrades in lighting, air conditioning, heat, and decor. Service areas were expanded to include an atrium with an attractive food court and a multilevel shopping area.

THE UNDULATING CEILING OF THE NEW FOOD COURT AT LAGUARDIA SUGGESTS WINDSWEPT CLOUDS.

A PRIVATE AIRPLANE IS DIRECTED TO THE RUNWAY AT LAGUARDIA.

RIGHT: TERMINAL OPERATIONS FOR NEWARK INTERNATIONAL AIRPORT ARE CONDUCTED FROM TERMINAL B.

BELOW: THE NEW FOOD COURT IN TERMINAL C OF NEWARK INTERNATIONAL AIRPORT PROVIDES A CAFÉ-LIKE RESPITE FOR TRAVELERS.

Newark International Airport's $1 billion Redevelopment Program was designed to feature a new International Arrivals Facility and a monorail to whisk passengers between the airport's three main terminals, long-term parking lot, and car rental facilities. The monorail will eventually link up with the northeast New Jersey corridor rail lines of Amtrak and New Jersey Transit. A Landside Access Project will include roadway, frontage, and parking improvements.

The $110 million International Arrivals Facility, which was completed in 1995, includes an expanded customs and immigration facility and a larger baggage claim area. Terminals A and B have also been modernized and Continental Airlines has added an extension to Terminal C, which was completed in 1988, to better serve its passengers. A two-building air cargo complex was completed in 1994.

TODAY, NEWARK AIRPORT STRETCHES OVER 2,000 ACRES, EMPLOYS 18,000 PEOPLE AND GENERATES $10.3 BILLION IN ECONOMIC ACTIVITY FOR THE NEW YORK–NEW JERSEY METROPOLITAN REGION. THIS INCLUDES $3.3 BILLION IN WAGES FOR SOME 110,000 JOBS DERIVED FROM AIRPORT ACTIVITY.

Air Cargo Flies High With Some Unusual Imports and Exports

The three major airports in the New York–New Jersey region distribute the largest and most diverse range of air cargo shipments in the world, some quite exotic.

At John F. Kennedy International, fresh flowers have become one of its most delightful imports. Fortunately for flower lovers, when it's winter in North America it's summer in South America. With skillful handling and transportation, roses, orchids, and other fresh flowers can be harvested in Ecuador and sold in U.S. florist shops within hours.

JFK also imports and exports animals. Vetport, an airport hotel for animals, is the only such facility of its kind in the country. Opened in 1957, the 1.25-acre site was first operated as Animalport by the American Society for the Prevention of Cruelty to Animals. Since 1992, it has been operated by a private veterinary practice. Each year, Vetport shelters thousands of animals en route to destinations around the world.

Vetport once arranged for 40 dairy cows from a Pennsylvania farm to stay overnight en route to China. Before boarding the plane, one bovine gave birth. Other guests have included a bobcat, monkeys, and many circus animals—elephants, giraffes, tigers, bears. One unusual guest was an American eagle that had been carried by a strong wind current across the ocean all the way to the Irish coast. The bird was nursed back to health at Vetport before being released to the wild.

Vetport also serves as a boarding kennel for dogs and cats of local residents, and is the home of the USDA's Beagle Brigade, the dogs used at airports to detect contraband plants and foodstuffs.

John F. Kennedy Airport's 321-foot control tower opened in 1994, an extraordinary piece of architecture with a distinct profile that seemed to presage a dramatic new era. It was but one of myriad improvements launched in the 1990s to bring a wide scope of enhanced airport services to a region that was redefining its image.

Numerous airlines—Delta, KLM and Northwest, Nippon Cargo, TWA, Tower, American, and British Airways—all upgraded or built entirely new facilities with investments ranging from $40 million to over $150 million each. The Port Authority earmarked funds for the preliminary design of a new International Air Terminal to replace the existing International Arrivals Building.

Roadway improvements and new ramps made it easier for travelers to reach and depart from their airport destinations.

CARGO HANDLERS AT JFK.

New Tower at JFK

Rising 321 feet into the air, the new air traffic control tower was not only the tallest in the East when it opened in 1994, but also one of the tallest in the world. It provides double the work space of its predecessor, built almost 40 years ago.

The tower's new location and increased height provide a better view of the runways and taxiways. Although closed-circuit TV has been an invaluable technology, a line of sight is preferred by Port Authority ramp control personnel as well as Federal Aviation Administration air traffic controllers. Ramp control workers are stationed on the tower's seventh floor, where they coordinate gate assignments for arriving international flights.

The tower complements an FAA plan to modernize the nation's air traffic control system. JFK is equipped with the latest communication, radar, and windshear alert, and flight data systems. All of the air traffic control equipment is supplied by the FAA, which has its offices at the top of the tower.

AIR TRAFFIC CONTROLLERS AT JFK'S NEW CONTROL TOWER DIRECT DEPARTURES AND ARRIVALS AT ONE OF THE WORLD'S BUSIEST AIRPORTS.

AN AIRLINE MECHANIC AT WORK.

LOADING FOOD SERVICE ITEMS ONTO A FLIGHT.

AN AIRPLANE BEING SERVICED.

A BAGGAGE HANDLER AT JFK INTERNATIONAL AIRPORT.

JFK'S PARKING FACILITY, WITH ITS SPIRAL RAMP, IS AN EXAMPLE OF FORM FOLLOWING FUNCTION.

A COGENERATION PLANT GENERATES ELECTRICITY FOR THE AIRPORT.

THE TWA TERMINAL
AT JFK IN 1994.

Those Captivating Cabbies

You arrive at Newark International Airport and hail a cab. A driver wearing a pressed suit and a chauffeur's cap gets out of his car, greets you with a smile and a friendly comment, opens the trunk and puts your luggage in without being asked, then walks to the passenger side to open the door for you.

After settling down in the spanking clean cab, you tell the driver that your destination is a certain Newark restaurant. He's never heard of it, so he pulls out a map and a telephone directory, and calls the restaurant on his cellular phone to ask for directions. Once under way, you ask the driver a question about the city. He gives you an accurate answer, then asks if you'd like to look at some tourist brochures, a special-events calendar, or a newspaper—or maybe you'd prefer to hear a cassette featuring the mayor's introduction to Newark.

A pipe dream? Well, not quite. Taxi drivers in Newark and Elizabeth, New Jersey, were urged to aim for this ideal in a training program originally dubbed "Jersey Gents and Ladies Too!" The class showed drivers that being courteous and helpful was in their own best interest—it yielded friendlier interactions and larger tips.

The seminar also covered Newark geography, places for visitors to know about, and the major annual festivals that take place in the city. Several thousand drivers in Newark and Elizabeth graduated from the program in the early 1990s. As a result, according to Newark's taxi bureau, complaints from passengers were cut in half. The program was so well-received, its principles have been applied to training cabbies and airport personnel at all Port Authority airports.

OPERATION ALTERNATIVE— A SUCCESS STORY AT THE PORT AUTHORITY BUS TERMINAL

To a great many people, the Port Authority Bus Terminal near Times Square is a gateway to New York City. For some, it is their first taste of the "Big Apple" and all it has to offer. For others, it is the primary hub where they find their way to work and back home each day. Whether occasional tourist or daily commuter, the Port Authority Bus Terminal is a key element in the New York experience.

Unfortunately, crime and other social problems had been on the rise in the Times Square area since the 1970s. Where the legitimate theater and fine movie houses once reigned over Manhattan's Great White Way, X-rated video stores and other "adult entertainment" crept in, and commuters frequently found themselves confronted with the homeless who saw the bus terminal as a convenient habitat and an ideal place to panhandle. The atmosphere of the entire neighborhood was in decline and something had to be done to restore its luster.

Consequently, in 1991, the Port Authority launched "Operation Alternative," a program that did much more than just enforce regulations prohibiting the use of public spaces as living quarters. It provided social service referrals to people in need. By its second year, Operation Alternative had aided some 22,000 homeless people, and had become a model for transportation facilities nationwide.

WITH THREE LEVELS CAPABLE OF LOADING 235 BUSES SIMULTANEOUSLY, THE PORT AUTHORITY BUS TERMINAL IS THE BUSIEST IN THE WORLD. SERVICE IS AVAILABLE TO 3,500 DESTINATIONS THROUGHOUT THE COUNTRY. ON A TYPICAL WEEKDAY, SOME 7,000 BUSES, CARRYING 182,000 PASSENGERS, USE THE TERMINAL. OVER 2 MILLION ARRIVALS AND DEPARTURES AND SOME 53 MILLION PASSENGER TRIPS WERE RECORDED IN 1996.

THE RUSH OF COMMUTERS AT THE PORT AUTHORITY BUS TERMINAL.

THE PORT AUTHORITY BUS TERMINAL AS IT LOOKS TODAY. THE AGENCY IS CONSIDERING SELLING THE SPACE ABOVE THE BUILDING FOR THE DEVELOPMENT OF COMMERCIAL OFFICES.

MAIN CONCOURSE LEVEL DURING CONSTRUCTION OF NEW RETAIL SHOPS.

THE PORT AUTHORITY BUS TERMINAL IS A PORTAL TO DESTINATIONS FAR AND NEAR.

LEISURE TIME LANES, ON THE THIRD FLOOR OF THE PORT AUTHORITY BUS TERMINAL, IS ONE OF NEW YORK CITY'S HOTTEST BOWLING ALLEYS.

Operation Alternative not only enabled many of the homeless to break their downward cycle, but it removed the atmosphere of anarchy that so often attracts other criminal activities such as drug dealing and prostitution. As a result, crimes of all kinds have declined dramatically at the bus terminal, and retail sales are booming. Indeed, the entire Times Square neighborhood is currently experiencing an astounding renaissance, and tourists are flooding back to experience its glittering lights, novelty, and excitement.

OPENED IN 1990, PATH'S $205 MILLION STATE-OF-THE-ART CAR MAINTENANCE FACILITY IN HARRISON, NEW JERSEY, WAS A SIGNIFICANT PART OF THE PORT AUTHORITY'S CAPITAL IMPROVEMENT PROGRAM BEGUN IN THE LATE 1980s. REPLACING AN EIGHTY-YEAR-OLD OUTMODED CAR SHOP BUILT BY THE H&M RAILROAD, THE FACILITY MORE THAN DOUBLED THE NUMBER OF CARS THAT COULD BE SERVICED AT ONE TIME.

EXPRESSRAIL

The Port of New York and New Jersey contended with growing competition from West Coast ports during the 1980s, as new markets emerged in Southeast Asia and the Far East. Port Authority studies indicated that cargoes from Asia bound for the Northeast could be handled more cost-effectively through the New York–New Jersey Port.

To better serve this growing market, the Port Authority began ExpressRail, an on-dock intermodal rail terminal located at the Elizabeth–Port Authority Marine Terminal, first opened on an interim test basis in 1991. It would lure not only goods destined for the Northeast, but also those bound for Eastern Canada and the Midwest.

ExpressRail proved a highly competitive option, using an all-water route to New York and faster rail service to inland regions. It also offered the first direct doublestack service to Chicago from the East Coast. ExpressRail offered same-day transfer between ship and rail, and second-morning service to points as far west as Chicago, shaving days off a shipment's travel time. Within a year of its opening, a permanent, larger facility was mandated.

THE PORT OF NEW YORK AND NEW JERSEY IS ONE OF THE LEADING U.S. PORTS FOR AUTOMOBILE IMPORTS AND EXPORTS. PICTURED ARE CARS AT THE AUTO MARINE TERMINAL ON THE JERSEY CITY–BAYONNE WATERFRONT.

THE PORT AUTHORITY INVESTED MORE THAN $19 MILLION TO DEVELOP EXPRESSRAIL, AN ON-DOCK RAIL TERMINAL THAT OFFERS FASTER SERVICE TO CARRIERS WITH CARGOES DESTINED FOR EASTERN CANADA AND THE MIDWEST.

PORT NEWARK CHANNEL WITH MANHATTAN'S SKYLINE TO THE NORTHEAST.

BELOW, LEFT: IN 1994, RED HOOK CONTAINER TERMINAL, LOOKING NORTH.

BELOW, RIGHT: CONTAINERS AWAIT SHIPPING AT THE ELIZABETH–PORT AUTHORITY MARINE TERMINAL.

ExpressRail provided a vital link between overseas shippers and the extensive rail network of the Northeast. Rail cargo handled by ExpressRail rocketed from 12,000 containers in 1991 to 102,500 in 1996. The Port of New York and New Jersey is the No. 1 port on the East Coast, and the gateway to the largest consumer market in the nation.

THE NEW YORK CITY PASSENGER SHIP TERMINAL, OPERATED BY THE PORT AUTHORITY FROM 1974 THROUGH 1996, HANDLES ARRIVING AND DEPARTING CRUISE SHIPS IN THE NEW YORK–NEW JERSEY PORT.

Jersey City Couple Wed Aboard a PATH Train

Terry Patterson and Charlotte Coleman were married aboard a PATH train in August 1994 by Jersey City Deputy Mayor William Macchi. As part of a joint promotion between PATH and the acclaimed Off-Broadway production Tony n' Tina's Wedding, *a gala reception was held at the Journal Square Transportation Center where local businesses provided flowers, beverages, a wedding cake, hotel accommodations, and a limousine. The wedding party then reboarded PATH for the ride into Manhattan to take in the performance of* Tony n' Tina's Wedding.

Executive Director Stanley Brezenoff

Stanley Brezenoff, a veteran public administrator, took the helm of the Port Authority in September 1990, succeeding Stephen Berger. The new executive director brought a reputation for having taken on some of the most difficult assignments in New York City government. He had filled a variety of deputy mayor posts under Mayor Edward I. Koch, eventually becoming First Deputy Mayor and serving as acting mayor during Koch's absence.

During his four years as executive director, Stanley Brezenoff helped to make the Port Authority a more cost-efficient and accountable organization. He maintained the capital program despite a lingering recession.

Brezenoff is, perhaps, most remembered for his actions during and after the terrorist bombing of the World Trade Center. His leadership of Port Authority staff, World Trade Center tenants, emergency personnel, and others who worked diligently to evacuate and rebuild the complex earned him the Commissioners' Special Award of the World Trade Center for Exceptional Service.

STANLEY BREZENOFF, EXECUTIVE DIRECTOR, 1990–1995

ABOVE: HOLIDAY PROGRAMS FEATURING LOCAL MUSICIANS AND CHORAL GROUPS ARE AN ENTERTAINING ASPECT OF COMMUNITY LIFE AT THE WORLD TRADE CENTER.

LEFT: THE AUSTIN J. TOBIN PLAZA OF THE WORLD TRADE CENTER IS A GATHERING PLACE FOR MANY IN THE LOWER MANHATTAN WORKING COMMUNITY. IN SUMMER PEOPLE EAT LUNCH AT THE OUTDOOR CAFÉ AND ENJOY MUSICAL PERFORMANCES ON THE OUTDOOR STAGE. BEHIND THE FOUNTAIN IN THE CENTER OF THE PLAZA, TOWER ONE (ON THE RIGHT) AND TOWER TWO (ON THE LEFT) FLANK THE VISTA HOTEL (NOW THE WORLD TRADE CENTER MARRIOTT). THE FIVE-ACRE PLAZA, CENTERED BY THE FOUNTAIN, CONNECTS THE TWIN TOWERS. THE SOARING PERSPECTIVE FROM THE PLAZA CAN ONLY BE DESCRIBED AS AWESOME. INDEED, VISITORS CAN FREQUENTLY BE SEEN POINTING THEIR CAMERAS SKYWARD.

ABOVE: LADY LIBERTY WELCOMES THE WORLD TO A NATION WHERE THE SKY IS THE LIMIT, AND THE WORLD TRADE CENTER IS ITS SILVER CROWN.

DWARFING EVEN THE HUGE WORLD FINANCIAL CENTER, THE TWIN TOWERS, ONE OF THE ENGINEERING WONDERS OF THE WORLD, DOMINATE THE ENTIRE SKYLINE FOR MILES. TOWER ONE OF THE WORLD TRADE CENTER IS TOPPED WITH THE REGIONAL TV BROADCASTING ANTENNA, WHICH ITSELF IS MORE THAN 30 STORIES HIGH. TOWER TWO'S WORLD-FAMOUS OBSERVATION DECK IS COMPRISED OF AN ENCLOSED OBSERVATORY ON THE 107TH FLOOR. A ROOFTOP PROMENADE ABOVE THE 110TH FLOOR IS, AT 1,377 FEET ABOVE SEA LEVEL, THE HIGHEST OUTDOOR VIEWING PLATFORM IN THE WORLD. THE OBSERVATION DECK OFFERS A FOOD COURT AND TWO GIFT SHOPS, ALONG WITH A CLOUD-TOUCHING PANORAMIC VIEW IN ALL DIRECTIONS. ON A CLEAR DAY YOU CAN SEE FOR 50 MILES.

The Attack on the World Trade Center

THE DAY THE BOMB STRUCK

FIRE AND EMERGENCY EQUIPMENT LINED UP FOR BLOCKS ALONG WEST STREET AND OTHER LOCAL STREETS TO BRING AN ARMY OF RESCUE WORKERS TO THE DISASTER SCENE.

Snow flurries drifted by the Windows of the World Trade Center on Friday, February 26, 1993, inspiring many of the building's 50,000 workers to remain indoors at lunchtime. Elevators raced up and down the Twin Towers, whisking thousands of noontime employees to sky lobbies, cafeterias, restaurants, and shops. Guests at the World Trade Center's Vista Hotel perused their menus. Just another hustle-and-bustle workday in New York City.

Then, at 12:18 P.M., it happened—a peculiar thud resonated throughout the superstructure from somewhere down below. The lights blinked, then went out. The first speculation was that an electrical transformer had exploded. Then it was thought that an accident had occurred on one of the subways running beneath the twin towers. Some even suspected a plane had hit the building.

As the electrical systems stopped, the building's usual background noise of air conditioning, office machines, and elevators left an eerie silence. People milled about waiting for some word about what was going on. It wasn't until smoke came billowing out of the elevator shafts that people realized that this was not a simple power outage but an emergency that would require evacuation of the building. A rumor began to spread—"It's a bomb!"

A CEILING JARRED LOOSE BY THE HORRENDOUS BLAST MIRACULOUSLY FELL WITHOUT INJURING ANYONE ON THE MEZZANINE LEVEL LEADING TO THE ESCALATORS AND PATH TRAIN PLATFORMS.

Most of the phones were dead, and the emergency communications center for the huge complex, which had been placed on the subterranean level as a protective measure, was destroyed by what turned out to be, in fact, a bomb. Not just a pipe bomb, but a bomb of tremendous power designed to destroy the main support beams between the two towers, presumably to bring both of them down.

The blast created a five-story crater that plunged through five underground levels. It immediately knocked out all fire alarms and emergency and intercom systems. Emergency lights initially went on, but flooding caused by ruptured pipes forced firefighters to call for a shutdown of power to protect the rescue workers searching in dangerous areas.

Those unfortunate enough to be stuck in the building did not know what to do. Cut off from all communications, they could only follow their instincts and the directions of those who took command. Thousands of people made their way down the smoke-filled stairways of the 110-story towers, feeling their way in the pitch dark, uncertain whether they were heading toward safety or greater danger. An occasional flame from a cigarette lighter held high like a torch or a beam from a miniflashlight provided a modicum of comfort to the claustrophobic. Hundreds were trapped in elevators, some for hours.

TV and radio transmitters located atop Tower One were knocked out, throwing virtually all television stations off the air for hours for viewers who did not have cable TV. Only Channel 2, New York's CBS affiliate, was able to resume over-the-air broadcasts because it had an auxiliary transmitter at the Empire State Building. Luckily, some of the telephones still worked. Those phones became a lifeline as TV and radio anchors assured those in the building in on-air conversations that help was on the way.

FIVE BASEMENT LEVELS COLLAPSED UNDER THE FORCE OF THE EXPLOSION, BUT THE VERTICAL SUPPORT COLUMNS HELD.

For hours after the blast, thousands of people streamed out of the buildings into the snowy February day—many without coats, faces covered with soot, gasping for breath. Shards of glass rained down on the street below as those still trapped inside sought fresh air by breaking windows.

Rescuers from the entire New York–New Jersey region converged on the buildings, making the joint response the largest in New York City's history. Port Authority police from all facilities joined rescue teams from the city and surrounding New Jersey counties. New York City's fire department alone responded with 63 fire engines, 51 ladder companies, 23 battalions, eight divisions, five rescue companies, two fireboats, 18 special units, and HazMat, a unit that handles hazardous materials.

The Building

Few buildings would have survived the blast endured by the World Trade Center. The design, unlike in most skyscrapers, makes use of hundreds of columns to form the tower perimeters. Groups of columns, in turn, converge into "super" box columns of high-strength structural steel, which descend into solid bedrock. These columns are strengthened further by diagonal beams that brace the building from windsway.

So resilient is this design, it deflected the bomb's force even at ground zero. While the parking garage floors around the super columns collapsed and fell into a crater five floors deep, even the super column six feet from the bomb sustained little damage.

Stories of Heroism Abounded During the Ensuing Days and Weeks...

• **RAYMOND ECHEVARRIA**, *a maintenance supervisor, was in the B-2 locker room when the blast buried him alive. As he lay trapped under the rubble for an hour, he managed to create a small hole for breathing, and used a piece of cinder block to bang on a fallen locker for help. Inexplicably, he started calling "Michael, Michael." He had no idea why he chose that name, but he continued to call it until his lungs filled with smoke and he started to pass out.*

Just before he lost consciousness, he heard a voice say, "I can hear you, but I can't see you." With his last ounce of strength, Echevarria stuck his hand through a hole in the wreckage. A fireman's flashlight shone on it, and a team quickly came to dig him out.

Echevarria was treated for a punctured lung, broken ribs, and a blood clot, none of which he can recall. What he does remember is waking up in intensive care and immediately wondering—Who's Michael? He thought the question might be answered when the fireman visited him in the hospital and said, "You don't know me," to which Echevarria quickly replied, "Yes, I do! I recognize your voice." But his name turned out to be Bob, not Michael. Echevarria lay in bed obsessed with the Michael mystery for days.

The answer came when it was discovered that one of the employees under his supervision became fearful that Echevarria might have been trapped in the locker room. **MICHAEL CAMPISI** *had run to a fireman named Bob and asked him to look for his boss.*

"I called his name," Echevarria says with emotion. "Out of 40 crew members, I picked him out."

VEHICLES IN THE PARKING AREAS CLOSEST TO THE BLAST WERE MANGLED BY THE EXPLOSION AND CRUSHED BY FALLING DEBRIS.

A DRESS REHEARSAL COLOR GUARD OF PORT AUTHORITY POLICE FROM VARIOUS UNITS WHICH RESPONDED TO THE BOMBING LED A CONTINGENT OF POLICE, FIRE, EMERGENCY MEDICAL SERVICES, TRANSIT AUTHORITY, AND PORT AUTHORITY PERSONNEL ONTO THE INFIELD OF YANKEE STADIUM FOR A PRE-GAME CEREMONY ON APRIL 18, 1993. THE CITY OF NEW YORK PAID TRIBUTE TO THEM BEFORE 57,000 LOCAL FANS.

- **PAUL IANNACONE** *and* **RICHARD PIETRUSZKI** *weren't where they normally work—the B-3-level stockroom—when the bomb exploded. For* **TOM MARTINEZ**, *fate was not so kind. Working in the stockroom when the bomb went off, Martinez was flung beneath a table. He sustained a back injury that would keep him out of work for three months. After coworker* **OLIVER BROWN** *helped him to safety, Iannacone and Pietruszki conducted a detailed search of the area to determine if anyone else was trapped or injured.*

  Working with a single flashlight, the two men crawled forward on their hands and knees in the pitch-black and smoke, patting the ground in front of them to make sure that they would not fall into any of the holes that had opened up. They gave up after an hour of searching without finding other survivors. They then sought out the FBI and local police to offer their intricate knowledge of the subgrade levels.
- **ED PICCINICH**, *manager of operations of the World Trade Center and his 12-man team were trapped in an office in the subgrade—the heat of the blast had welded shut one door, while the second was blocked by tons of debris from collapsed cinder block walls.* **BOB RAFFERTY**, *a security coordinator, quickly corralled the staff into his office, the only space that offered protection against the enveloping smoke. Piccinich grabbed the flashlight and crawled forward to determine whether their last chance for escape was still available—the exit to the executive parking lot. Reaching the parking lot, Piccinich saw that the blast had ripped open the bottom portion of the emergency door. With Rafferty's help, he was able to safely evacuate the employees through the opening.*
- *Building mechanic* **FRED FERBY**, *working in the subbasement, was thrown against a wall by the blast. Buried in the wreckage, he dug his way out. Hearing his coworkers' cries for help, he found a flashlight and searched for them, pulling two from the wreckage of the collapsed ceiling and leading them to safety.*
- *Supervisor* **ED STRAUSS** *was sitting at the operations desk on the B-1 level when the ceiling collapsed and the subterranean office was plunged into darkness. Finding a flashlight, he searched the rubble for the injured and helped clear the truck dock for the arrival of emergency equipment. When emergency personnel arrived, Strauss reentered the building with firefighters to obtain the necessary door keys. He advised firefighters of the best way to gain access to various areas, information that expedited the evacuation of the towers, and eliminated the need to chop through dozens of doors that had been locked for security reasons.*
- *Port Authority employees assisted their colleagues, many in wheelchairs. Two agency lawyers,* **DONALD BURKE** *and* **MICHAEL DRISCOLL**, *carried fellow attorney* **KATHLEEN COLLINS** *and her wheelchair down 66 floors.*
- *A pregnant WCBS-radio transmitter technician was among those saved in a police helicopter rescue off the top of Tower Two.*

Engineers With Long Memories

"At about the 58th floor, the elevator stopped," said Vincent Miller, trapped with seven others in an elevator halted by the blast. "We did not hear an explosion or feel a shock. We pressed emergency buttons and got a recorded message that said the call had been received. When smoke began to fill the elevator we realized something was wrong and we had to think fast."

But these were no ordinary elevator passengers. Among them were five Port Authority engineers, all experts in the inner workings of the building. The group included Chief Engineer Eugene Fasullo, one of the agency engineers involved in the building of the World Trade Center. The emergency power came on but the car did not move. The engineers began to attack the problem systematically, by first pulling open the elevator doors. Faced with a two-inch-thick gypsum-board wall, they tried to kick through it. Then, using make-shift tools—car and house keys—a few of them attempted to make a hole. Others, looking for another means of escape, opened and removed the cover door of the manual-control panel and used it as a hatchet to cut through the remaining gypsum plank. Finally they cut a one-foot square hole that opened into an access area with a supply of fresh air.

"Then the lights went out for good," said engineer Dominick Montalbano. "We used the night-light in our beepers and a book of matches for lighting as we proceeded to cut through the elevator-shaft wall to escape." After opening a small hole in the gypsum they heard a sound like breaking glass when they hit tile in the women's bathroom. By continuing to chop away with the control-panel door, they managed to make a hole big enough for the party to escape.

In the first hours of the crisis, the international press corps gathered to cover one of the major news stories of the year. The story was broadcast to cable TV subscribers around the world. Reporters converged on people as they poured out of the building, seeking first-person accounts from rescuers, victims, and witnesses. Subsequent days saw the news media focus on the enormity of the devastation with pictures of a canyon of twisted steel and broken concrete.

The blast killed six people, four of them Port Authority employees who had decided to have lunch together in the mechanical engineering office that served as the emergency control room for the WTC complex. Perhaps it was a choice inspired by the snow. Perhaps they were getting some extra work done, or they had decided to enjoy each other's company on a Friday afternoon. When the ferocious blast leveled the office, Steven Knapp, William Macko, Robert Kirkpatrick, and Monica Rodriguez Smith, who was expecting her first child within the month, were all killed. John DiGiovanni, a dental equipment salesman who had parked his car in the garage, was crossing the parking area when he was killed. After the evacuation, Wilfredo Mercado, a purchasing agent for the Vista Hotel, was missing. After an extensive search using a canine squad, his body was found 17 days later after five feet of debris had been cleared.

In addition to the deaths, 15 bystanders, 35 police officers, 88 firefighters, and one Emergency Medical Services worker were injured by the blast. More than 1,000 people suffered from smoke inhalation, almost half of them needing to be treated in hospitals.

What was, perhaps, most amazing was the truly heroic response of the agency's entire staff in coping with this emergency. Within hours, engineers and other staff members were assessing the damage and pulling together teams to get the complex back in order. Temporary facilities were set up in nearby warehouses, stores, and office buildings to get support services up and running. The Port Authority's Medical Office promptly dispatched personnel for trauma counseling to help employees and tenants cope.

For many employees, the emergency brought them closer together. They helped each other overcome what had been a bewildering mystery for several days—who did this and why? By the time the answer came, they were already on a determined course of action to prove they would overcome this cowardly attack and do so with amazing efficiency and speed.

PATH

The PATH terminal at the World Trade Center is located beneath Tower One. Although part of the ceiling collapsed and some walls were blown in, the station was immediately closed for another reason. The PATH train tracks ran around the periphery of the crater caused by the blast; there was concern that running the trains would destabilize the equilibrium of the debris below the hotel. Before PATH could be opened again, seismographic equipment (the type used for earthquake measurements) was placed at critical locations around the crater. Test trains were run, at lower speeds than normal, starting with the track farthest from the blast. At 6 P.M. on Sunday, February 28, the engineers concluded that PATH and the nearby subway systems could be reopened. PATH crews managed an astoundingly fast clean-up of the platforms and turnstile mezzanine, where ceiling and wall panels had been dislodged. Miraculously, by Monday morning, the usual stream of PATH commuters poured into the concourse.

THE IMMEDIATE TASK WAS TO STABILIZE THE PERIMETER OF THE CRATER TO PREVENT MOVEMENT OF THE RUBBLE.

The Restoration

Port Authority staff worked quickly to begin restoring the World Trade Center. Engineers and others with knowledge of the building reported in to assist wherever they could. Engineering calculations were started the evening of the blast. Faced with an enormous chasm and an avalanche of rubble under the Vista Hotel, the workers first needed to shore up the perimeter to avoid cave-ins.

Port Authority Chief Engineer Eugene Fasullo stood with two contractors at the crater's edge, deciding on the best way to erect emergency bracing. They determined that the only way to get the equipment, workers, and temporary steel bracing into the area was from the top. Engineers and contractors cut holes in the plaza and the floor of the Vista Hotel, and lowered the men on "spider rigs," platforms lowered by cables. Steel bracing was then delivered through the holes.

A command center was set up on the concourse in Tower One, in a former restaurant called the Big Kitchen. For the next six weeks, Port Authority staff and contractors worked around the clock to restore the towers and accommodate the needs of tenants. They faced the gargantuan task of reconstructing damaged floors and supports, restoring the communication and safety systems, and cleaning out mountains of rubble.

The design for restoring concrete floors and fabricating steel supports began hours after the blast. Scaffolding was erected, and the painstaking task of removing enough wreckage—enough to build a substantial skyscraper—began. Clearing the tons of rubble was a risky venture, particularly in the beginning. The debris was supporting the weakened structural columns, and there was fear of destabilization. One Port Authority construction manager quipped, "We had to create our own carefully controlled version of the game pick-up-sticks."

Another massive task was restoring the chillers used to air-condition the towers. Because the chillers were buried under tons of concrete and steel, engineers were unable to determine how much they were damaged; new temporary backup chillers were erected outside on Liberty and Vesey Streets at the same time that the chillers at level B-5 were being salvaged and repaired. It was a race to get the air-conditioning system operating by summer, but it was up and running on time.

Three days after the bombing, one third of the World Trade Center was open for business, including many concourse retailers and the Commodities Exchange. Some tenants in the towers would have to wait only three weeks before they could return to their offices. To demonstrate that residents of the region would not be intimidated by terrorism, New York Governor Mario Cuomo and his staff led the return to the World Trade Center by moving back into their offices in Tower Two two weeks ahead of schedule.

The Investigation

Dogged investigative work by the Federal Bureau of Investigation; Port Authority Police; the New York City Police Department's Bomb Squad, Arson Explosion Squad, Auto Crime Division, and Emergency Services Unit; and the U.S. Treasury Department's Bureau of Alcohol, Tobacco, and Firearms turned up leads to the bombing suspects two days after the blast. It was the kind of crime investigation one would expect to find in a Sherlock Holmes mystery.

In a workroom set up close to the investigation site, a Ford Econoline 350 van identical to the one used in the bombing was parked on blocks so that workers could slide underneath and examine it. It was used as a prototype against which pieces of the van used in the bombing were identified by cross-matching. Traces of chemicals found on those parts were analyzed to confirm theories about the bomb's components and how the explosive was detonated.

Two days after the blast, a mangled piece of chassis bearing a partial vehicle identification number was traced to a yellow van rented by Mohammed Salameh, who was arrested four days later when he went back to the van rental agency for a third time in an effort to retrieve his rental deposit, claiming that the van had been stolen. Shortly thereafter, Nidal Ayyad, a chemical engineer who used his position to purchase critical components, was arrested. Ahmad Ajaj and Mahmud Abouhalima, who had fled the country directly after the bombing, were also captured and indicted for the crime. After a five-month trial and just one year after the bombing, each of the four defendants was convicted on each of the 38 charges brought against them. Ongoing investigations led to the arrest of Sheik Omar Abdel-Rahman, an exile wanted for crimes in Egypt, and several members of a terrorist ring alleged to be planning to blow up other area landmarks including the Holland and Lincoln Tunnels and the United Nations. In October 1995, the Sheik and nine radical followers were convicted of conspiring in a "war of urban terrorism" against the United States through a series of bombings and assassinations. A worldwide search for the alleged mastermind of the World Trade Center bombing, Ramzi Yousef, concluded with his return to the United States to stand trial.

VEHICLES DESTROYED BY THE BLAST ARE REMOVED FROM THE PARKING GARAGE.

The Memorial on the Austin J. Tobin Plaza

On a spring day in 1995, hundreds of people filled Austin J. Tobin Plaza to dedicate a fountain between the twin towers, directly over the blast site, as a memorial to those who died in the bombing. The fountain's gentle waters flowing over polished stone symbolize healing.

As a coverlet was removed to unveil the fountain, bagpipers played "Amazing Grace," and family members of the victims gathered around the memorial. Many, visibly shaken, felt compelled to touch the stone. Flowers were placed around the edges, a practice carried on to this day by visitors.

For many, the Memorial Fountain has become hallowed ground. Its inscription reads:

> On February 26, 1993, a bomb set by terrorists exploded below this site. This horrible act of violence killed innocent people, injured thousands, and made victims of us all. This fountain is dedicated to the memory of those who lost their lives:
>
> John DiGiovanni
> Robert Kirkpatrick
> Steven Knapp
> William Macko
> Wilfredo Mercado
> Monica Rodriguez Smith and her unborn child

THE MEMORIAL FOUNTAIN'S OUTER RING, MADE OF REJOINED PIECES OF JAGGED GRANITE, SYMBOLIZES REBUILDING FROM THE DESTRUCTION.

FOR FIVE WEEKS IN THE FALL OF 1993, TIBETAN BUDDHIST MONKS CREATED A SYMBOL OF PEACE FOR THE WORLD TRADE CENTER BY PAINTING A WHEEL OF TIME IN THE LOBBY OF TOWER ONE. CALLED A MANDALA, A MEDITATIVE OBJECT DEPICTING THE UNIVERSE THAT IS USED TO PROMOTE HARMONY, IT WAS MADE ENTIRELY OF COLORED SAND. AFTER COMPLETING THE PIECE, THE MONKS SWEPT THE SAND INTO VASES, FORMED A PROCESSION TO THE HUDSON RIVER, AND CEREMONIOUSLY OFFERED THE SAND TO THE RIVER.

The Port Authority Moving Into the Millennium

CUNARD'S *QUEEN ELIZABETH II* SETS SAIL FOR A TRANSATLANTIC TRIP TO SOUTHAMPTON, ENGLAND, FROM THE NEW YORK CITY PASSENGER SHIP TERMINAL. ON HER WAY OUT SHE SURVEYS THE WORLD TRADE CENTER, WORLD FINANCIAL CENTER, AND BATTERY PARK CITY.

"Is the Port Authority too big?" That compelling question was posed by executive director Austin Tobin in his weekly report to the commissioners in 1947. Not surprisingly, he concluded that "serious questions can be raised...as to whether or not the Port Authority is at all as big as the two states intended it to be when they created it." The Port Authority, he wrote, might even be criticized for being too small for the tasks of rehabilitating, modernizing, and developing the terminal and transportation facilities in the port region.

Forty-eight years later, New Jersey Governor Christine Todd Whitman and New York Governor George E. Pataki asked an updated version of the same question: Has the Port Authority grown too big over the last several decades? Concluding that it had, the governors gave the Port Authority Board of Commissioners a mandate: review every facility and service with a view toward possible privatization.

From a public policy standpoint it makes sense for the Port Authority to capitalize on private sector proficiency. It frees the agency to deploy more of its resources and expertise on the things it does best—coordinating and defining critical transportation systems for the region.

CONTEMPORARY VIEW OF THE HOLLAND TUNNEL TOLL PLAZA.

In 1995, the Port Authority announced a plan to refocus the agency on its basic mission of providing tunnel, bridge, aviation, and port facilities and services. The newly appointed executive director, George J. Marlin, and the Port Authority Board of Commissioners believed that the agency's energy and focus would be weakened by maintaining businesses outside its original mandate—particularly in an environment of limited dollars and enormous demands on its transportation responsibilities.

The agency stepped up the privatization of its assets. It sold the Vista Hotel to the Host Marriott Corporation following a complete building renovation that had been under way even before the World Trade Center bombing. The renovation resumed after the sublevel was repaired, which resulted in a beautifully refurbished and marketable property.

Several buildings at Yonkers Industrial Park and land at the Elizabeth Industrial Park have also been sold. The Newark Legal Center is being considered for divestiture, as are the Brooklyn piers. The Port Authority also began looking at privatization options for the World Trade Center.

GEORGE J. MARLIN

Two Executive Directors: George J. Marlin and Robert E. Boyle

George J. Marlin became the Port Authority's executive director in February 1995, bringing with him 17 years of municipal bond experience. Marlin set about getting the agency back on course, redirecting the agency's resources toward its basic transportation mission.

On March 1, 1997, he was succeeded by Robert E. Boyle, the former president and chief executive officer of the Jacob K. Javits Convention Center in New York City. Boyle transformed the Javits Center from a facility with high costs, chronic labor problems, and the influence of organized crime into one of the premier convention centers in the world.

ROBERT E. BOYLE

The New York and New Jersey region is the mecca of art, fashion, and culture. It is the center of telecommunications, advertising, media, and design. It is the financial capital of the world. The region's desirability as a business center was uncontested for decades, but competition has grown dramatically over the past 15 years. As other regions market their advantages as places for companies to locate or do business, it has become even more critical for the Port Authority to provide state-of-the-art transportation facilities and services.

As we head toward the new millennium, the Port Authority is addressing issues that are basic to the region's vitality. The port will be dredged to serve a dynamic shipping industry. The airports are being brought up to 21st century standards to ensure that the region will retain its ability to attract and better serve tourism and industry. Improved customer service and convenience at transportation facilities is an essential component to enhance the quality of life of residents and visitors.

MANHATTAN'S "TOP" RESTAURANT, WINDOWS ON THE WORLD, REOPENED IN THE SUMMER OF 1996, OFFERING HAUTE CUISINE IN A MULTILEVEL PENTHOUSE. DINERS CAN CHOOSE FROM AN ECLECTIC SELECTION OF INTERNATIONAL DISHES AND WINES AND LIQUORS FROM THE RESTAURANT'S CELLAR IN THE SKY.

Public-Private Partnerships at the Port Authority

The private sector has always had a powerful presence at the Port Authority, not only in the construction of its facilities but in the management of its operations as well. The marine terminals at Port Newark and Elizabeth are privately operated by the tenants. Private operators run the Windows on the World restaurant and the Observation Deck at the World Trade Center. At the airports, most of the airline terminals, parking lots, food and other retail shops, and travel information counters are privately run, as are some cleaning and maintenance functions and bus and taxi dispatch services. At the Port Authority Bus Terminal, private enterprises include the bus lines, information and travel booths, and retail operations.

Privatization via the leasing or sale of facilities has been part of the Port Authority's history. The Union Motor Truck terminals were leased to private companies and eventually sold. After the World Trade Center was completed, the Port Authority Building at 111 Eighth Avenue was returned to the private sector. Seven World Trade Center was built by the private sector, without Port Authority capital investment. Twenty-two years ago, the operation of Teterboro Airport was turned over to a private airport operator for 30 years.

The Port Authority has often joined forces with the private sector to construct facilities. Oftentimes the private company would eventually take over the operation and management of the facility. In the 1980s, the Teleport was developed in partnership with the City of New York and a private firm, which now operates, maintains, and oversees the facilities and services. The Port Authority developed a program for ferry service from lower Manhattan's Battery Park to Hoboken, New Jersey, and then awarded a contract to operate the service to a private firm.

More recently, the agency built the financially successful Essex County Resource Recovery Facility in partnership with Essex County, the City of Newark, and a consortium of private companies, which will operate the plant until 2015. At JFK, a cogeneration plant developed to supply the airport with electricity is operated by a private firm under a 25-year agreement with the Port Authority. The Port Authority also plans a $150 million project financed by the private sector to develop 110 acres at JFK and 60 acres at Newark International for airport cargo facilities.

STATIONS THAT SPARKLE AND IMPROVED AMENITIES ARE PART OF THE NEW EMPHASIS ON SERVICE FOR PATH. SIMILAR IMPROVEMENTS ARE UNDER WAY AT THE BRIDGES, TUNNELS, AIRPORTS, AND BUS TERMINAL.

IMPROVING REGIONAL TRANSPORTATION

AIRPORTS

With 80 million airline passengers traveling to and from the region in 1996, and an ever-booming demand for cargo capacity, it became essential that almost half of the Port Authority capital budget be invested at the three major airports.

New terminals are being built, and older ones are being redesigned to make flight connections easier. New access roadways and better signage will make travel around the airports less difficult. Amenities such as new restaurants and boutiques are playing an increasingly important role in wooing the traveler. Business services, such as fax and copier machines and on-line computer services, are now being offered, as are accommodations for the disabled.

JOHN F. KENNEDY INTERNATIONAL AIRPORT REDEVELOPMENT

Once the crown jewel of the world's airports, JFK is being readied to regain its original sparkle. Almost $5 billion in Port Authority and private sector funds will be spent by the year 2001 in a major airport overhaul and modernization.

In the largest public–private partnership ever created at an airport, a private consortium will design, build, operate, and maintain a new International Air Terminal, Terminal 4. A symbol of the airport's renaissance, the terminal will feature soaring glass walls and 1.4 million square feet of open-design

John F. Kennedy International Airport

John F. Kennedy International Airport is located on Jamaica Bay, in the southeast section of Queens County, 15 miles by highway from midtown Manhattan. The original construction of the airport cost $60 million. By the middle of 1996, the Port Authority's capital investment in the airport was $2.2 billion. The current redevelopment program consists of Port Authority and tenant construction and expansion programs, including construction of the new Terminal 1 on the site of the former Eastern Air Lines terminal, and expansion and renovation of their facilities by American Air Lines, British Airways, and Delta Airlines. The Port Authority program includes a quadrant roadway system, new utilities, a new air traffic control tower, a new parking garage, a redeveloped Terminal 4 (the International Air Terminal), and a light-rail system which will connect the terminals to parking, rental cars, and subway and rail lines.

space, improved check-in and security areas, faster processing through Customs and Immigration, and additional airplane gates. Amenities include food courts with a variety of moderately priced eateries, a retail mall, and a large duty-free section.

Another new terminal, Terminal 1, is scheduled to open in 1998. It is the first airline passenger terminal to be erected at JFK since the completion of the British Airways terminal in 1971. A joint venture of its prime users—Air France, Japan Airlines, Korean Air, and Lufthansa—the project is the first limited partnership of foreign carriers to develop, construct, and operate a multi-airline passenger terminal in the United States.

In the area of safety, a new foam arrestor bed, the first in the nation, was installed in 1997 to prevent aircraft from overshooting the runway.

AN ARTIST'S RENDERING OF TERMINAL 1, CURRENTLY UNDER CONSTRUCTION AT JFK.

THE NEW CONTROL TOWER AT JFK, COMPLETED IN 1995, IS EQUIPPED WITH STATE-OF-THE-ART ELECTRONIC EQUIPMENT FOR FAA OPERATIONS. IT IS THE SECOND TALLEST CONTROL TOWER IN NORTH AMERICA AFTER DENVER INTERNATIONAL'S.

LaGUARDIA AIRPORT REDEVELOPMENT

More than $800 million has been invested by the Port Authority and the airlines for the redevelopment of LaGuardia Airport. LaGuardia's redevelopment program began in 1992, with the opening of the USAir Terminal. The new building greatly expanded the capacity of the airport, which had outgrown the arc-shaped Central Terminal Building that originally housed all the airlines. The USAir Terminal was built by a public–private partnership between the airlines and the Port Authority, like the earlier renovation of the landmark Marine Air Terminal for general aviation facilities, and the adjacent Delta Shuttle Terminal.

By 1994, parking garage improvements, a new taxiway, additional aircraft parking space, and new internal roadways helped the airport to better handle the boom in air travel. The $200 million renovation of the Central Terminal Building resulted in a three-level, skylit atrium and retail mall; expanded ticketing, arrivals, and baggage areas; and new escalators and elevators. The redevelopment program also includes reconfiguring and widening roadways, modernizing airline gate and waiting areas, and improving runways and taxiways.

DECORATIVE GRILLWORK GRACES THE OUTER ROADWAY SIDEWALKS AT LaGUARDIA AIRPORT.

LaGuardia Airport

LaGuardia Airport is located in the Borough of Queens, eight miles from Manhattan, bordering on Flushing Bay and Bowery Bay. Originally built at a cost of $40 million, the airport has benefited from some $1.5 billion in additional Port Authority and airline improvements.

LaGuardia Airport employs some 9,000 people, and generates another 63,000 jobs and nearly $5.7 billion in economic activity.

Welcome
m-vindo
Willkommen
Center
Bienvenue!
Welcome
U.S. Immigration
& Naturalization
Service
Baggage Claim
EXIT
38
39
40
41
42

A MORE SPACIOUS CUSTOMS AREA AT NEWARK INTERNATIONAL AIRPORT IS THE CENTERPIECE OF THE NEW INTERNATIONAL TERMINAL.

A proposed high-speed ferry will shuttle LaGuardia travelers to and from several Manhattan locations, providing views of New York's unforgettable skyline, harbor, and bridges.

NEWARK AIRPORT REDEVELOPMENT

Continental Airline's Terminal C opened in 1988. Extensive modernization of Terminal A and the construction of a new International Arrivals Facility in Terminal B followed in the 1990s. New shops and restaurants offer a variety of products and services to the traveling public. Floor-to-ceiling windows in the Immigration Hall in Terminal B provide panoramic views. The New Jersey landscape rolls to the Hudson, and Manhattan's spires punctuate the horizon. Planes large and small glide by in an aeronautical ballet, each landing and takeoff creating an exciting performance. The new customs hall can process 3,000 passengers per hour, sending most on their way in less than 30 minutes.

Two new cargo facilities are also part of Newark International's redevelopment.

In 1997, the Port Authority Board of Commissioners authorized a much-needed runway extension that will reduce delays at Newark International Airport. Runway 4L-22R will be extended 1,800 feet to the southwest and 1,000 feet to the northeast, offering much more operational flexibility.

Traffic congestion and pollution has been reduced by an automated monorail, which offers fast, frequent service throughout the airport. Opened on May 31, 1996, the 1.9-mile-long system offers driverless trains that operate around the clock every day of the year. Among the high-tech features is a heated guideway that permits unimpeded operations in icy weather.

THE SIGNATURE ARCHES OF NEWARK INTERNATIONAL AIRPORT FORM A DISTINCTIVE ARCHITECTURAL PATTERN UNDER A PORTICO TO SHELTER ARRIVING TRAVELERS.

Faster Trips to the Airports

Although the Port Authority has improved traffic flow at the three airports, getting there has always been a challenge to people driving on the metropolitan area's heavily traveled highways. This is especially true for roads leading to JFK.

A plan was approved in 1996 to provide reliable public transportation to JFK. The Port Authority plans to build a $1.5 billion 8.4-mile automated light-rail line to connect the airport's terminals, car rental facilities, and long-term parking lots with existing subway and commuter rail lines in Queens. Because the system will link up with the Long Island Rail Road and subway lines at Jamaica Station, it will enable travelers from Manhattan, Brooklyn, Queens, Nassau and Suffolk counties, and New Jersey to reach JFK entirely via mass transit. Travel at the airport itself will also improve, with the time to travel around the two-mile loop of terminals taking only a few minutes.

The new monorail at Newark International Airport was designed to be linked with local mass transit systems. A one-mile extension of Newark Airport's monorail to a new station west of the airport will enable people to reach the airport from the Northeast Corridor Line, which is used by Amtrak and New Jersey Transit commuter trains. New Jersey Transit is building the airport station and Amtrak is providing the track work on the line. New Jersey Transit also plans to build a nine-mile trolley extension to connect the airport to the Newark City Subway's 12 stations.

NEWARK INTERNATIONAL AIRPORT'S $354 MILLION MONORAIL IS A SLEEK, HIGH-TECH TRAIN OFFERING FREE, FREQUENT, AND FAST SERVICE. PASSENGERS WITH CONNECTING FLIGHTS OR THOSE USING LONG-TERM PARKING OR RENTAL CAR LOTS CAN AVOID THE TRAFFIC CONGESTION ON AIRPORT ROADWAYS BY RIDING THE MONORAIL FROM ONE TERMINAL TO ANOTHER.

Newark International Airport

Newark International Airport is located about 16 miles from Manhattan, in New Jersey's Essex and Union Counties. Built at a cost of $8.2 million by the City of Newark with an additional $15 million invested by the U.S. government during World War II, the airport has since been enhanced by more than $1.6 billion in Port Authority improvements.

Newark Airport's current $1 billion development program includes a new International Arrivals Facility, the modernization of two terminals, a new monorail system, the extension of Runway 4L-22R, and improvements in airport access and airport roadways. Newark International employs more than 18,000 people, and generates another 110,000 jobs and $10.3 billion in economic activity.

POPE JOHN PAUL II'S HISTORIC OCTOBER 1995 VISIT TO THE UNITED STATES BEGAN AT NEWARK INTERNATIONAL AIRPORT. HIS PRESENCE REQUIRED THE UTMOST IN SECURITY MEASURES.

Airports Roll Out the Red Carpet

From popes to presidents, the Beatles to the Bolshoi Ballet, the Brooklyn Dodgers to Princess Diana, luminaries come to the New York–New Jersey metropolitan area after passing through the Port Authority airports. The degree of effort, teamwork, and coordination involved in providing security, as well as handling the increased traffic caused by fans and the media, is truly daunting.

Take, for example, the October 1995 visit by Pope John Paul II. When he arrived at Newark International Airport, the Pope was met by President Clinton and several cabinet members, scores of local officials, and 500 members of the world press. Some 3,500 people, including 2,000 schoolchildren, clamored for a chance to greet the pontiff. Planning for the papal visit took six months. More than 100 phone lines, along with fax and computer equipment, had to be installed to transmit accounts of the event throughout the world. As with all special events, tickets, badges, parking stickers, and accommodations were prepared for the media. Bleachers, platforms, and sound systems had to be set up for the official ceremonies.

Because the Pope was deemed a target for a potential terrorist attack, the highest security arrangements were put in place. An escort of armored cars, emergency personnel, and a motorcycle brigade of police officers rode as part of his entourage. Sharpshooters were stationed atop buildings along the motorcade route, and frogmen were even positioned underwater to ward off a possible marine attack.

Almost immediately on the heels of the papal visit, the United Nations General Assembly celebrated its 50th anniversary. Some 200 presidents, kings, and other world leaders made their way to the U.N. via JFK.

Mid-August to the end of October 1995 was a period of high terrorist alert. The largest security contingent ever assembled at an airport required the involvement of security forces, including the Secret Service, Immigration, the FBI, the Drug Enforcement Agency, New York City Police, and specially trained bomb-sniffing dogs. The degree of security provided for each visiting VIP was carefully planned.

While airport operations continued as usual during this time, 120 special flights were handled. Some of the dignitaries arrived on commercial flights, but delegations from many countries arrived on unscheduled flights in various types of aircraft, from small Gulfstreams to large B747-400s.

VIPS AND CELEBRITIES ARRIVING AT PORT AUTHORITY AIRPORTS THROUGHOUT THE YEAR REQUIRE RED-CARPET TREATMENT—AND TIGHTENED SECURITY—AT ALREADY BUSTLING FACILITIES. THIS PHOTO SHOWS THE KUWAITI DELEGATION DISEMBARKING AT JOHN F. KENNEDY INTERNATIONAL AIRPORT IN OCTOBER 1995 TO TAKE PART IN THE U.N.'S 50TH ANNIVERSARY CELEBRATION.

N.Y. Jet Explodes; 229 Aboard

Flight to Paris Plunges in Flames Into Ocean

TWA Flight 800 Crashes Over Long Island Sound

On the evening of July 17, 1996, one of the worst air disasters in United States history took place above the waters off Long Island, claiming the lives of 230 passengers and crew members. TWA Flight 800, bound for Paris, left JFK airport at 8:30 P.M. Ten minutes later, just beyond Westhampton Beach, the plane exploded into flames and plunged into the ocean. Debris scattered over a five-mile radius. Witnesses described the event as a powerful midair explosion. They saw a bright flash, then a ball of fire descending from the sky trailing black smoke as it plunged into the waters below.

A herculean rescue effort began with a flotilla of boats and helicopters from the U.S. Coast Guard, Navy, and National Guard and local law enforcement agencies, supplemented by dozens of small privately owned pleasure craft. The Port Authority's helicopter ferried emergency personnel from the closest Coast Guard base to the crash site, and assisted in the search for survivors. Beneath a moonless sky, the search was hampered by heavy haze. Hovering at times only 200–300 feet over the murky water, the pilots dropped flares to assist the small boats that targeted their lights to illuminate the scene. Throughout the night and for the next several days, police and fire rescue teams from New York City and elsewhere in the region joined in the search. FBI and National Transportation Safety Board personnel immediately took over the investigation, which centered first on a bomb but did not rule out mechanical failure.

Grieving relatives and friends of the crash victims poured into the TWA terminal waiting for news. Port Authority employees helped comfort them. Port Authority staff set aside a safe and secure place for the victims' families to gather, and arranged to have the airport's Ramada Inn serve as headquarters. In the ensuing days, Port Authority staff and JFK chaplains set up offices at the hotel, and arranged transportation for families traveling to and from their hotels. They also assisted those relatives still flying in, and helped organize memorial services for the victims, held on Sunday, July 21, and Monday, July 22, 1996.

There is no charge to ride the monorail, which travels between terminals, parking lots, and car-rental facilities. The trains and the stations are climate-controlled, with sheltered canopies stretching the length of the parking lots. The monorail is accessible to people in wheelchairs; and audio announcements in the cars and stations identify the route direction, arrivals, and departures.

WATERFRONT DEVELOPMENT

THE HOBOKEN PIERS

Hoboken's piers hark back to a bygone era and the once-bustling docks fell into disrepair. Containerization and the use of cargo vessels with enormous capacities demanded more upland space, causing abandonment of the urban docks.

Hoboken residents sought to reclaim their waterfront. After ten years of community squabbles over what should be done with the piers, the City of Hoboken and the Port Authority agreed in 1996 to collaborate in the transformation of the waterfront from a deteriorating eyesore into an attractive residential and commercial community. Private developers are providing an estimated $600 million for office and residential buildings, a hotel, restaurants, retail stores, and recreational areas, including a marina and fishing pier, a soccer field, and athletic courts. The Port Authority will supply $75 million for land acquisition and infrastructure improvements.

BELOW: THE COMMUTER FERRY LAUNCHED IN 1994 FROM HUNTERS POINT TO EAST 34TH STREET IN MANHATTAN IS AN IMPORTANT ELEMENT IN THE EVOLVING $2.3 BILLION DEVELOPMENT OF QUEENS WEST. THE FERRY IS OPERATED BY NEW YORK WATERWAY.

LEFT: A RENDERING OF THE QUEENS WEST WATERFRONT DEVELOPMENT AT HUNTERS POINT (IN THE FOREGROUND). THE DEVELOPMENT WILL OFFER A STUNNING VIEW OF THE UNITED NATIONS COMPLEX AND THE MANHATTAN SKYLINE.

NEW JERSEY TRANSIT'S HOBOKEN TERMINAL, A NEWLY RESTORED BUILDING, SERVES AS A HUB FOR COMMUTER TRAINS, PATH, AND FERRY CONNECTIONS ACROSS THE HUDSON.

ERIE
LACKAWANNA
NY WAT

TAKING A FERRY FROM THE HOBOKEN FERRY TERMINAL TO THE WORLD FINANCIAL CENTER IN DOWNTOWN MANHATTAN IS AN ENJOYABLE WAY TO COMMUTE.

The Hoboken Ferry links the Hoboken waterfront with downtown and midtown Manhattan. Adjacent to the Hoboken piers is the landmark Hoboken Terminal, a spectacular beaux arts confection built for the old Delaware, Lackawanna & Western Railroad. An architectural delight, it still functions as a transportation center for New Jersey commuters taking PATH and New Jersey Transit. Hoboken's "green palace" has a stately passenger concourse with 16 skylights, stained glass windows, coffered ceilings, cut stone designs, and ornamental copper. The building, which offers ample space for commercial uses, is the planned site for a new museum.

QUEENS WEST

Stretching some 70 acres along the East River directly across from the United Nations building, Queens West will be a mixed-use development made up of residential buildings, a new hotel, and some 2 million square feet of office space. In the mid-1980s, the Port Authority joined the New York State Urban Development Corporation and the New York City Economic Development Corporation to develop this site at Hunters Point, once a manufacturing area. Groundbreaking took place in 1994.

Queens West includes a waterfront esplanade of 50 acres of park and recreation areas as well as community centers, an early childhood center, and small retail shops. Easy access to Manhattan is available via subway and ferry, and to points east via subway connections to the Long Island Railroad.

HOWLAND HOOK REOPENS

Howland Hook on Staten Island celebrated a reopening in September 1996 that was 10 years in the making. Run by a private operator, the facility contains 2,500 linear feet of berthing, 147 acres of space for container storage, and seven container cranes. Able to handle some 425,000 containers annually, it is the largest-capacity terminal on the New York side of the harbor.

Once a rail-to-ship coal terminal for the Baltimore & Ohio Railroad and a shipping facility for scrap metal in the early half of this century, Howland Hook was later rebuilt by American Export Lines as a marine terminal.

At the behest of the City of New York, which purchased the property in 1973, the Port Authority leased the marine terminal in 1985. Investing some $50 million in its redevelopment, including $4 million for dredging, the Port Authority is working with the city's Economic Development Corporation to rejuvenate the Staten Island North Shore Railway to serve Howland Hook and with the New Jersey Department of Transportation to establish a railroad link to points west in 1997.

A New Mission Statement for the Port Authority

REFLECTING THE AGENCY'S CURRENT PHILOSOPHY, THE PORT AUTHORITY BOARD OF COMMISSIONERS ADOPTED A NEW MISSION STATEMENT IN 1995:

"TO IDENTIFY AND MEET THE CRITICAL TRANSPORTATION INFRASTRUCTURE NEEDS OF THE BISTATE REGION'S BUSINESSES, RESIDENTS, AND VISITORS: PROVIDING THE HIGHEST QUALITY, MOST EFFICIENT TRANSPORTATION AND PORT COMMERCE FACILITIES AND SERVICES THAT MOVE PEOPLE AND GOODS WITHIN THE REGION, PROVIDE ACCESS TO THE REST OF THE NATION AND TO THE WORLD, AND STRENGTHEN THE ECONOMIC COMPETITIVENESS OF THE NEW YORK–NEW JERSEY METROPOLITAN REGION."

PRESERVING A FIRST-CLASS PORT

Harbor dredging of Port of New York and New Jersey has become more crucial as larger ships require deeper channels to reach the docks. The port competes with such natural deep-water harbors as Norfolk and Halifax. If carriers were to bypass New York, the East Coast's busiest containerport would be relegated to second-class status. Thousands would lose their jobs, and importers and exporters would transfer their operations elsewhere. Consumers would pay higher prices for goods due to higher land transportation costs.

How to dispose of the dredged silt became a subject of fierce debate between shipping interests and environmentalists. In 1996, a breakthrough in the dredging impasse was reached when the governors of New York and New Jersey agreed to take the lead in planning a dredging strategy for the New York–New Jersey harbor. Disposal techniques being discussed include finding beneficial uses for the dredged silt at upland disposal sites, storing the silt in below-the-ocean-floor pits or on containment islands built in Newark Bay, and developing decontamination technologies.

Despite obstacles, by the mid-1990s the Port Authority managed to push through dredging of the Kill Van Kull and Newark Bay channels, and berths at the Brooklyn Piers and the Red Hook Container Terminal.

One of the Port Authority's primary concerns is to preserve the thousands of port-related jobs and the $20 billion in economic activity that the shipping industry generates in the region each year.

POSTSCRIPT—THE YEARS AHEAD

The Port Authority, still in perpetual motion, is moving ahead with transportation and trade innovations. The E-ZPass electronic toll collection system, already introduced at its tunnels and bridges, and "intelligent" systems for traffic management and information will make travel easier. Other contributions to regional mobility include the light-rail system to JFK International Airport, scheduled for completion in 2002, and Newark Airport's monorail, which will be extended to the Northeast Rail Corridor by 2000. PATH's fleet of cars and its signal system will be reconditioned, and planning and investments for the maritime terminals will ensure that the Port of New York and New Jersey maintains its global preeminence. The agency is also developing and enlarging its presence on the World Wide Web. Internet users can access the Port Authority's home page at http://www.panynj.gov for information and resources that are expanding almost every day.

Seventy-five years after the Port Authority was created, its agenda of renewal, modernization, and expansion of its transportation and trade facilities remains worthy of the vision of its founders.

The 9.5-Million-Square-Foot Paint Job

It will be one of the largest paint jobs in the world. The monumental repainting of the George Washington Bridge, which will take 10 years to complete, will seal the steel superstructure against the elements for another quarter-century.

In years past, lead was a common component in paint, so an equally huge project entails the safe removal of all of the lead-based paint. Using special enclosures with high-tech ventilation and dust-collection systems to protect workers and the community, the enormous span will be stripped by abrasive blasting before being repainted with three coats of paint made of epoxy, zinc, and urethane.

ON JUNE 28, 1995, THE PORT AUTHORITY ISSUED ITS 100TH SERIES BOND, BRINGING TO $8 BILLION THE AMOUNT OF MONEY BORROWED SINCE THE FIRST CONSOLIDATED BOND WAS SOLD ON DECEMBER 10, 1952.

Port Authority Time Capsules

1921

- The Port Authority is created by The Port Compact and by a congressional consent resolution signed by President Harding.

1924

- The States of New York and New Jersey authorize the Port Authority to build, operate, and maintain the Outerbridge Crossing and the Goethals Bridge.

1925

- Legislation is passed in the two states authorizing the Port Authority to build, operate, and maintain the Bayonne and George Washington Bridges.

1927

- The Holland Tunnel is opened by the New York State Bridge and Tunnel Commission and the New Jersey Interstate Bridge and Tunnel Commission.

1928

- The Outerbridge Crossing and Goethals Bridge open.
- Newark Airport is opened by the City of Newark.

1930

- The States of New York and New Jersey pass legislation authorizing the Port Authority to operate the Holland Tunnel.

1931

- The States of New York and New Jersey pass the Bridge and Tunnel Unification Act, which grants to the Port Authority control, construction, and maintenance of all interstate bridges and tunnels in the Port District.
- Construction of the Midtown Hudson Tunnel—the Lincoln Tunnel—is authorized.
- The George Washington Bridge opens.
- The Bayonne Bridge opens.

1932

- Union Inland Freight Terminal No. 1 begins operation in the new Port Authority Commerce Building.

1933

- The Port Authority's general offices move to the Commerce Building (later called the Port Authority Building) from 80 Eighth Avenue.

1934

- Construction of the Lincoln Tunnel begins.

1937

- The first tube of the Lincoln Tunnel opens.

1939

- LaGuardia Airport is opened by the City of New York.

1944

- The State of New York transfers its Grain Terminal properties in Brooklyn to the Port Authority.
- The City of New York requests that the Port Authority finance and construct a bus terminal in mid-Manhattan.
- A landmark decision by the United States Court of Appeals holds that Port Authority bonds are exempt from federal income taxation.

1945

- The North Tube of the Lincoln Tunnel opens.
- Construction begins on the Union Motor Truck Terminals in New York and Newark.

- The first of five domestic and four overseas Port of New York Trade Development Offices opens in Chicago.

1946

- At the request of the City of Newark, the Port Authority presents its proposal to develop Newark Airport and Seaport.
- At the request of the City of New York, the Port Authority presents its proposal to lease, develop, and operate LaGuardia and New York International Airports.

1947

- Under a lease with the City of New York extending to 1997, the Port Authority begins to develop and operate LaGuardia and New York International Airports.
- The Port Authority submits its proposal, at the request of the City of Hoboken, to finance the rehabilitation of Hoboken's federally owned and operated piers and to lease and operate them.
- The Port Authority enters into a lease with the City of Newark to develop and operate Newark Airport and Seaport through 1997.

1948

- The Port Authority begins the development and operation of Newark Airport and Seaport under a lease with the City of Newark.
- New York International Airport opens.

1949

- The Port Authority purchases Teterboro Airport.
- The New York Union Motor Truck Terminal opens.

1950

- The Port Authority Bus Terminal opens.

1951

- The Newark Union Motor Truck Terminal opens.

1952

- The Port Authority signs a lease with the City of Hoboken and the United States Maritime Administration to assume responsibility to rehabilitate and operate the Hoboken piers.
- The Port Authority board of commissioners adopts a resolution establishing a new issue of Consolidated Bonds to finance future Port Authority construction and refunding.

1953

- A new Passenger Terminal Building at Newark Airport is dedicated, marking the 25th anniversary of the airport and the golden jubilee of powered flight.

1956

- The Port Authority begins operation and development of the Brooklyn Piers.
- The International Air Cargo Center, the world's largest, opens in New York International Airport.
- The West 30th Street Heliport opens.
- The Hoboken–Port Authority Piers open.

1957

- The Third Tube of the Lincoln Tunnel opens.
- The International Arrivals Building and airline wing buildings at New York International Airport open.

1958

- The Port Authority acquires property to develop the Elizabeth–Port Authority Marine Terminal.
- Pier 11, the first of the new Brooklyn–Port Authority Piers, opens.
- The Port Authority purchases marine terminal property at Brooklyn's Erie Basin.

1959

- The Air Cargo Center at Newark Airport opens.

1960

- A major expansion of the Port Authority Bus Terminal begins.
- The Downtown Manhattan Heliport opens on the East River.

1962

- The States of New York and New Jersey pass legislation authorizing the Port Authority to acquire and rehabilitate the Hudson & Manhattan Railroad and to develop a World Trade Center on the west side of lower Manhattan.
- The Port Authority Trans-Hudson Corporation acquires title to and begins operation of the Hudson and Manhattan Railroad System.
- The Elizabeth–Port Authority Marine Terminal, the world's first all-container port facility, opens.
- The six-lane lower level of the George Washington Bridge opens.

1963

- The George Washington Bridge Bus Station opens.
- The Port Authority Heliport and Exhibit Building at the New York World's Fair opens.
- New York International Airport is rededicated as John F. Kennedy International Airport.
- A reconstruction program at Newark Airport begins .

1964

- A new passenger terminal and control tower at LaGuardia Airport open, completing a major portion of the airport's rehabilitation program.

1965

- The Port Authority Grain Terminal ceases operation.
- The lease between the City of New York and the Port Authority under which the city operates LaGuardia and John F. Kennedy International Airports is extended to December 2015.

1966

- Construction of the World Trade Center begins.

1970

- The World Trade Center opens in lower Manhattan.

1972

- The "Port of NY Authority" is renamed "The Port Authority of New York and New Jersey."

1973

- The Central Terminal Area's Terminals A and B at Newark International Airport open.

1974

- The New York City Passenger Ship Terminal opens.

1975

- The Journal Square Transportation Center opens.
- The Observation Deck at the World Trade Center opens.

1979

- Foreign Trade Zone No. 49 at Port Newark/Elizabeth opens.

1981

- The North Wing of the Port Authority Bus Terminal opens.

1982

- Bathgate Industrial Park opens.

1984

- The States of New York and New Jersey pass legislation enabling the Port Authority to initiate mixed-use waterfront development projects to foster economic growth in Hoboken, New Jersey, and Hunters Point, Queens.
- The Industrial Park at Yonkers becomes a Port Authority facility.

1985

- The Port Authority leases the Howland Hook Marine Terminal from the City of New York.

1986

- The Teleport opens in Staten Island.

1987

- The rebuilt Downtown Manhattan Heliport opens.

1988

- The Port Authority concludes public- and private-sector agreements for commuter ferry service between Hoboken and lower Manhattan.
- The Central Terminal Area's Terminal C at Newark International Airport opens.

1989

- The Auto Marine Terminal in Jersey City/ Bayonne opens.
- Elizabeth Industrial Park opens.
- The Port Authority board of commissioners authorizes work to begin on a major redevelopment program at JFK.
- The Newark Legal Center opens.
- A redevelopment program at Newark International Airport begins.

1990

- The Essex County Resource Recovery Facility in Newark, New Jersey, becomes operational.
- A new PATH Car Maintenance Shop and yard facility in Harrison, New Jersey, opens.

1991

- An $11 million berth expansion project at the Red Hook Container Terminal is completed.
- ExpressRail on-dock rail service at the Elizabeth–Port Authority Marine Terminal, offering double-stack container service, begins.
- A new toll plaza and new roadways at the Holland Tunnel are completed.

1992

- The New York Union Motor Truck Terminal and the Erie Basin Marine Terminal are sold.
- The Delta Ferry Service between LaGuardia Airport and Manhattan is initiated.
- A redevelopment program at LaGuardia Airport begins.

1993

- The World Trade Center is bombed by terrorists.

1994

- Groundbreaking ceremonies are held for the Queens West Waterfront Development. Ferry service from Manhattan is launched.
- The FAA begins operations from a new 321-foot-high control tower at JFK.

1995

- Dredging is completed at the Howland Hook Marine Terminal, paving the way for the opening of the facility for the first time in 10 years.
- The Port Authority and the City of Hoboken sign *Principles of Agreement* that set the stage for the transformation of the Hoboken South Waterfront.

1996

- The new ExpressRail facility opens at the Elizabeth–Port Authority Marine Terminal.
- The region's first airport monorail begins service at Newark International Airport.

Bibliography

Ammann, O.H. "George Washington Bridge: General Conception and Development of Design." American Society of Civil Engineers, Paper No. 1818.

Arend, Geoffrey. *Air World's Great Airports—Newark 1928–1952.* New York: Air Cargo News Inc., 1978.

Arend, Geoffrey. *Great Airports—Kennedy International.* New York: Air Cargo News Inc., 1978.

Arend, Geoffrey. *Great Airports—La Guardia, Celebrating 50 Years, 1939–1989.* New York: Air Cargo News Books, 1990.

Arend, Geoffrey. *Great Airports—Worldwide.* New York: Air Cargo News Books, 1988.

Auletta, Ken. *The Streets Were Paved With Gold.* New York: Random House, 1979.

Bard, Erwin W. *The Port of New York Authority.* New York: Columbia University Press, 1942.

Bird, Frederick L. *A Study of the Port Authority.* New York: Dun & Bradstreet, 1949.

Bunker, John G. *Harbor & Haven, An Illustrated History of the Port of New York.* Woodland Hills, Calif.: Windsor Publications, Inc., 1979.

Butterfield, Roger. *The American Past.* New York: Simon & Schuster, 1996.

Caro, Robert A. and Edwin C. Hargrove. *The Power Broker: Robert Moses and the Fall of New York.* New York: Knopf, 1974.

Clifton, Daniel, editor-in-chief. *Chronicle of the 20th Century.* New York: Dorling Kinderley Publishing, Inc., 1995.

Cohen, Julius H. *They Builded Better Than They Knew.* New York: Julian Messner, 1946.

Doig, Jameson W. "To Claim the Seas and the Skies: Austin Tobin and the Port of New York Authority," from *Leadership and Innovation.* Baltimore and London: The Johns Hopkins University Press, 1990.

Doig, Jameson W. *Expertise, Politics, and Technological Change. The Search for Mission at the Port of New York Authority.* Journal of the American Planning Association, Vol. 59, #1, Winter, 1993.

Doig, Jameson W. "Politics and the Engineering Mind: O.H. Ammann and the Hidden Story of the George Washington Bridge," from *Building the Public City, The Politics, Governance, and Finance of Public Infrastructure,* edited by Perry, David C. Urban Affairs Annual Review. Thousand Oaks, Calif., London, New Delhi: Sage Publications, 1995.

Doig, Jameson W. *Empire on the Hudson.* Draft paper, January 1995.

Glennon, Lorraine, editor-in-chief. *Our Times, The Illustrated History of the 20th Century.* Atlanta: Turner Publishing, Inc., 1995.

Hornberger, Eric. *The Historical Atlas of New York City.* New York: Henry Holt & Co., 1992.

Jackson, Kenneth T., editor. *The Encyclopedia of New York City.* New Haven, Conn. and London: Yale University Press, New York: The New York Historical Society, 1995.

Morris, James. *The Great Port.* New York: Harcourt, Brace & World, Inc., 1969.

The Port Authority of New York and New Jersey. Annual Reports, 1921–1996.

The Port Authority of New York and New Jersey. Archival materials from Port Authority Records, 1921–1997.

The Port Authority of New York and New Jersey. *Art for the Public—The Collection of the Port Authority of New York and New Jersey*. New York, 1985.

The Port Authority of New York and New Jersey. *A Chronology of the Port of New York Authority: 1921–1967*, by the Public Affairs Department. New York, 1967.

The Port Authority of New York and New Jersey. *The Compact Between the States of New York and New Jersey; By Which the Port of New York District and the Port of New York Authority With Certain Powers, Were Created.* New York, 1921.

The Port Authority of New York and New Jersey. *The Diary* (now *P. A. Today*), a Port Authority employee publication. New York, 1938–1997.

The Port Authority of New York and New Jersey. The Executive Director's Reports to the Commission. New York, 1942–1972.

The Port Authority of New York and New Jersey. Goldberg, Daniel B. *A History of the Port of New York Financial Structure.* New York, 1964.

The Port Authority of New York and New Jersey. *Metropolitan Transportation.* Comprehensive Planning Office. New York, 1963.

The Port Authority of New York and New Jersey. *The Story of the Port of New York Authority*. New York, 1967.

The Port Authority of New York and New Jersey. *Via-Port Magazine.* New York, 1949–1990.

Trager, James. *The People's Chronology*. New York: Henry Holt & Co., 1992.

Photo Credits

All photos courtesy of the Port Authority with the following exceptions:

CHAPTER I
Pages 12 and 13. South Street Seaport Museum
Page 16. Museum of the City of New York
Page 17. Museum of the City of New York
Pages 18–19. Museum of the City of New York

CHAPTER III
Page 39. Corbis-Bettmann
Page 40. Corbis-Bettmann

CHAPTER VI
Pages 116–117. New York Daily News (LAG 5660)
Page 118 (bottom). UPI (LG 3371; LG 20)
Page 120. G. Arend/Air Cargo News Inc. (VI 17 LAG)
Pages 122–123. Daily Mirror (LAG 1341; LG 21)
Page 144. Fairchild Aerial Surveys (CP 76-6/1/29)

CHAPTER VII
Page 160. Corbis-Bettmann
Page 161. Corbis-Bettmann

Index

A

B

C

D

E

F

G

H

I

J

K

L

M

N

O

P

Q

R

Y